SHORT COURSE SERIES

WORLD TRADE PRESS®

Professional Books for International Trade

THE SHORT COURSE IN INTERNATIONAL TRADE SERIES

A Short Course in International Business Culture

A Short Course in International Business Ethics

A Short Course in International Business Plans

A Short Course in International Contracts

A Short Course in International Economics

A Short Course in International Intellectual Property Rights

A Short Course in International Joint Ventures

A Short Course in International Marketing

A Short Course in International Marketing Blunders

A Short Course in International Negotiating

A Short Course in International Payments

A Short Course in International Trade Documentation

A SHORT COURSE IN

International Marketing

3rd Edition

Approaching and penetrating the global marketplace

Jeffrey Edmund Curry, MBA, Ph.D

Published in arrangement with World Trade Press by

ATLANTIC
PUBLISHERS & DISTRIBUTORS (P) LTD

7/22, Ansari Road, Darya Ganj, New Delhi-110 002
Tel: 40775252, 23273880, 23275880, 23280451; Fax: +91-11-23285873
E-mail: orders@atlanticbooks.com; Web: www.atlanticbooks.com

World Trade Press
800 Lindberg Lane, Suite 190
Petaluma, California 94952 USA
Tel: +1 (707) 778-1124
Fax: +1 (707) 778-1329
USA Order Line: +1 (800) 833-8586
E-mail: sales@worldtradepress.com
www.WorldTradePress.com
www.WorldTradeREF.com (international trade and logistics)
www.BestCountryReports.com (business travel, communications and culture)
www.GiantMapArt.com (Giant maps for building lobbies, conference rooms and education)

A Short Course in International Marketing
By Jeffrey Edmund Curry, MBA, Ph.D.
Short Course Series Concept: Edward G. Hinkelman
Cover Design: Ronald A. Blodgett
Text Design: Seventeenth Street Studios, Oakland, California, USA
Desktop Publishing: Steve Donnet

ISBN 978-81-269-1250-6
First Indian Reprint 2009

This edition is for sale in Indian sub-continent only.

This book is dedicated to the memory of my parents.

Library of Congress Cataloging-in-Publication Data
Curry, Jeffrey E., 1953–
A short course in international marketing : approaching and penetrating the global marketplace / Jeffrey Edmund Curry.
p. cm. — (The short course in international trade series)
Includes bibliograhical references.
1. Export marketing. I. Title. II. Series.
HF1416.C87 2009
658.8'48—dc21 09-17796
CIP

Printed in India at Chaman Enterprises, 1603, Pataudi House,
Darya Ganj, New Delhi-110 002

INTRODUCTION

EVERYTHING MUST BE MADE AS SIMPLE AS POSSIBLE BUT NOT ONE BIT SIMPLER. — ALBERT EINSTEIN

THE INTERDEPENDENCE OF MARKETS: WHO NEEDS WHOM?

A great deal of emphasis has been placed on the need for companies to pay attention to the global economy, even when they operate on a seemingly domestic basis. This call for a larger perspective has come about because very few businesses can truly say that they're unaffected by conditions outside of their home market. The corner restaurant in New York notices the rise in prices when coffee crops are bad in South America, an office supply shop in Buenos Aires feels the effect of a transportation strike in Europe, and a Beijing computer manufacturer knows exactly when the price of microprocessors has jumped in the United States. Large companies go so far as to hire personnel to track the markets that will affect them the most. Many would say that all of this interdependence is the result of advancements in transportation and communication. The real cause, however, is an increase in the effectiveness of international marketing.

Those companies that have done the best in the global arena are those that have released themselves from any emotional attachment to the schemes that made them a success domestically in order to see each new marketplace as a distinct entity. This is not to say that some aspects of domestic plans can't be used internationally; many times the new market will demand elements of the old mixed with the new. The key to success is a reliance on proper research and analysis. Whereas some functions of management (sales, human resources and even some manufacturing processes) may be described as "art," marketing (whether domestic or international) is science. The stakes are far too high and the pace much too quick to rely on guesswork, intuition, or gut feelings. Entering a new market far from home without a detailed plan is akin to building a skyscraper without a blueprint—possible, but highly improbable.

The goal of this text is to give the reader a grounding in marketing and its application to international business. The book is directed at novice marketeers as well as those experienced in domestic applications but new to the global marketplace. The former group will discover that marketing is much more complex than it first appears; the latter will find that much of their acquired skill is readily transferable after reasonable retooling. All will see that the boundaries between domestic and international marketing are, at times, quite solid and on other occasions somewhat hazy.

The realities of the international marketplace will be stated as such, often bluntly so, and no theory will be promulgated without concrete examples. The contents are meant for practical application, not theoretical discussion. Readers will also find that culture and cultural distinctions are at the heart of international marketing. A company's ability to access and appeal to those societal distinctions will spell the difference between long-term profits and short-term failure. The continued desire of societies to retain their individuality, coupled with an increased awareness of the effect of commerce on culture, has given rise to the specialization of the international marketeer.

THE LACK OF HOMOGENEITY: ONE WORLD, MANY WALLETS

The world may be becoming more cosmopolitan, but homogeneity is centuries, if not millennia, away. No longer will the developing world accept the products of their richer neighbors willy-nilly, nor do the industrialized powers show any less resistance to the encroachments by the powerful American and Japanese technoliths. Even at the top of the commercial heap, emotions run high on the topic. The United States, for its part, was just as resentful of Japanese auto manufacturers as Japan was of U.S. rice producers. The desire to exclude foreigners from "traditional" markets is as much an economic fear as a cultural one.

This book will delve extensively into the cultural concerns intrinsic to the international, and sometimes even the domestic, marketing process. Throughout, guidelines will be presented for formulating a marketing strategy. Cultural analysis, research planning and a marketing plan outline will give the reader a step-by-step program for assembling a cogent scheme for international business. A marketing audit is also supplied to help with long-term planning.

"Culture shock" is a common malady among world travelers. It is this author's goal to provide sufficient information to prevent the reader from suffering the decidedly more expensive consequences of "market shock."

Jeffrey Edmund Curry
San Francisco, California

TABLE OF CONTENTS

CHAPTER 1

Marketing Basics

LIVE TOGETHER LIKE BROTHERS AND DO BUSINESS LIKE STRANGERS. — ARAB PROVERB

THE WORD MARKET derives from the Latin *mercari* meaning "to buy or trade" (hence merchant) and that infinitive finds its roots in *merx,* which means "goods." The "market" is anywhere that goods or services may be sold or traded. Nowadays, it can range in scope from a simple open-air exchange of farm products to a description of an entire economy (as in the European Market) or a nebulous commercial function (like the stock market). The term also covers specific ethnic, cultural, religious, national, political, or social groups. People may purposely group themselves together as a market (e.g., NAFTA) or they may come together by circumstantial default (e.g., adults 21 to 30 years old). As will be seen later, all markets can be subdivided or segmented into smaller and smaller groups, all the way down to individuals if so desired.

Marketing versus Sales

For some inexplicable reason, marketing is constantly linked to sales in a way that no other function of management seems to be. Many people, including top executives, confuse the terms on such a regular basis as to render them interchangeable. This erroneous matchup is true for both domestic and international companies. To promulgate the belief that marketing is something that only salespeople do (as in the sales and marketing department designation) is exceedingly dangerous. The problem seems to stem from a misunderstanding about the difference between a process and a result, as well as from the failure to understand the centrality of marketing to all management functions. Sales occur when goods or services are "given over" to a customer in exchange for money or another valuable consideration. It's the end result of the marketing process.

Marketing describes the whole commercial process that creates (through promotion) the interest that the potential customer demonstrates prior to a sale. The role of sales is to capitalize on that interest to the point where there's a successful exchange. Once a sale is complete, a company must provide follow-up service in an effort to maintain satisfaction and promote future sales. Many large companies have begun to officially demarcate and prioritize these functions by instituting a marketing department, within which is a subdivision called the sales and service department. Smaller companies and solo entrepreneurs must have an equally clear distinction and understanding of all the areas covered by the term marketing.

Effective Marketing: Binding the Buyer and Seller

Sales transactions are the goal of marketing and they serve as the basis for the relationship between the marketeer and the consumer. No one enters the marketplace, buying or selling, without the expectation of some type of gain. Even the briefest transaction creates a relationship, however small, between the buyer and seller. The marketing plan is a detailed scheme of how a company will designate, access, sell to, and service a specific consumer group. When done properly, it will create the environment for transacting business in a way that is mutually "gainful" for both sides. The degree of care that's taken to assure this mutual gain will dictate the length of the relationship. Taking advantage of a customer on the first go-around makes for a brief, and often acrimonious, relationship, while the extraction of a reasonable profit and the offer of follow-up services results in larger, longer-term relations. Both extremes are regularly planned and executed, though companies utilizing the former have little staying power. The binding relationship between the buyer and seller that's created by effective marketing tends to last longer—and to be set up more quickly—as the speed of information in the marketplace increases. Good reputations can be quickly gained but just as quickly damaged or lost forever as the pool of informed and demanding consumers grows larger everyday.

Role of the Marketing Plan: The Action Budget

As is true of many activities in life, gain rarely appears without pain or, more precisely, effort. The burden of this effort is greatest on the selling side and is therefore the responsibility of the marketeer. Product, price, promotion, distribution, and postal service must all be thoroughly designed during the market planning process and controlled in compliance with that plan after its implementation. As hard as it may be for other management personnel within a company to accept, all of their actions must be directed by and subservient to the marketing plan. To return to the construction analogy from the introduction, to build a building the carpenter, the electrician, the bricklayer, and the glazier must all practice their arts within the confines of an architectural blueprint. In fact, the ability to produce results within those restraints is the measure of their professionalism. This is not to suggest that the primacy of marketing acts as a straightjacket on the other activities of management. The marketing plan is simply an action "budget" and, like its financial counterpart, is subject to change during the course of the company's lifespan. Many ongoing internal and external factors (some controllable, some not) affect marketing, and adjustments must be made accordingly. The marketing audit process (Chapter 16) analyzes the need for adjustment and is nothing more than the matching of a planned budget against "actual" costs. When applied to finance, these planning and auditing processes are recognized and valued by any professional manager. However, it's rare that marketing is seen in the same matter-of-fact light.

Marketing is often taken to be some sort of intuitive mechanism that requires a "feel" for a specific market or product line. The result has been that the number of high tech, telecom, and financial services marketing specialists are now a legion.

The fact is that marketing is very much akin to accounting in its procedures and equally universal in its applicability. Just as accountants are "good with numbers," marketeers are proficient with consumer-related data. Once the methodology of marketing has been grasped, it can be applied to any business.

WARNING: Whether using internal or external marketing staff, there is no substitute for current information and recently analyzed approaches. A professional marketeer can develop profitable strategies for any product.

Marketing Potential: Today and Tomorrow

Market potential—the ultimate size and profitability of a market—can vary greatly and will be affected by factors both within and without of the control of the marketeer. A good portion of this text will deal with these variants, but at this point the reader should recognize that marketeers must view all markets in the short-, medium-, and long-term. Additionally, markets can compete with each other for the attention of the marketeer, and the relative potential of those markets (international ones in particular) must be weighed before expensive resources are allocated. After being first entered or penetrated, markets will move through progressive stages. There's no set period of time for their maturation, which will occur when demand consistently absorbs allocated supply, with pricing objectives met.

Companies usually seek to control their own status in any particular market, though there are an intrepid few that allow the marketplace to dictate their positioning. This position can remain static or change drastically, up or down, over the course of a market presence. Positioning a product against its competition is heavily linked to image. The recognizability of an established brand name can go a long way toward allowing an established company to pre-position a proven product in a new market or to position a new product in an old market. A company may labor for decades to establish a brand name (e.g., Volvo in automotives) or it may become an overnight sensation with worldwide recognition (e.g., Google). It's a matter of timing and consumer demand.

The Role of Marketing in Business: The Rudder of Commerce

Marketing is the targeting, acquisition, and retention of customers over a period dictated by the life cycle of the product (goods or services) under consideration. In many ways this is a simple statement, but one that belies extensive research and complex analysis. Marketing is the initial movement of ideas that results in a saleable product. Surely good ideas are rampant in the marketplace but customers, flush with money and eager to spend, often go home empty-handed. Products heralded as the "greatest thing since ———" soon find their way to the rubbish heap. Is this the result of quality problems? . . . Sometimes. Government intervention? . . . Occasionally. Hyperbolic advertising? . . . Usually. Consumer fickleness? . . . Often. Poorly planned marketing? . . . Always.

The rush to enter the marketplace is most often quickly followed by rejection; the successful are begrudgingly described as "lucky" by those who fail. There's little doubt that "being in the right place at the right time" leads to success in the marketplace. However, luck is no more involved in business than it is with other complex human undertakings. The trajectory of the NASA Pathfinder spacecraft led to it being accurately placed within the orbit of Mars and then successfully landed on its surface. Time and place had been carefully planned and those plans methodically exercised. Variables and risks were calculated, deemed reasonable, and then overcome; logic, logistics, and long-term thinking were all brought to bear. NASA's success proved the Aristotlean postulate that the educated tend to be "luckier." Marketing functions under the same rubric.

Marketing Functions: Five Classic Functions and a Forgotten One

After creating or finding a market, a company can exploit it quickly by maximizing profit on a per-product basis, or it may choose to pursue a process of maximizing market share. This latter process requires that the company secure the greatest amount of consumer purchases possible through careful pricing and quality control in an effort to establish a long-term relationship with the customer. Over time, prices will be increased and costs reduced with an eye toward taking profit once competitors have been driven from the field or at least had their share of the market reduced. The acquisition of market share is subject to the rigors of finance ("Can we wait this long to make money?"), opportunity ("Are the consumers ready, willing, and able to buy our product?"), and the competitors' strength ("Will they fight back?").

Traditionally, marketing has been broken down into the following processes.

CONTACT

This is the seeking out of prospective consumers and it may be based on a variety of determinants. Time, distance, media, and the overriding factor of access to finance can make this initial function extremely difficult. No matter how useful and desirable the product may be, improper handling of the initial contact can keep a company out of the marketplace indefinitely.

MERCHANDISING

Once potential customers have been located, goods and services must either be developed from scratch or customized. For the purposes of international marketing, merchandising is the process of bringing the right product to the right place at the right time in the right quantity at the right price. Ultimately, the consumer determines what's "right."

PRICING

The price of a product is often the determining factor when a purchase is made and is always a key to profit. It's also part of a strategy of seizing market share. Setting a proper price will determine how long any company will stay in the marketplace. When a company practices price competition, it consciously uses price as the major means of attracting consumers. It's not unusual for consumers (at both the wholesale and retail level) to buy based entirely on price, regardless of the efforts of the marketeer to promote quality or service.

PROMOTION

Once a product and its price have been developed, customers must still be convinced to favor it over a competitor's offering. There are four types of promotion used to support marketing efforts: paid advertising, personal selling (one-to-one), public relations (press releases, articles), and supplemental efforts (coupons, sweepstakes). All promotion, but especially advertising promotion, is open to overstatement and misrepresentation. Successful and ethical marketeers devise advertising that keeps customer perception closely aligned with product or service reality. Promotion is taken up in detail in Chapter 11.

DISTRIBUTION (A.K.A. DISTRIBUTION CHANNELS)

Although this is often associated with the movement of physical products over distances, it is, in reality, the process of putting the consumer and the product (whether goods or services) together. In its strictest sense it means the extent to which consumers have access to a product compared to the total number of possible access points. In a larger sense, distribution encompasses all of the participants in the delivery of a product, any product, from the marketeer to the consumer. Participants include retailers, wholesalers, agents, shippers, customs brokers, manufacturer's representatives, advertising agencies, media buyers and a plethora of other middlemen who act on the behalf of the marketeer. And there's a great deal of overlap among their functions.

To make the above processes truly comprehensive we add human resources.

HUMAN RESOURCES

The internal marketing that occurs at every company when they attract, hire, train and retain employees is directly reflected in the ability to market externally to the public. All employees, from the mailroom to the conference room, must be selected for their ability to contribute to the company's external marketing efforts. Transactions don't take place between companies and faceless consumers but between flesh-and-blood human beings. It is essential that sellers understand, communicate with, and value buyers. This purely human aspect of marketing is the basis of every successful company, whether they actively acknowledge it or not. While it has been determined that other animals on the planet can "make" things, only human beings bring their wares to market.

The Hierarchy of Effects: Why and How Consumers Buy

Every marketing effort has a series of stages it must progress through toward the ultimate consumer transaction. This "hierarchy of effects" is the same whether the end-user is a single consumer or a large corporation.

PRODUCT AWARENESS

The potential consumer must be made aware of the existence of a product. This can be accomplished through promotion, advertising, active research, or the much ballyhooed "word of mouth." This last source of awareness, where one happy customer sings a product's praises to other consumers, is always thought of as optimal. It may be optimal, but it takes a long time for its effects to be felt.

PRODUCT AFFINITY

Awareness doesn't always result in a desire to buy. Marketeers must take great pains to ensure that a product and the company create a favorable impression on the consumer. Being useful isn't enough; being useful and attractive is. Keep in mind that the term *useful* will be defined by the perceptions of the consumer. Agreeing with that perception isn't as important as understanding it.

PRODUCT PREFERENCE

A product may be the first of its kind in the marketplace but it will not be alone for very long. Even strong copyrights and patents don't prevent competition. A marketeer must make the consumer prefer one product over another once the affinity effect has been achieved. It might be price, it might be quality, it might be service, or it might just be the color of the package. Whatever makes the customer favor a product over its competition must be pursued. Being equal isn't being competitive. Being better is.

PRODUCT CONFIDENCE

Consumers rarely purchase anything that gives the impression of unreliability. Although there are many cases of products being purchased that were "too good to be true," their presence in the marketplace is short-lived. Today's marketeers are very aware that consumers are increasingly savvy. Beyond the legal ramifications of fraud, marketeers must realize that "they can't sell water as wine" for very long. Obtaining and retaining the consumer's confidence in your product not only precedes a successful transaction but also lays the groundwork for establishing the brand identity.

PRODUCT PURCHASE

Once they know you, like you, prefer you, and believe in you, consumers are ready to open their wallets. Oddly enough, the transactions don't always occur. Some companies unconsciously make it difficult for consumers to consume. Excessive paperwork, lack of credit financing, poor delivery schedules, or slow processing can all contribute to failure at this point. If you don't make the purchase process easy, prepare for a return to "square one" and an uphill battle.

Common Marketing Mistakes: Pay Attention or Pay the Price

Customers are the major concern of marketeers; the product being offered can take any form, commodity or service, without significantly changing the governing rule of the relationship. The rule is quite simple: the cost to the customer must reflect the customer's *perceived value* of the product. All businesspeople (perhaps all people) understand the primacy of this rule, and yet the failure rate in commerce is staggering. It's the marketeer's job to understand the perception of cost and value when approaching customers, thereby avoiding commercial calamity. Here are some common failings.

UNIVERSALITY

Group A accepted the product readily, therefore Groups B, C, and D will be equally receptive.

This approach is quite common when moving from a smaller to a larger marketplace or from a domestic to an international one. While human cultures and sub-cultures have many things in common, consumer behavior isn't one of them. Marketeers must only find large enough groups bearing similar behavior to make the effort of the transaction worthwhile. Even giant companies like Coca-Cola, McDonalds, and Toyota have recognized that universality is impossible, and they repackage their products accordingly.

PERSONALIZATION

I think my product is great and so will you.

This is similar to universality in wrong-headedness, but on a much smaller scale. Patent offices are overflowing with ideas that seemed perfectly useful to the inventor but were savaged in the marketplace—if they got there at all. Services suffer a similar fate, as can be seen in the reception consultants often receive in the marketplace as they discover that their services, once highly valued by a previous employer, have little or no open market value. Similarly, the Internet is awash in unprofitable products and services that seemed like great ideas to someone, somewhere.

PRICE BLINDNESS

People will be willing to pay big money for this.

Many good ideas and products price themselves out of the market or slow down the pace of their success by entering at too high of a price point. For example, the commercial real estate market in developing economies chronically suffers from overpricing compounded by overbuilding. Eventually, though begrudgingly, prices are adjusted downward, but it's usually too late to salvage the market. Consumers and real estate developers often have very different ideas about how much "a view" and "location" are worth. The desire for good products should not be confused with the ability to pay.

QUALITY DEFAULT

For this price, it's the best we will (can) do.

Consumers in the developing, industrialized and technological markets all have very different views about quality—above and beyond cultural requirements. The difference in hotel service quality between Hong Kong and its close neighbor on the mainland, Shenzhen, is considerable although the price differential is slight. Hong Kong leads the world in hospitality, while its neighbor says "good enough" with the foreseeable effect on sales.

CULTURAL MYOPIA

These people just don't get it.

Marketing books and case histories are rife with examples of marketing blunders, most of them due to a poor understanding of the targeted culture. Such mistakes are most costly for the big international firms, but the problem isn't confined to them alone. For every Chevrolet Nova that didn't sell in Latin America (*no va* means "doesn't move" in Spanish), there's an optimistic rancher still trying to figure out why no one wants to buy ostrich meat in Germany (Germans like to eat pork). Marketing failure and sloppy cultural research walk hand in hand.

PACKAGING PLOYS

The product speaks for itself.

While this may be true, its "language" may be unintelligible to many. Even domestically, regional differences can cause customers to misinterpret the nature or value of a product. Communication is the responsibility of the sender, not the receiver. From the wood-paneled offices of a high-priced lawyer to the size and shape of boxes for children's toys, the package is often as important as the product.

POOR TIMING

How were we to know that the ______ trend was over?

You can use a product from either the goods or services sectors to fill in the blank of the preceding sentence. There's always some person or company that gets their product to the market just as consumer interest wanes. Failure here is the result of being blinded by your own preparatory activity to the exclusion of the impending realities of the marketplace.

WARNING: No one is so busy or so destitute that they cannot pay attention.

Found versus Created Markets: Discovering and Inventing

Many people say that markets are found, while others believe they're created. Both are correct. So-called market-driven businesses regularly find markets—by taking the commercial pulse of the general public to determine what's desired and then striving to produce the requisite goods or services. In this case, consumer demand determines what products will be supplied. This can be best exemplified by the practicality of personal computer products. Until engineers developed practical software programs (e.g., spreadsheets, desktop publishing, word processing), computer sales were minimal. After marketeers found out what consumers wanted, sales skyrocketed.

At other times (though rarely so nowadays), products are developed first and then attempts are made to convince the public that it needs them. The new product, at least initially, may appear to have no practical value. Such a product-driven company (like deodorant manufacturers in the 1950s and 1960s) creates an artificial demand through advertising in the hope of supplying the new long-term "need." By equating cleanliness with lack of body odor in numerous ad campaigns, marketeers caused millions of people worldwide to believe in the need for deodorants. Created markets such as this (now given the far more luxurious name of "personal care products") eventually come to demand "improvements" (e.g., simple deodorants became anti-perspirants), and even found markets are refined, whether requested or not (e.g., gigabyte-eating software upgrades).

In the late 1980s, marketing managers ceased to refer to product- or market-driven companies and changed the nomenclature to push and pull, respectively. Some products had to be pushed through the distribution system toward the consumer (created), while others were pulled through (found) by demand. As will become clear, all international markets are a varying mixture of both types.

CHAPTER 2

Elements of the Marketplace

IT IS NOT ENOUGH TO AIM, YOU MUST HIT.
— ITALIAN PROVERB

FEW COMPANIES enter the international marketplace directly. For the most part, they move from domestic markets into exports and then into a full-fledged international presence. This applies to both goods and services. It may take decades to reach the international scene or it may be a matter of months. Today, any company that markets itself via the Internet achieves almost instant global access, even when its wares are directed at a domestic market. The process of "testing the waters" locally before jumping into international seas is the same for a small manufacturer as it is for a financial consultancy or even a high-tech "hyper company." Many of the lessons learned at home will serve the company abroad.

Elements of Domestic Marketing: Starting at Home

Many companies are quite content to operate on a very local scale. Their active marketing may not extend beyond a radius of a few miles. Other companies may expand their horizons to a few cities, a province, or even their entire country. All of this is considered to be domestic marketing. Every company goes through the same planning process, some companies more consciously than others, when entering the domestic or international marketplace. Following is a list of the major elements of marketing.

MARKET ASSESSMENT

This is the part of the process where opportunities are initially assessed. It can be as simple as observing that groggy commuters have no place to buy coffee before boarding the morning train or as complex as recognizing the potential demand for satellite TV dishes in remote farming communities.

MARKET ORIENTATION

After the initial assessment, a company must set its basic objectives by deciding which products to bring to market at what price and which customers to pursue. At this stage, the company should also consider how much of the market they wish to control and over what period of time. Researching and objectively analyzing the competition is a major part of this process.

STRATEGY DEVELOPMENT

Once objectives are set, a strategy must be developed to attain them by the most cost effective means available. Strategy has three subprocesses that must be dealt with.

- **SEGMENTATION**

Segmentation is the targeting of specific groups with specific products. A marketeer realizes that different people and groups of people will require different products or modifications to products. Recognizing the extent of those requirements will determine the level of success and longevity available to a company. No matter how good your coffee is, it will not satisfy someone looking for a cup of tea. (Segmentation will be covered in detail in Chapter 9.)

- **PENETRATION**

Penetration is the part of planning that deals with a company's ability to get access to consumers. Just because you see a market doesn't mean that you'll be permitted entry. A company may struggle and be rejected or merely be unable to overcome the regulatory or financial obstacles placed in its way. Penetration requires not only willingness but also resources.

- **POSITIONING**

Positioning is the way customers perceive a company's product in relation to that of its competition. It may be based on quality, size, price, brand recognition, packaging, and a host of other "subjective" features. A company may choose to *control* their positioning or only *react* to the fickleness of the marketplace. Positioning will determine a company's "share" of the market. A shop offering "the best cup of coffee in town" could charge a premium price and maintain a small customer base, or it might offer a wide-range of beverages at lower prices hoping to get as big a share as possible. The local café and Starbucks both must consider positioning or the consumer will do it for them.

IMPLEMENTATION

Once the strategizing has stopped, the hard task of plan implementation begins. Here the tactics of packaging, pricing, promotion, sales, advertising, and distribution must all be activated. The number of perfectly good products that never made it to market is so large as to be an embarrassment to all who wear the title of marketing manager. As is true of all management tasks, planning is easier than implementing, and implementation requires considerable planning of its own.

CONTROL

Many products have reached market, chalked up a few years of sales growth, and then nosedived into the dustbin of marketing failures (e.g., BetaMax videotape, Atari computers). The inability to maintain continuous control of product quality, modification, distribution, and image are the leading factors for such failure. Controls and the ability to monitor performance must be planned as thoroughly as strategy and, like implementation plans, be in place before the product is brought to market. Remember, you can't build a levee in the middle of a flood.

STRATEGY ANALYSIS

As feedback in the form of customer satisfaction, profit tallying, brand recognition, and market share statistics pour into a company's data collection apparatus (from a filing cabinet to a computer), proper analysis must be made.

Preplanned strategies must be "tweaked" or totally revised, and tactics continually evaluated. Even the smallest domestic market has sufficient dynamism to preclude stagnation. Look behind, plan ahead!

Elements of Export Marketing: Setting Your Sights on New Horizons

There are many reasons to consider exporting to a foreign market. A domestic market may be saturated (automobiles), a product may have reached the end of its useful cycle in the domestic market (computer software), a sudden demand from a foreign market may present itself (foodstuffs), or a company may just be looking for new territories. Whatever the reason, a certain degree of domestic success has usually preceded the decision. Beyond the normal market planning procedures listed above, the following elements must be taken into account when exporting.

REGULATION

All nations regulate their imports. And even when demand is high in the target country, government regulation can prevent your exports from reaching the customer. In some cases, restrictions have been put in place to protect product quality and the safety of the population. Regulation can become protectionist as governments favor domestic producers. This can be politically or culturally based (e.g., Japan's restrictions on rice imports) and may require extensive maneuvering to circumvent legally. Also, all countries put controls on their own exports for many of the same reasons (e.g., the United States' security restrictions on computer exports). The first area for research when considering exporting is the thorough investigation of the regulatory atmosphere.

LICENSING

Part of the regulatory process may involve the actual licensing of your company for exporting (or importing). This is above and beyond the regulations regarding the products. Governments are very sensitive about not only what crosses their borders but also who will profit from the transactions. Licensing is considered a form of control and taxation beyond import/export duties.

DISTRIBUTION

One of the most difficult parts of exporting is the development of distribution channels. If you turn your product over to local distributors, you'll have to relinquish a degree of control over merchandising and quality assurance. If you maintain your own distributorship, it can be a very expensive learning process to adapt to the practices of a foreign land. Though many large companies may be able to afford to operate their own distribution channels, local governments often frown on that possibility—especially in emerging markets, where distribution charges are the only means to add value to imports. For some markets, the internal movement of products (including legal and financial services) can be as sensitive an issue as the actual importation. When they find they can't directly control distribution, many companies will either make frequent trips to the target country to do quality checks or open a representative office for that purpose.

FINANCING

International transactions often require the extension of credit. Part of the difficulty of exporting is the degree of trust that must be exhibited between buyer and seller. The buyer is reluctant to pay in advance because the seller holds the product on distant shores, and the seller is loathe to extend credit and ship to a stranger. Until a firm relationship between importer and exporter is developed, most will use letters of credit (L/C) and correspondent banks as neutral intermediaries in the credit process. In some cultures, importers are quite upset when a foreign exporter will not accept their word as a bond, but such trust is unrealistic during the initial phase of long-distance relations. Keep in mind that even with a correspondent bank as intermediary, governments may short-circuit the process for reasons that may benefit the importer.

EXCHANGE RISK

Even when financing goes well, there will be a "lag time" between when a trade is contracted and when the money arrives. During that period, the value of the transaction currency can change. As the summer and fall of 1997 clearly showed, currencies can quickly devalue, particularly so in the emerging markets. Both importer and exporter take a degree of exchange risk, so each tries to ensure use of a payment method that benefits their position. Exporters like to be paid in the hardest currency available (Japanese yen, European euros, U.S. dollars), while importers like to pay with weaker currencies. Exporters must take great care to specify the currency of payment. Simply contracting at 50,000 dollars with an Australian importer can be a very costly mistake, as they can choose among U.S., Canadian, Hong Kong, or Australian dollars as payment.

NOTE: Some countries (e.g., China and Vietnam) have currencies that can't be converted on the international market, so all payments by their importers must be made in foreign currency. Exchange rates can be affected by a whole host of variables and should be thoroughly investigated before contracts are signed.

LEGAL STATUS

For all of the economic unions, tariff treaties, and trading blocs that have come about in the last to decades, local governments still exert a great deal of power over the import/export process. When a trade goes wrong, and some do, legal recourse for the exporter can be as variant as the number of foreign markets. In some major markets, like China, foreigners have virtually no legal status and will be unable to seek redress for the illegal activities of importers. Others, like Great Britain, provide substantial protection for foreign companies. No matter how good the trade looks on paper, research your legal position in the importer's country *before* contracting.

Decision-Making for Entering International Markets: Taking Aim

The following checklist will help in the making of initial decisions about entering the international marketplace. It can be used for import/export companies, service businesses, manufacturers, and those considering joint-ventures with foreign partners.

DECISION-MAKING CONCERN	YES	NO
1. Have I researched the target market for potential competitors?	❑	❑
2. Has the target market exhibited interest in my product?	❑	❑
3. Has the potential size of the target market been quantified?	❑	❑
4. Will the foreign government permit import of my product?	❑	❑
5. Will my government permit the export of my product?	❑	❑
6. Will I be able to get my price?	❑	❑
7. If exporting, can letters of credit be secured?	❑	❑
8. Can proper insurance be obtained in the target market?	❑	❑
9. Is the target infrastructure capable of handling my product?	❑	❑
10. Will the foreign government give us fair treatment?	❑	❑
11. Can I control distribution?	❑	❑
12. If I have to use local distributors, are they trustworthy?	❑	❑
13. Can I maintain the quality of my products overseas?	❑	❑
14. Can we maintain control (rather than give it up to a local partner or agent)?	❑	❑
15. Does the foreign government promote imports?	❑	❑
16. Does the foreign government have a convertible currency?	❑	❑
17. Will I be permitted to travel freely in the target market?	❑	❑
18. Has my legal status in the foreign country been researched?	❑	❑
19. Have the regulatory and licensing processes been investigated?	❑	❑
20. Does the foreign tariff code treat us fairly?	❑	❑
21. Does my domestic tariff code treat us fairly?	❑	❑
22. Does the foreign market allow us to promote and advertise our imported products?	❑	❑

While a "no" answer to any of the above questions doesn't automatically eliminate the potential for success, it should certainly give the reader cause for reflection before proceeding.

Commonality and Conflict: Reading the Target

Like shooting an arrow, wanting to hit the target market is much easier than actually doing it. What appears to be a simple task turns out to involve great skill and preparation. This is true of both domestic and international marketing. Although it shares a great deal in common with its domestic variant, international marketing takes the archery analogy several steps further.

THE TARGET IS ALWAYS MOVING

The international marketplace is extremely dynamic, some may even say volatile. Just a brief look at the purchasing power of China or Brazil five years ago should give a good idea of how quickly a marketeer must react. New products, new competitors, and the nouveau riche flood the marketplace at various times, all frantically searching for each other.

NO TWO TARGETS ARE EXACTLY ALIKE

What one culture finds fascinating another finds boring. A popular brand name in one country is a swear word in another. A fair price here is gouging over there. The "bull's eye" isn't always in the center.

EACH TARGET MAY REQUIRE A SPECIFIC ARROW

Cultures may share a desire for a general type of product, such as automobiles or air conditioners, but the specifics will vary greatly—size, shape, color, voltage, or numerous other modifications may be required. The change could be as small as a switch from red to blue or as large as redesigning the chassis. If you want access to the market, you may have to retool.

THE DISTANCE TO EACH TARGET IS DIFFERENT

Doing business directly across your border has one set of problems. Doing business on the other side of the world has another set entirely. Communications, logistics, and quality control all require greater attention as distance increases.

NOTE: Effectiveness decreases in proportion to the distance from the domestic market. Stronger bowmen—and larger companies—are better at hitting distant targets.

THE CROSSWINDS CHANGE WITHOUT NOTICE

Besides the changes brought about by consumer volatility, factors such as politics, war, climate and religion can all wreak havoc on your aim. Because they're all taking stage outside of your regular physical and cultural boundaries, you're less likely to be able to predict their arrival.

NOTE: Maintaining a constant flow of information from the foreign market will assist in predicting these "windage" problems.

CHAPTER 3

The Dimensions of International Marketing

SHEAR THE SHEEP, BUT DON'T FLAY THEM.

— DUTCH PROVERB

MARKET WISDOM is millennia in age and prodigious in size. Like the preceding aphorism, the best of this wisdom is the result of clear-headed observation filtered through common sense. Keeping marketing in perspective requires the practitioner to look both backward at the forces that shaped today's markets and forward to where those forces are propelling new prospects. Many marketeers fail to realize that much of the groundwork and research have already been laid for them; they're best advised to view the future by standing on the shoulders of those who preceded them. "Don't reinvent the wheel, put new tires on it" is a common saying in marketing, one that admonishes the listener to learn from history, not repeat it before moving forward. This chapter will give the reader essential background for understanding the complexity and scope of international markets.

Defining Market Conditions: Money Talks

Human beings have always traded among themselves, with each side of a trade believing they stood to gain by the transaction. Originally goods were traded for other goods (my two chickens for your pail of milk) in a process called bartering. Eventually, goods were traded for services (my two chickens in exchange for your medical recommendations). Much of what went on in the marketplace was (and still is) a matter of perception. I believe your pail of milk is of greater value to me than my two chickens and therefore I'm willing to relinquish the chickens. You, of course, believe the opposite.

Money soon came along to replace the barter and it became a medium of exchange. Money also created a wider range of bargaining options (it's very difficult to make change with a live chicken). Money originally had some intrinsic value (gold, silver, copper); it gradually came to serve as a promissory note for the delivery of goods and services. Once everything was "priced" in terms of money (rather than chickens or milk), a new burden of proving value was placed firmly on the seller. The buyer had a set value for money and the seller had to prove that a product was worth that monetary value. Although there were extreme cases where buyers had to convince sellers that money has value (e.g., war-ravaged economies), the marketplace demanded (for the most part) that the seller do the convincing and the buyer the believing. Sellers would bring products to market hoping to attract buyers equipped with money. This was the birth of marketing, but it wasn't an equal relationship. The sellers might do a great deal of talking, but money always had the last word.

The Dawn of Exchange Rates: Money "Walks"

For many centuries, there was no guarantee that a single country would have a single currency. Localities minted specie or printed their own scrip, thereby complicating both the concept and practice of the marketplace. When different localities traded, both the value of the products and the currency were open to discussion. Even the amount of precious metal in coins was subject to dispute. In many ways, the burden of proving value was redistributed almost back to the level of bartering. National currencies put an end to this for internal trade purposes and reburdened the seller with all marketing responsibilities. Once trade across national borders or among city-states became prevalent, the old questions of value were resurrected. Since no nation was willing to give up its right to print or mint its own money, currency exchange rates had to be agreed upon. Gold and silver figured prominently in international trade due to their seeming universal value but, as happened before, purity was always in question.

Over time there was a movement toward the use of paper money for international trade. This made currency supply and transport easier, but without the backing of precious metals (as is the case today), paper scrip was valued (or backed) only by the "full faith and credit" of the issuing country. A powerful country could say that its paper money was worth more than a weaker country's scrip. This led to "strong" and "weak" currencies and onto the latter day nomenclature of "hard" and "soft" (for use when describing a nation's ability to back their scrip). The marketing of a nation's goods and services is heavily tied to this currency valuation. The "power" behind a currency is purely economic as many of the strongest currencies come from militarily weak but economically vibrant nations (e.g., Germany and Japan). Having only military power means little in international trade, as is evidenced by the almost eternal weakness and longtime inconvertibility of Russia's ruble.

One of the hardest of the "hard" currencies, the U.S. dollar, is issued not just by the only military superpower but by the world's largest economy. Emerging markets tend to have the weakest currencies and their markets can suffer enormous swings of value, as was seen in Southeast Asia at the end of the 20th century. This huge devaluation greatly affected the ability of Malaysian, Indonesian, Korean, and Thai companies to sell their products internationally at a profitable price. Sudden drops in their respective currency value, some as high as 40 percent, made goods from these countries very attractive to foreign buyers. However, when paid in foreign hard currencies, these nations' exporters received far less in payment for products that had been priced in their local currencies, due to exchange rates. Foreigners with strong currency got a lot more for a lot less. This effect unfortunately ricochets to the stronger economies, because their own products or raw materials are now priced far above the buying power of emerging Asia's consumers and manufacturers. Marketeers worldwide had problems until currencies and prices found a new equilibrium.

This effect on marketing created by currency fluctuation comes into play among even the strongest economies. The constant wrangling over trade deficits and surplus between the top economies, China and the United States, for instance, is a major problem for their marketeers. Currency rates will determine when, what, and how companies can bring products to the international marketplace. Political and cultural influences weigh heavy on marketing as well. It's important to understand that the determination of "value" for both product and currency is the oldest (and most visible) of the forces still at play in the international marketplace and one that ultimately reflects the other underlying forces.

International Business: Who's Playing, Who's Winning

International business takes place at many levels of commerce, with success and failure being distributed throughout the roster. Below is a listing of the types of companies (large, medium, and small) that have the largest involvement in international trade. The reader needs to understand the marketing process from both sides of the transaction, as each will act as both marketeer and target during their time in the marketplace.

- EXPORTERS These "sellers" are the backbone of international trade, as they bear the burden of proving value. Though generally associated with the shipping of goods, countries also export services, as the "service economies" of the United States and Great Britain are known to do to great success. Exports can run the gamut from mangoes to movies, shellfish to software, or coffee to cameras; the scale of operations can be massive or minuscule. If you're selling on the international scene, regardless of size, you are an exporter.
- IMPORTERS These are the "buyers" at the other end of the transaction, although they may not be the "end-users." Like exporters, they come in all shapes and sizes and frequently act as exporters as well. Because they hold the money end of the trade, all marketing efforts are ultimately directed at them. Even if it doesn't say so on your business card, if you're buying products internationally, you're an importer.
- FREIGHT FORWARDERS AND SHIPPERS These very capital-intensive service providers move products among the globe's nations by land, sea, and air. Even other services (such as software companies and movie studios) rely on freight forwarders and shippers to move the physical goods (computers and projectors) necessary to ultimately deliver the service. This highly competitive business can include enormous sea shipping lines, shipping brokers, consolidators, couriers, airmail delivery, railways, trucking companies, or even a cross-border bicycle cart. If exporters are the backbone of international trade, then freight forwarders and shippers are its arms and legs.
- TRANSPORTATION Whereas some companies move products, the transportation business moves people. Few doubt that the enormous rise in international trade is due in great part to the revolution in transportation. Trips that took weeks or months only a few decades ago now can be measured in hours or days. Operating abroad is no longer a long-distance affair as foreign companies regularly visit their representative offices in target markets. Though airlines and

airplane manufacturers are the main beneficiaries, other transporters such as railways have profited as well. Many emerging markets use international transportation as a welcome source of "hard" currency, and every country seeks the prestige of having its own national airline.

- HOSPITALITY Hospitality and tourism as an overall industry is now the world's largest employer, with one of every ten people on the planet involved in its operations. Not only does this new colossus of hotels, airlines, and restaurants supply travelers with diversion, but it also feeds the demand for international products through exposure. Once sampled on vacation or business trip, a product can be marketed in the visitor's home economy as a symbol of sophistication. All nations track their visitors via immigration statistics and savvy marketeers have a ready supply of new targets. Emerging markets build hotels before they even put in a telephone system as a means of securing hard currency from visitors. Tourism is so important to most nations that it's a primary focus of antigovernment groups: Kill tourism, kill the economy.
- TELECOMMUNICATIONS International business lives and breathes "information flow," and telecommunications is the pipeline. The marketing of "telecom" services and hardware has exploded in the last decade and yet still seems to be feeding an unquenchable demand. The internal development level and potential of a market is now measured in "teledensity" or telephones per 100 people. Moving information has become just as important as moving freight or people, and international calls are another source of hard currency for developing nations.
- INFRASTRUCTURE Bridges, roads, seaports, airports, waste disposal, potable water, flood control, and power plants are all key factors in the development of international business. The companies that market the goods and services necessary for their acquisition are usually the first ones into emerging markets, as well as key players in the developed world's effort to remain ahead of the pack. It's a simple formula: No infrastructure, no access to markets.
- ADVERTISING Advertising, along with its related services (such as media buying and graphic design), has taken on global proportions. Advertising agencies now have multinational offices and worldwide contracts. Though lucrative and acknowledged as essential to international business, many countries put severe restrictions on how this driving force in marketing can ply its trade. Advertising foreign goods in a local market is not without peril. It's often the unfortunate target of a government's or subculture's wrath and can be the flashpoint for greater problems.
- ENTERTAINMENT Music, videos, movies, theater, games, radio, television, newspapers, magazines and book publishing all fall under the entertainment industry title. It's one of the leaders in global marketing and, like advertising, can be the target of considerable resentment and censorship. Marketeers must take care not to have their entertainment product viewed as a form of cultural imperialism. Entertainment is a service that helps fill the coffers of many trade leaders (United States, Great Britain) but is slyly left out of trade deficit bickering. Without a doubt, entertainment is big business internationally.
- TECHNOLOGY The United States and Japan are the undisputed leaders in this marketplace. Manufacturing may be done worldwide, but the ideas flow primarily

from the two big players, with the United States dominating in both hardware and software. Technological advancement is the external yardstick used to measure an economy and "computer literacy" marks the stature of a national workforce. Every nation wants to get into this market.

- CURRENCY TRADERS Currency trading represents the biggest single market in actual value in the world. The equivalent of more than two trillion U.S. dollars changes hands daily worldwide, with the market open twenty-four hours a day, seven days a week. Many international banks make more from their arbitrage trades (the price differential between two markets for the same commodity—in this case, currency) than they do from commercial loans. This trading drives prices, exchange rates, and purchasing power with very little, if any, government oversight. Though often denounced by the governments of floundering economies, currency traders operate in the ultimate free market. It's a highly technical business with large international companies employing their own arbitrage departments to protect their profits from international sales.
- BANKERS With all of the money floating around the globe, someone has to keep track of it. Beyond just issuing letters of credit, bankers provide both the security and financial acumen needed for trade and were thus one of the first services offered to cross-border traders. Banks were the original issuers of paper money, although most currency now moves across borders electronically. Government-run national banks (e.g., Bank of Namibia), international banks (e.g., Credit Suisse), and local banks (e.g., VietCom Bank) all contribute to, and receive profits from, international business. Money is the blood of commerce and banks are the arteries through which it flows.
- MANUFACTURERS Manufacturers of all nations make the stuff of which marketing sings the praises, and they make a lot of it. Manufacturers can range in size from major automotive producers to peasants doing piece-work. Even the marketer of services relies on manufactured goods to deliver the physical component of the product. From computers to cosmetics to sunglasses, manufactured goods are still the greatest focus of international marketing and will be for some time.
- FOODSTUFFS This group includes agriculture, aquaculture, food processors, food chemists, and food geneticists. While some nations show declining populations, the world as a whole is expanding. Subsistence feeding is a concern in China and India (each with over a billion people), while Africa is constantly plagued with famine. Alarmingly, North Korea's continual bout with starvation is a major security concern for regional governments. More developed economies demand increasingly sophisticated foodstuffs, with no end to demand in sight. As will be seen in Chapter 6, food can be a serious cultural issue for marketeers, and no one should doubt its importance to international commerce and world peace.
- MEDICAL "Wealth makes health." There's a clear correlation between a nation's coffers and its coffins. Medicine production and medical services are one of the globe's largest businesses (only recently surpassed by hospitality) and they are concentrated in the high-end economies. Marketing "life" is a fairly easy task, and demand always outstrips supply. Marketeers need only set the right price.

- FINANCIAL SERVICES Like entertainment, many of the world's top economies neglect to include this in their published trade figures, concentrating on merchandise instead. It includes such multibillion dollar (yen, mark, pound etc.) industries as credit cards, business consultancy, "back office" accounting, and securities brokerages. This industry keeps international business flowing in an orderly fashion. There will be nothing but growth in this area.
- LEGAL SERVICES Some countries are law bound (France), some are overly litigious (United States), and others find commercial law bothersome (China). The attractiveness of joining the World Trade Organization (WTO), as well as sundry trade treaties (NAFTA, APEC, MercoSur), has given rise to a blossoming of international legal services. The new requirements for standardizing many aspects of international trade, along with the penalties for noncompliance, will provide decades of work for barristers, lawyers, and their support staff in Brussels and other centers for international commercial courts. Law firms are multinational now, though many countries restrict the role that foreign practitioners can play in domestic courts. Though potentially evoking somewhat more resentment than financial services, the legal profession is in an international "bull market."
- INFORMATION SERVICES Telecommunications may launch the satellites, lay the optic fiber, and sell the modems, but other companies supply the information. Database assemblers, search engines, statistical researchers, and archivists are all examples of information services. The Internet and its service providers (ISPs) have made databases available internationally, and marketeers were the first to take advantage of them. This element of the business depends on telecom and sophisticated infrastructure to function globally, and every economy (even totalitarian ones) realizes that information is critical to commerce. The old phrase was "No news is good news." The modern equivalent is "No news is no business." Believe it.

CHAPTER 4

International Trade

NO NATION WAS EVER RUINED BY TRADE.

— BENJAMIN FRANKLIN

ON THE TIME SCALE of human existence, the development of the nation-state is relatively new, and international trade probably commenced as soon as national borders were determined. As cultures (ethnic and political) bound themselves together, it was just a short additional step to start protecting their possessions and another quick leap to covet those of their neighbors. Flash ahead a few centuries and you find import tariffs and currency valuation. This chapter will look at the underlying motivations for international trade and some of the very human issues that govern those motivations. Marketeers must understand these larger scale incentives before approaching a target market.

Growth of International Markets: The Grass is Always Greener

Even the most prosperous countries seek to exchange goods and services with their neighbors. In fact, the greater the level of prosperity, the greater link to high performance in the global markets. It could be said that if a nation isn't competitive on the international stage, that nation is chasing mediocrity. Long gone are the days when self-sufficiency was measured by the amount of shelter, food, and water a nation could garner within its own borders. Minerals, fuels, services, technology, manufacturing processes, and education have been added to the "essentials," with no single nation having enough of what it now perceives itself to need.

It's an accepted fact that transportation and communication have had a great deal to do with the increase in cross-border trading. Travel abroad is no longer an experience limited to a few economic and political elites. Once a general awareness of another nation's products is in place, demand can be readily sparked. International marketeers have been this spark and have led the drive toward the globalization of business. Though feared by many and resented by some, globalization is an irresistible tide that shows no sign of ebbing. The explosive growth in international trade that has occurred in recent years has raised millions of people out of poverty, though millions more wait their chance.

Pride, Prosperity and National Industries

International trade is not without its detractors and many of the nay-sayers have reasons that aren't completely based in the rationale of economics. Viewing globalization as a threat to homegrown prosperity is a universal pre-occupation of demagogic politicians and competition-fearing businesses. Foreign companies are portrayed as predatory and conniving while domestic firms are painted as having the country's best interests at heart. This ploy can work because most nations (perhaps all) have a sense of national pride about certain products.

Some industries (such as auto production and steel smelting) are considered benchmarks in a nation's advancement. These "prestige" industries are sometimes put into production very early in development as a show of pride to neighbors. By way of example, Indonesia's attempt at creating a "national car" seemed to analysts as a bit premature in a country that is primarily agrarian. The move has taken a toll on the economy, and it's made it difficult for foreign auto manufacturers to market their own wares here, as the Jakarta government seeks to coddle its infant producer.

Industrial pride isn't restricted to the emerging markets, as can be seen in Great Britain's intransigence in the face of "mad cow disease" and the effect on its exports. Beyond the economic loss of destroying thousands of diseased cattle, much time was lost seeking to assuage the hurt pride of an industry so intrinsic to the country that "John Bull" is a national symbol. British beef is highly protected by government sanction and is a continual source of controversy between the United Kingdom and its continental counterparts. National pride, not dispassionate commercial thought, continues to protect Japan's farmers, France's vintners, the United States' microchip makers, Brazil's coffee growers, and virtually everything in China.

NOTE: Marketeers must understand and take advantage of this pride factor when attempting to enter a market. It can't be eradicated but it can be out-maneuvered. No market is completely closed or completely open. A marketeer's job is to find a place to put "the thin edge of the wedge" that will pry things open.

Absolute and Comparative Advantage

I CAN DO ANYTHING YOU CAN DO . . . MAYBE BETTER

An educated and energetic workforce can produce any product if given the raw materials necessary. Yet most nations buy finished goods and services from each other rather than the components to produce their own. This is due to the fact that the exporting nation has an advantage over the importer for a particular product. The exporter may simply do it better and in greater quantity, as is the case in Vietnam's importation of Danish brewing equipment for local beer production. Vietnam could produce their own equipment but not at the same price as Denmark. This is an example of a "comparative advantage." Other times, as occurs when Sweden imports Indian tea, sometimes a country simply can't produce a reasonably priced product at all, in this case due to geography, thereby relinquishing "absolute advantage" to a foreign marketeer.

Absolute advantage can be the result of climatic, educational, or developmental factors but is usually the result of the economies of scale that the exporter brings to bear. Anyone can make microprocessor chips if they're willing and able to invest the trillions of yen necessary, but why not use those resources elsewhere? Marketeers love to find and exploit absolute advantage, but it's not all that common.

Comparative advantage, on the other hand, is quite common and is at the root of most international marketing plans. When the United States decided to buy 9mm Italian-made pistols to supply its military officers, they did so after being convinced by the Beretta Company that this weapon was better than any U.S.-made product at the same price. Comparative marketing advantage may take the form of quality, quantity, price, delivery, warranty, or service and can be maintained as long as the marketeer remains vigilant.

WARNING: Absolute and comparative advantage will get you into a market, but staying competitive is the only way to survive long-term. The Swedish may never grow tea, but the Vietnamese can eventually out-brew the Danes.

Coproduction and Trade: Buying Apples with Apples

International marketeers were quick to realize that countries often sell each other the same products. This is true for automobiles, textiles, shoes, music, foodstuffs, and, in the long-term, potentially any product. In many ways, this coproduction is the means by which nations determine comparative advantage as consumers decide which companies produce the best products for the best price. As the reader will see in the next chapter, governments (usually at the behest of troubled producers) often interfere in this "natural selection" process with tariff and trade restrictions. At this point the reasons but not the reactions to coproduction will be discussed.

Much coproduction is the result of fine-tuning the demands of consumers (which, as noted in Chapter 2, is referred to as segmentation). Shrewd marketeers can pinpoint the demands of consumers right down to the individual buyer or a major sub-group. Hence, although the United States produced and consumed much of the world's automobile supply in the 1970s, U.S. consumers were successfully targeted by Japanese manufacturers during that period as being ripe for market penetration. The Japanese took advantage of U.S. factories' inability to quickly and cheaply meet the demand for more fuel-efficient autos in response to OPEC's oil price increases. The overall U.S. automobile segment was subdivided into luxury, midprice, compact, and sub-compact, with the Japanese concentrating on the lower end to seize market share. At first just sold as imports, Japanese cars quickly became a major, if not dominant, feature in the U.S. car market; eventually, the Japanese built manufacturing plants inside their new market. Over time, U.S. companies did the same thing in Asia and Europe, while European manufacturers responded in kind with a concentration on the luxury segment.

Coproduction usually takes place between countries on good political terms and only involves products that a nation doesn't deem vital to its economic or military security. It should be stated that the word vital is interpreted against a backdrop of great political change, as can be seen in many nations' present-day coproduction of military goods. Culture also plays a big role in deciding which products a nation will reserve for itself, but this too can change very quickly. In China, for example, the move from Mao suits to Armani suits was lightning paced. A marketeer should understand that very few markets are so saturated that another subsegment can't be exploited, nor does any market remain closed forever.

NOTE: Being an astute observer of global economic, cultural, and political scenes is mandatory for success. Garnering and interpreting information are daily, if not hourly, processes. The spinning of the globe has produced its own "information slipstream" and international marketeers thrive in it.

Trade Among Nations: Out of Balance, Out of Sorts

The choice of which products to market abroad will depend a great deal on how your own nation views its trading partners and how those partners see themselves in relation to your domestic market. Understanding the "balance of trade" will not only affect your ability to penetrate a market but determine the long-term viability of your goods or services in the targeted segment.

Some nations buy more from foreign countries than they sell, some sell more than they buy from abroad, and a rare few have roughly equal amounts in each category. The United States regularly runs overall "trade deficits" (buys more) with its partners while its major rival and trading partner, Japan, continually has "trade surpluses" (sells more) when matching exports to imports of goods and services. The disparity between the two largest economies dispels the notion that deficits are always bad and that surpluses are necessarily good.

The United States spurs its economic growth via internal consumption and is the foremost "consumer society" in the world, with its citizens having a very small rate of savings (less than 15 percent) and a high rate of spending. Japan takes the opposite tack, preferring to maintain its markets with exports and downplaying consumerism (at least compared to the United States). Japanese citizens regularly bank upwards of 30 percent of their income. Because of this differing approach to foreign products, most of the world's marketeers, especially the Japanese, head straight for the U.S. market because of its ease of entry and consumer potential. Japan, meanwhile, continues to protect its producers with formal restrictions and informal distribution controls, although it has become somewhat more attractive to foreign firms as these restrictions have subsided. Additionally, while Japan's per capita income is slightly higher than the United States', the internal purchasing power of its currency is considerably less. Which market has the greatest long-term potential when viewed by a foreign firm? It should be clear that the respective governments of the two countries have made themselves extremely attractive to foreign marketeers through differing methodologies.

NOTE: No nation likes to be seen as a dumping ground for another nation's inferior or outmoded products, and all countries believe in reciprocity of trade. However, reciprocity isn't equality, and too much inequality has major ramifications for international marketeers of all levels.

CHAPTER 5

The Role of Governments

AN OPPRESSIVE GOVERNMENT IS MORE TO BE FEARED THAN A TIGER. — CONFUCIUS

MARKETEERS MUST UNDERSTAND that the world's markets are overseen by governments, and even "free" markets are subject to considerable legislation. Ideally, those governments set policies based on what they believe will serve the greatest number of their people to the greatest extent. Trade and its regulation are a source of tax income for governments, which also recognize that physical security is tied very closely to economic security. Not only does a strong economy generate funds for military expenditures but it also, via international trade, creates a bond of codependency that strengthens every nation through alliance. It's clear from history that trading partners often become military allies in times of trouble. It's equally clear from history that economic benefits that can't be won at the conference table are often decided on the battlefield. Marketeers must understand both the role of governments in trade and the motivation for that role.

Sovereignty, Prestige and Security: Our Market, Our Rules

The maintenance of national borders is the single-most-important element that separates international trade from domestic trade. Geography aside, no country applies the same level of restriction within its borders as it does when dealing with its neighbors. The ability to maintain, protect, and restrict entry across (or exit from) national borders isn't merely symbolic; it's a legal requirement of a nation's sovereignty. Failure to do so leaves it open to claims that it's not a country at all and is therefore subject to control by other parties.

Some countries have very tight control of their borders (Russia, China), making them military and commercial checkpoints. Others (Canada, the United States) take a far less stringent approach to the movement of people and products across their borders. The former examples believe themselves to be in great danger from foreign intervention, while the latter exhibit an almost recklessly open approach to foreigners. The difference in approach has a great deal to do with each country's view of their international prestige. Countries at the top of the economic heap tend to flaunt openness as a challenge to would be opponents. Lesser economies seek to protect every possible area of vulnerability by keeping foreign traders at bay.

The formation of the European Union (EU) has essentially consolidated many smaller, weaker economies with a few strong nations to form a larger "country" with a new centralized government. This new entity has free-flowing internal state borders and a restricted periphery facing nonunion members. Beyond simply forming a trading bloc similar to NAFTA (Mexico, Canada, United States), the EU has formed an entirely new entity out of dozens of separate (and formerly sovereign) economies that will eventually (they hope) have a single currency. Snidely nicknamed "The United States of Europe," it was formed solely to advance its membership's ability to compete in international trade, as the commercial well-being of almost 500 million people was at stake. Political sovereignty issues within the EU may be disputed for some time to come.

Populations always hold their governments responsible for the overall economic prosperity of a nation. So great is this responsibility that most revolutions have economic dissatisfaction at their base. Governments, in their turn, set customs duties and other cross-border trade restrictions based on their understanding of domestic and international markets, as well as on their ability to control currency flows. While there's little disagreement as to the general movement toward "market economies" throughout the world, each country has its own take on the philosophy.

Each nation's approach to their domestic and foreign markets is dictated by its requirement for border sovereignty, the belief in its own prestige, and a need to secure its physical and economic well-being. Marketeers must respect each government's individual responsibility to its people, both from a legalistic (their country, their rules) and a commercial angle (their demand, my supply).

NOTE: While no government is perfect, some do a better job than others of promoting international trade. Individual marketeers will waste a great deal of time and energy on a moral crusade, attempting to change a government's view on a particular trade topic. Let the big corporations and trade organizations handle these problems. Your job is to find out where your product fits into the current scheme and to exploit that segment.

Host Government Trade Barriers: You Can't Do That Here

The host government of your target market can throw up a vast number of roadblocks to your success—some of them quite arbitrary in appearance. Here are some government-formulated obstructions to look out for when researching a new foreign market.

TARIFFS

Import tariffs are the means by which a government, in the form of a customs office, controls the in-flow of foreign goods across its borders. It's a form of taxation and a source of revenue for the state. Rather than banning a certain product outright or letting it outcompete local producers, a nation makes its import prohibitively expensive, thus eliminating widespread acceptance. All nations have a sliding scale of tariffs for various categories of products and trading partners, with its "normal" rates often being referred to as Most-Favored-Nation (MFN) status. Imports from foreign countries held in disfavor pay in multiples of MFN rates proportional to that disfavor. Many emerging markets have rather arbitrary tariff rates, which they blame on the fluid nature of their economic development. Tariffs are subject to much political influence and favoritism. This aspect must be calculated into the total pricing portion of a marketing plan.

INSPECTIONS

No one disputes a government's right and duty to protect its citizens' health and welfare. This is certainly the case with foodstuffs, medical equipment, and farm animals. However, some inspections are performed with an eye toward delaying your product from reaching the marketplace. This can be a very important factor when it comes to perishable goods or those that are particularly time sensitive (e.g., publications). By slowing down the import process, governments protect their home producers without actually having a formal trade restriction. This tactic, like other nontariff barriers, is usually put into practice by economies seeking to diminish domestic consumption levels of foreign products until homegrown producers feel the playing field is level.

IMPORT LICENSING

Like inspections, import licensing is a legitimate function of government, whereby the product must be formally licensed by the importer's government and a fee paid by the importer. Where inspections control the product quality, licensing is used to control those involved on both sides of the transaction. It's a process subject to arbitrary rulings, and licenses are withheld (or "reconsidered") at the first sign of disgruntlement by local producers or bureaucrats. When used as a barrier, the granting of licenses is such an expensive and potentially corrupt practice that some goods in great demand end up being smuggled.

DISTRIBUTION

Distribution will be considered at length in Chapter 10 but warrants some consideration here. In a larger sense, distribution is every aspect of the network that exists between the original seller and the end-user. Many marketeers have found that all of their plans came to naught simply because local governments placed inordinate restrictions on distribution or because local distributors are inefficient. Often, the distribution layers are so thick that consumers can't afford the product once it has passed through the sundry middlemen and their add-on charges. Many international marketeers have found this to be a common problem in Asia, especially in highly developed Japan.

ENVIRONMENTAL CONTROLS

Increasingly, governments are protecting the environment within their borders, and much of that control takes place *at* those borders. Restrictions on packaging (amount, size, recyclability), product content labeling (chemical proportions), and pollution controls can be placed on foreign exporters before licensing will be granted. While every country has environmental standards, strictness is in direct proportion to wealth. Advanced economies (like Great Britain and Germany) are famous for their concern about their domestic well-being, as much of their environments were polluted by their former industrial emphasis. Their environmental "impact studies" and "green" product packaging requirements can drive a product from market as easily as bad pricing. Research and preparation are the keys to avoiding this problem, which often occurs after a product is in the marketplace, when lawsuits are filed by environmental activists. Emerging economies, eager to attract investment, are far more lax, but "environmental colonialism" is fast becoming a rallying cry in the developing world.

TECHNOLOGY TRANSFERS

A target company can insist that any joint venture, product importation or manufacture under license with a foreign marketeer must ultimately involve a transfer of technology (physical, process design, managerial, or otherwise). It's a way to "catch up" with competitors without expensive research or investment. Most developing markets insist on technology transfers if a product is to be sold within their national boundaries. There may be a "grace period" of several years while the transfer takes place. These same markets have the least stringent patent and copyright protection so theft or domestication is inevitable.

NOTE: Coca Cola's refusal to reveal its recipe to its local partner in India kept the beverage giant barred from that gigantic market for many years. As is true of business travel, if you can't afford to lose it, don't bring it with you.

CUSTOMS DELAYS

Even once a product is licensed it can be held at customs without a stated cause for extended periods. Software, music and videos are usually a target of this practice, and you can rest assured that illegal copying is rampant. Customs may also hold perishables for the purpose of bribery or to protect local markets. The only way to combat this is to solicit the involvement of embassy personnel in advance of the importation.

LOCAL PARTNERSHIPS

It's not unusual for a government to require the use of a local partner to represent your product or to "invest" in your business. At times, the local is declared to be the majority partner, regardless of the size of their investment. By mandating that a local receive a piece of the action, the government maintains local control of the business and hopes to gain a management education for its population as a form of technology transfer. Part of a solid marketing plan in such an environment requires the studied selection of the right partner. Keep in mind that in some countries (Indonesia, China, Vietnam), the government will *assign* a partner for certain industries.

LOCAL CONTENT REQUIREMENTS

If your plans include the construction or purchase of manufacturing plants overseas, you'll find that most governments require that you use some local companies as parts suppliers. No matter how efficient it may be for your business, you will not be allowed to simply import all the parts from your headquarters. While this requirement can be planned for, little can be done if local suppliers raise prices. This can occur when they're ready to push you out of the market and take over your facility, so vigilance and good government connections are required.

CONTRACT LANGUAGE

Contracts with foreign firms are typically binding in the dialect of the locality in which the contract will be executed. (Although you may have signed a translation as well, it's meaningless and unenforceable.) Before you sign anything make sure your own translators have gone through the document thoroughly. From one end of the economic scale to the other, local courts favor local businesses.

QUARANTINE

This process applies mostly to goods (such as live animals or foodstuffs) that are suspected of carrying disease or infestation. The goods are held at a controlled location until inspectors can determine whether they pose a health threat. Although the word *quarantine* literally means "40 days," there's no set time limit for the holding process on an international level. Some countries may use the quarantine process to hold materials they believe have deleterious cultural ramifications. Books, movies, tapes, periodicals, and CDs are some notable targets, with religious fundamentalist and politically isolated nations being the most regular practitioners of such quarantines.

QUOTAS

An import quota is a non-tariff barrier imposed by a government to restrict the quantity of imports it will take from certain national markets or exporters. It is also a means of keeping all of its trading partners happy. For instance, Government A will allot 20 percent of its entire importation of a product to each of five trading partners. This process can also be used to protect local producers from foreign trading practices (lower the quota of the most competitive exporter) or as a punishment for political problems between rival powers (lower or eliminate an entire nation's quota). Even the best marketeers can expect to suffer if their home government conflicts with the host officials.

NOTE: Poor economies see absolutely no advantage in granting foreign companies the same trading rights they're reserving for themselves. Marketeers from these foreign markets must realize that the quotas set by their home governments can be used as a countermeasure to pry open a target foreign market. Having good political connections at home is as important as having them abroad.

ANTI-DUMPING LAWS

These laws were instituted to prevent foreigners from selling products at extremely low prices into a market to drive out competition. This is called "dumping." Local competitors are the first to cry "foul," hoping to tie up a foreign firm in court, and the tactic usually works quite effectively. Only countries with sophisticated commercial law can use this type of legislation. The remainder resort to any and all of the tactics listed above to protect market share.

WARNING: It's surprisingly easy to prove "dumping," due to the widespread access to trade information. Your overseas competitors are well aware of what it costs you to produce and distribute a product. Selling "under cost" is a dangerous tactic in an information society.

Home Government Intervention: You Can't Do That There

It's rare for a country to attempt to stop its local companies from exporting. Even when they permit a steady outflow, governments maintain oversight and taxing rights. Marketeers, however, may have just as difficult a time handling their own government as they will the overseas variety. As is true of import laws, not all export requirements are written down in all countries and are therefore subject to "negotiation" and arbitrary enforcement. Research and good governmental relations are keys to keeping your product in the export pipeline.

EMBARGO

While there's much debate as to whether embargoes accomplish their political goals, there's little doubt that they have a disastrous effect on exporters. Blockade running is rarely part of anyone's marketing plan and long-term risk is high. Some (like the U.S. embargo of Cuba) are ignored after several years while others (the U.N. embargo of Iraq) are more stringently, though not completely, enforced.

NOTE: Marketeers must be aware of the political environment they work in and be prepared to calculate, as well as manage, risk.

NATIONAL SECURITY ISSUES

Some goods are considered too strategic militarily and economically to be freely marketed to other nations, regardless of the profit potential. These may include nuclear materials, strategic minerals, chemicals, computer chips, technical manuals, or military surplus. Countries that have these restrictions delineate them quite clearly, and violation is a criminal offense.

EXPORT TARIFFS

Governments tax exports primarily as a source of revenue and use the process as a means of promoting or punishing particular industries. These tariffs are, like import duties, a means of controlling flow and controlling businesses. Export duties can be highly negotiable in some countries and should be thoroughly investigated during the market planning stage. Many countries have set up export processing zones for foreign manufacturers, so that goods produced domestically for export will not be tariffed. These zones promote investment and job creation while protecting domestic manufacturers from direct competition.

EXPORT LICENSING

Like export tariffs, licensing is a flow control. It's often used as a means of denying a rival economy access to both raw and finished products without instituting a full embargo. Keep your eyes open and avoid political crossfire.

ANTI-REROUTING MEASURES

When embargoes and quotas are in place, exporters often try to reroute their products through less controversial areas and have the "country of origin" changed in the paperwork. Getting caught practicing this tactic can get an exporter in serious trouble with his home government.

JOB PROTECTION SENTIMENTS

Governments will often clamp down on their exporters when they detect that the products being exported will result in job losses for the domestic market. Heavy machinery and high-tech manufacturing equipment can be targeted. If export tariffs on your products don't exceed the gain from taxes derived from the potentially lost jobs, expect government intervention.

Formal and Informal Restrictions: Protecting Prosperity

Discussed above are the very formal and, for the most part, straightforward means by which governments control the marketing of their domestic producers, as well as that of foreign companies. Beyond these codified restrictions, there are a host of constraints—neither codified nor necessarily government enforced—that can affect the marketing of your product in foreign lands. These informal barriers (listed below) are more difficult to detect and, in many cases, harder to overcome than their more official counterparts.

PUBLIC RELATIONS

The number of public relations fiascoes committed by international companies is large, legendary, and the subject of several books. From poorly translated brand names to the lack of locally hired management personnel, bad public relations (and even worse, press relations) can sidetrack the best of products. Often these public relations disasters are engineered (or at least exacerbated) by market competitors, who make appeals to some or all of the other issues listed in this section.

NATIONALISTIC

Competitors, host government officials, and political activists are not beyond raising the cry that your marketing efforts are "bad for the nation," that they threaten its continued survival or strength. This barrier was used to restrict Australian wines in France, British movies in Argentina, and virtually any major Japanese product in the United States during the 1980s. It's a very powerful force and a difficult one to control.

RELIGIOUS

Religion plays a greater factor in business every year, with much of it centering around Islamic beliefs regarding profit taking and interest rates. However, many Christian fundamentalist groups have flexed their muscles as of late (e.g., the Disney boycott), with marked results. Because religion carries such an emotional impact, pure reasoning and factual presentation will do little to get your product back on track.

ETHNIC

As can readily be seen in Bosnia or Burundi, ethnic conflicts that are centuries old still burn hot. Belief that your product is ethnically dangerous or inferior can stymie your marketing efforts whether the accusations are true or not. Nestlé faced cries of racism over its sales of baby formula in Africa while many of the marketing problems faced by the makers of the Yugo were based on the fact that few people believed the Yugoslavians were capable of building a proper automobile. Overcoming ethnic stereotypes takes years of work and enormous amounts of money.

SOCIETAL

Some societies have a structure that simply will not accept certain products—at least right away. It may be a matter of taste (light beer in Germany) or social restriction ("adult" movies in Iran). Marketeers must often approach a market several times before they're permitted entry. Some industries are bound by edict not to promote foreign products. Canada's radio broadcasters, for example, are required by law to limit the playing of foreign-produced music as a means to promote Canadian culture.

SCIENTIFIC

Product lines that are radically innovative may have a difficult time overcoming the skepticism of the target market. Medicines, therapies, business software, securities, and the like suffer intense scrutiny (mostly justified) when entering foreign markets. It's best to assemble your proof beforehand and tailor its delivery to the target market.

ETHICAL

"End Apartheid" and "Remember Tiananmen Square" were both used as rallying cries to affect the marketing and profit generation of many products from South Africa and China as well as from companies that traded with them. Although both eventually resulted in some formal legislation, the ethical considerations started as grassroots, informal restrictions.

WARNING: It's a series of quick leaps from ethical concerns to political rancor to restrictive legislation. If a marketeer waits to take action at the end of the process, it may be too late.

ENVIRONMENTAL

Water pollution, endangered species, and alleged man-made global warming are very emotional concerns of very vocal groups, who often look for international companies to pillory. They are well-organized and zealous. If your product has any potential ill effect on the environment, you can expect major market resistance, even without restrictive legislation, once such effects are brought to light. Environmental action groups enlist anyone they can in their effort and are unabashed when it comes to emotionalizing an issue.

NOTE: Nine-year-olds wearing "Save the Dolphins" buttons did as much to reform tuna fisheries (and affect buying habits) as any law. Beware, and be aware of, self-righteous consumers. They carry their wallets next to their hearts.

EDUCATIONAL

Sometimes the greatest informal barrier is the educational level of large sectors of the target market's population. Massive sections of the globe are still illiterate and many more are innumerate. It's not unusual for a controlling government to wish the situation to remain in stasis. Even when educational levels aren't this low, many products, from cars to computers, have their own particular "learning curve." Training must be part of your marketing plan when educational levels are key to a product's acceptance.

Trading Blocs: The Invisible Handcuff

In the last few decades, nations have bound themselves together in non-military regional alliances that are designed (at least ostensibly) to promote trade. However, those that join such trading blocs have recognized the interdependence of trade among their immediate neighbors and use the blocs to prevent outside marketeers from having regional free-flow. Blocs essentially restrain foreign traders from assailing the weaker members by protecting them with numerical strength. Deal with one, deal with all. Unlike Adam Smith's famous natural market forces, which act as the "invisible hand" to move all markets to eventual equilibrium, blocs work as regional handcuffs to control and sometimes eliminate trade in certain products.

International marketeers need to be aware of the membership and goals of such trading blocs, so that their plans can be tailored not just to a single country but perhaps to an entire region. Listed below are some of the major trade organizations.

1. APEC (Asia-Pacific Economic Cooperation)
2. ASEAN (Association of Southeast Asian Nations)
3. NAFTA (North American Free Trade Agreement)
4. MERCOSUR (Argentina, Brazil, Paraguay, Uruguay, Chile, Bolivia)
5. FTAA (Free Trade Area of the Americas)
6. OPEC (Organization of Petroleum Exporting Countries)
7. EU (European Union)
8. SAARC (South Asian Association for Regional Cooperation)
9. SAPTA (South Asian Pacific Trade Association)
10. CIS (Congress of Independent States)
11. AFTA (ASEAN Free Trade Association)

The WTO and International Intervention: One World, One Court

One of the most influential international governmental bodies to affect marketing has been the World Trade Organization. As an outgrowth of the General Agreement on Tariffs and Trade (GATT), the WTO and its enforcement arm, the World Court, have been set up as an oversight body to rule on international trade disputes. Countries and companies accused of unfair trading practices can be brought before the court for trial and potential punishment (usually fines).

Membership in the WTO isn't open to every nation, as there are certain guidelines that must be met prior to acceptance. The greatest benefit is the low (if any) tariffs on trade among association members. The goal of the organization is the eventual removal of all import/export tariffs. The membership and their companies must also conform to Generally Accepted Accounting Principles (GAAP) as laid out by the WTO, so that each nation's "books" may be accurately compared with those of other members. Many countries have been denied membership over this issue, as it greatly affects the valuation of national assets.

The effect on marketeers is that they can no longer just be concerned with local court rulings in the targeted markets (though such courts usually have little enforcement capability over foreign nationals). The stakes are much higher nowadays and the WTO has a very wide reach. Market or membership banning is a possibility for egregious violators, and business deals can easily become international political problems (as happened with France's Total oil venture in Iran). Commerce usually comes out on the short end when politicians become involved; marketeers are forewarned to steer clear of WTO violations. The organization is still nascent, so it's best to keep current with their rulings and legislation.

Overseas Risk Management: Read The Map . . . and Heed It

Marketing abroad can be a very risky pursuit as the legal landscape in some countries is extremely fluid. Laws are sometimes uncodified and even when they are, interpretation can be arbitrary. Governments certainly have the right, and in many cases the duty, to intervene in businesses or trade being conducted by foreign nationals. However, there are some other governmental activities that go beyond the law (or at least blur it) for which the international marketeer must be prepared.

DOMESTICATION

Entering a new market with a new product can often perplex local authorities who, not seeing the potential, may initially grant a marketeer carte blanche to operate. Success does attract attention, so it's not unusual, especially in the emerging markets, for successful foreign companies to suddenly discover that they have a new partner. The partner may know absolutely nothing about your business and may bring nothing in the way of investment. Regardless, the government may insist that as much as 51 percent of the company be put under the control of the new associate or that the associate at least be given veto power over company decisions.

It can be the result of government greed, pressure by competitors who feel you were given a "sweetheart" deal, or sudden xenophobia with accompanying fears of exploitation. Multimillion dollar projects can be forced into renegotiation well after a project has been active, as happened to the Enron hydroelectric project in India; antiforeigner sentiments forced the American company to shut down construction while the deal was restructured to favor local partners. Local governments usually wait until a company is too committed to walk away before using the domestication ploy.

TAXATION

Governments of all sizes and economic standings view business as a source of tax revenue. Unlike the tactic of domestication, taxation allows the government to receive a portion of a foreign company's operation directly, without the sham of a proxy. Some authorities lure foreign businesses with initially low tax rates or "grace periods," with the full intention that once the company has been committed and is operating successfully, tax rates will soar almost to the point of being confiscatory.

EXPROPRIATION

During periods of extreme political stress or due to inordinate levels of greed, governments will take over a foreign company outright. The former motivation still occurs quite regularly in war-torn countries (such as those in eastern Europe or central Africa). The potential is always there for any company operating in foreign territory, war-torn or not, when internal or international political tempers rise. The latter cause for expropriation has rarely been seen since the early 1980s and has been usurped by the somewhat more subtle domestication.

SPONSORED COMPETITION

Like domestication, sponsored competition puts a favored local company or person under a government aegis. These "competitors" are given substantial financial and distribution aid in the hope that they'll unseat the foreign firm that first brought the product to market. Often, these sponsorships are further aided by technology transfers that were mandated by the government as part of allowing the foreign company to operate within its borders. Transfers are handed over directly to local companies that will exploit them without paying fees or royalties.

In a variation on this tactic, local partners have also been known to siphon off funds and materials from a joint venture with a foreign firm, in order to set up a competing company. Local government officials then turn a deaf ear to the complaints or lawsuits brought by the foreigners.

BRIBERY

Government officials seeking bribes from foreign firms is a worldwide problem. It can take the form of a storefront shakedown by the local police, special "processing fees" by customs officials, or "requests" for campaign donations for incumbent politicians. Bribery in some economies becomes the grease that makes the wheels of commerce turn more easily. Anyone engaged in international marketing must be prepared to deal with both the seemly and unseemly versions of such requests.

RISK MANAGEMENT

In all of the cases stated above, marketeers have to learn how to manage risk. The first step is recognizing potential risk through proper pre-entry research (Chapter 8). Once the level of risk has been determined in a particular market (it exists to some degree in all markets), the best possible preventative is engendering and maintaining good "relations" with the pertinent government officials. Marketeers should realize that *realpolitik* can become *machtpolitik* very quickly if a foreign company falls into disfavor with a host government. Risk management is an ongoing process and requires eternal vigilance.

CHAPTER 6

The Role of Cultural Forces

CUSTOM RULES THE LAW. — LATIN PROVERB

THE MOST IMPORTANT factor in determining whether your product, be it goods or services, is compatible with a particular market is the proper and thorough understanding of the target culture. Cultures can be painted with very broad strokes or minutely dissected. The more layers that are peeled away, the greater the market segmentation available. It's truly a case in which knowledge is power—marketing power. Because this book deals with international marketing, "culture" will be viewed as the total pattern of human behavior embodied in a nation-state and its internal subdivisions.

Language: The Importance of Communication

VERBAL

Most of the world's national boundaries are set along linguistic perimeters. Often, these perimeters have a physical form (a mountain range, a river, an ocean) that permitted the language to develop in solitude and kept it separate from neighboring tongues. Once travel over those boundaries became possible and desirable, so did trade, and the first marketing problem was confronted almost immediately: communication.

A loaf of bread may be *pan, bahn mi, brot,* or *mianbao* depending on where one travels. Once the name is settled upon, trying to trade for a loaf of bread brings on a whole host of other problems and nomenclature. Establishing a common value for goods is best served by speaking a common language. Though pointing and pantomiming may work when exchanging milk for bread in the short run, modern marketeers have neither the time nor the inclination for such activity.

While English has become a default language for doing global business, it's just that—something used in the absence of a better tool. Wise marketeers learned early on in their careers that speaking the local language, to some degree, gave them a marked advantage over less polyglot competitors and provided genuine insight into their target market. Besides enabling the foreign businessperson to present products and establish value, language opens the door to the interior of the target culture. First-hand assessment of all the motivational factors present (including those that trigger purchases) in any given society can only come about after the language has been mastered.

Social interaction can take place on a more intimate level (once translators are taken out of the loop), and foreign marketeers can be introduced to all of the nuances that make up a social fabric. Festivals, parties, art, literature, music, and even food take on greater meaning and, most importantly for our purposes, marketing significance. For some nations (e.g., France, China, Brazil,) language is seen as the essence of the culture without which no other aspect of that culture can be truly understood. This is true to a large degree for all cultures.

A great deal about interpersonal relationships is revealed by language. For instance, egalitarian cultures like the United States make no linguistic distinction between intimate and formal relationships in matters of address. You are *you,* whether I've known you for five minutes or five decades. In Spanish, the formal *usted* is used until familiarity permits the use of *tu*. The rule in French and German is equally stringent. This speaks volumes about these four societies and about how they'll accept strangers—or their products. Asian languages reveal similar relationship undertones with their vast number of honorifics involving extensive reference to gender, age, family relationship, and rank ("esteemed older sister," "number one son").

Names are, of course, important in every language and for marketeers, brand names are paramount (see Chapter 9). Arriving in a new market with a great new product that's saddled with a bad brand name could spell disaster. Even established international companies have problems with their names: Siemens is rarely spelled correctly anywhere but Germany, and few people in east Asia can pronounce Nestlé properly, nor can Westerners pronounce Hyundai. Understanding the importance of language was surely key in naming the Bic Pen. Luckily its inventor, Mr. Bich, had some savvy marketeers.

PHYSICAL

Gestures, carriage, proximity of speakers, eye contact, and smiling all play key roles in a culture's use of language. Like the words themselves, the physical aspects of communication all play a big part in negotiations and advertising for an international marketeer. What passes for acceptable movements in one culture may be considered uncouth in another or even overtures to physical violence.

- GESTURES Cultures around the globe have gained the reputation for "speaking with their hands" as well as their tongues. These gestures may emphasize particular points of the conversation as well as show the emotional intensity of the speaker. And the same gestures often have different meanings within different cultures. In France, for example, the shoulder shrug expresses a lack of interest in or disgust with the subject matter at hand. That same gesture in the United States means the person doesn't understand or has no comment. In China, a shoulder shrug is almost never seen as a linguistic nuance and is considered a form of chiropractic therapy. Finger pointing is another gesture common to many cultures and spurned by others. In France, the gesture is emphatic and the digit is often poked into the chest of the opposing speaker or alternately pointed skyward in an allusion to high-mindedness. In the United States, finger pointing is either a beckoning or the prelude to an accusation. In China, as in most of Asia, it's considered the height of rudeness, as people rarely wish to be singled out in public.
- CARRIAGE Marketeers (like everyone else) will be judged by their posture when negotiating or selling, as "carriage" is a physical representation of a person's self-esteem. Carriage also plays a large role in product advertising if the depiction of consumers is involved. As with gestures, carriage may be interpreted differently by different cultures. A casually dressed, unshaven male slumped in a chair may indicate a Silicon Valley millionaire programmer in the United States or a top-

flight artist in France. In China, that same carriage means poverty and spiritual disharmony. Marketeers are "on" all the time when they're working overseas. It's best to present an image that's most favorable to the target market.

- PROXIMITY Each culture has its own rules about "personal space." Understanding that space is essential to a full understanding of a culture. Russians, for instance, are an outgoing people who tend to stand very close to business counterparts, often touching them lightly during conversations and exchanging hugs during greetings. The Japanese are far more reserved; they keep business conversations quite formal and counterparts at some distance. Argentinians begin with very formal and distant posturing but quickly warm, reducing distance as the conversation (or negotiation) progresses. The Russians will be offended if you're standoffish, the Japanese will go into shock if you hug them, and the Argentinians will think you presumptuous if you're too informal at first.

NOTE: Marketeers must be able to change styles as easily as they change time zones if they wish to compete internationally. Before a market accepts your product, they have to accept you.

- EYE CONTACT Eye contact, or the lack thereof, can greatly affect a marketing effort when face-to-face meetings are involved. In advertising as well, the eyes of the pictured subject, and where those eyes look, can make or break a product. (One reason the Marlboro Man is so universally recognized is that diverse cultures all read positive, but different, messages into the cowboy's distant stare. Some see serenity, others ambition, and still others independence.) In some cultures, "looking someone in the eye" is a sign of honesty and disclosure; in others, it may provoke a fight or be interpreted as an invitation for intimate relations. Steady, direct eye contact early in a relationship (business or otherwise) is considered disrespectful in many cultures, especially when elders are involved.

NOTE: "Looking" and "seeing" are separate functions when conversing. Often, you'll be shown more by not looking.

- SMILING Businesspeople from the United States are always being derided for their constant smiling and cheery faces, while the Japanese have been saddled with the image of frowning inscrutability. The former aren't universally chipper, nor are the latter solidly glum. Smiles are an expression of business and cultural traditions. Americans, who have had great success with few setbacks, believe that work should be fun. The equally successful Japanese, having brought their nation back from near destruction, see business as a very serious matter.

LESSON: Products advertised with smiling faces or humor may produce the wrong reaction in the targeted market. Every culture has specific topics that it feels warrant a serious tone.

TRANSLATION

Marketeers can't master every language needed to operate on the international scene; at some time or another, they'll have to use translators. This will be a key issue during negotiations. (Greater detail on this topic can be found in a related text, *International Negotiating*, World Trade Press, 2009). Here are a few tips for choosing the right translator and for handling translated materials.

- Translators should either be natives of or highly experienced in the target market. They must act as both cultural and linguistic interpreters and can be essential in filling in the gaps of your cultural research.
- During negotiations, hire your own translators rather than using those supplied by counterparts. You have to be able to trust the translators' insights and recommendations above and beyond their actual translations.
- Brief translators thoroughly on your marketing goals and any technical terms necessary for getting your points across. Translators are an extension of your marketing plan and must be well-informed.
- All written materials (letters, faxes, emails, business cards, presentation charts) and advertising collateral should be translated and then reviewed by a native speaker other than the original translator. Poorly translated materials can cause irreparable harm to your marketing effort—by making it appear sloppy or by insulting your target market.

A FINAL NOTE ON LANGUAGE: Every culture appreciates an attempt to learn some of their language. Even when a counterpart speaks your language well, you (as a smart marketeer) should learn a few phrases of a counterpart's language to emphasize your interest in the culture. Don't worry about making a few mistakes. All the current trade "experts" have made lots of them.

Local Customs: Faux Pas, Vrai Pas (False Step, True Step)

Long ago, successful marketing people saw the close connection between custom and customers: The way to turn people into customers is to make your product part of their customary actions. Sometimes whole industries are created around a custom (Halloween costumes) and at other times, customs are created around a product (Valentine's Day cards). In both cases, marketeers took advantage of the basic human need for ritual. Cultures distinguish themselves by their rituals, even when they share a common language. By no stretch of the imagination would anyone believe that a product that was successful in Spain would automatically be a hit in Mexico. The markets are as distinct as Germany and Italy.

Gathering knowledge about local custom is best done up close and first hand. (More about research will be discussed in Chapter 8.) Getting "on the ground" information is well worth the cost that it may entail. If your first trip to a new country is for the purpose of selling a product rather than investigating the *potential* to sell one, you may be disappointed. Unless you arrive with the cure for cancer, your chances of success are quite minimal. You have to learn how, why, and when the target market goes about its business in order to make your product fit.

Traditional holidays, vacation periods, mythology, work schedules, use of color, purchase decision makers, gender roles, standard buying patterns, age demographics, views on foreign merchandise, and family structure all dictate to some degree how goods and services are consumed. Marketeers must also be informed about customary behaviors, as such knowledge will be vital during negotiations. Understanding the motivations of counterparts when cutting a deal may well be the key factor in a successful contract negotiation. Knowing when to bow, shake hands, or make a toast may not change the quality of your product, but it will keep you on good terms with the marketplace until you have a chance to sell.

EXAMPLE: When first-hand information would have helped: "Nine Lives Cat Food" has never sold well in Hispanic cultures. They believe their cats have only seven lives!

History: Bearing the Burdens of the Past

Every country and culture, whether it's as ancient as India or as young as the Czech Republic, has a history that will greatly affect both the market and the marketeer. A market that has been heavily exploited in the past by foreigners (or even colonized) will turn a predictably skeptical eye toward any overseas company seeking new sales territory. It may even refuse products that could greatly benefit the society. Understanding that history will enable a marketeer to approach the culture in a more subtle manner, and it will certainly cause an adjustment of schedule. On the other end of the spectrum, a culture that has been marked by independence for some time will have few fears of foreign operations and may find the subtle approach far too lackluster and slow.

Marketeers may bring their own burdens to the process and should take care to separate themselves, at least emotionally, from their personal and cultural history. Oftentimes, this includes racial prejudices that are difficult to shake, earlier political disagreements that have never been fully settled, or old, unhealed war wounds.

Let's look at the race issue first. Companies with Caucasian marketing personnel returning to postapartheid South Africa are generally plagued with a feeling that they "owe" something to the new black majority government. It's a completely self-generated debt as the government is, in reality, overjoyed that investment has returned after the long embargo. However, this joy doesn't prevent South African companies from taking advantage of their counterparts' guilt feelings when it's time to cut a deal.

On the political front, the relationship between Vietnam and the United States is a prime example of two sets of marketeers misinterpreting each other's history and culture when it came time to do business. Following in the wake of the bloody two-decade war that ended in 1975, the United States and Vietnam finally reopened trade in 1994. The Vietnamese assumed that the American business community would heap investment on them to make up for past wrongs, while the Americans thought they would be welcomed as the saviors of Vietnam's floundering economy. Most of America's marketeers sent to Vietnam were small children during the war, and the conflict had little bearing on their lives. Vietnam's decision makers, on the other hand were primarily veterans of the conflict and saw it as the key element of the relationship. Neither side paid attention to the other's view of history and the results were decidedly disappointing for almost everyone.

LESSON: Marketing success and failure are much like history. They keep repeating themselves.

Education: Getting the Market Ready for Your Product

Certain goods and services require that the end-user has attained a specific level of education. One of the factors that continues to perplex (especially those marketeers from Western, developed economies) is that so many countries place restrictions on who and how many people can be educated. In some cases, it runs along gender lines, with women receiving little more than basic reading, writing, and math skills; many orthodox Islamic and Confucian countries follow this path. Other nations distribute education via a class or caste system and make it absolutely taboo for lower social echelons. Still others (as is true in many parts of Africa) mandate that education be portioned out on the basis of tribal ethnicity.

Marketeers should recognize that beyond these clear-cut examples, nations of all stripes have educational disparities. It may be the result of unequal opportunity, interest, or outcome, but the effect on marketing will be the same: not everyone will be able to fully utilize or understand your product, at least initially. Acknowledge that fact and plan accordingly.

Religion: God and the Marketplace

Though fundamentalist governments use religion as a tool to keep supposedly corrupting products out of their marketplaces, religious feelings among individual consumers and groupings must also be a consideration. Movies and books are regular targets of religious controversy, but services like banking and childcare can also cause rancor. Islam views banking, at least the standard loan/interest-cost type, as a form of usury forbidden by the Koran, while strict Christian sects see commercial childcare as an assault on family life.

Goods also can suffer from either religious backlash or simple neglect. Jewish communities, with hygiene concerns about pig products, will be unlikely pork barbecue consumers. Nor will Hindus, prone to cremating their dead, find much use for hermetically sealed metal caskets. Buddhism, though more philosophy than religion, has few serious practitioners who flock to meat-intensive fast-food dining. Selling chrome polish to the Amish, dance lessons to Baptists, or electric shavers to the Sikhs will be similarly disastrous.

RELIGIOUS SEGMENTATION

Some religious groups hold enormous sway within a culture even when their numbers put them in a minority nationwide. Catholics in the United States, for example, influenced restaurant menus with their strictures on eating meat on Fridays; fried fish and clam chowder are still standard Friday features on many menus, decades after the Vatican lifted the restrictions. Similarly, Jewish holidays regularly affect buying patterns in major European and North American cities, and Islam's Ramadan is showing signs of similar influence. Chinese and Vietnamese communities dispersed around the globe have similar economic influence with the celebration of the Lunar (Tet) New Year. Lastly, the worldwide celebration of Christmas has become, for many Christians and non-Christians alike, much more of a marketing event than a holiday of religious significance.

International marketeers may find that moving into a new country with a proven product will require a great deal of customization to avoid religious turmoil. This will be true for both small operators and global giants. When McDonald's set its sights on breaking into the Indian market in the mid-1990s, the corporation soon realized that the Hindu interdict against eating beef would make most of the fast-food giant's menu untenable. In place of the famous Big Mac, the company created a new item—the Maharajah Mac, made with religiously acceptable mutton. In another major bow to religion, Turner Broadcasting (founders of the global CNN) made concessions to the Indonesian government when attempting to market the twenty-four-hour-a-day Cartoon Channel. Because the nation is primarily Islamic, the company wisely agreed to eliminate all Porky Pig cartoons from its Indonesian satellite broadcast.

HOLIDAY MARKETS

Entering any market will require some adjustment to religious activity, if only from the viewpoint of buying patterns. Religious holidays can greatly promote spending, as is the case with Christmas, or cause a slowdown, as happens during Ramadan's fasting periods. Some holidays and practices can promote the purchase of specific items (Easter flowers, Lunar New Year cakes) or just a sudden increase in the purchase of general products (new clothing for parties, fuel for traveling). The hospitality and tourism industries are greatly affected by religious holidays and marketeers with products related to those industries need to be highly sensitive to this issue.

NUMEROLOGY

The proper timing for entering a market may also be dictated by religious beliefs or holidays. Numerology still plays a large role in the developing world; the day of the week or month or even the year can be viewed as being particularly auspicious, or not, for starting a new venture. If your company or product line has numbers in its name, you may find that local acceptance is based on those numerals. The widespread acceptance of 555 cigarettes in China or 333 beer in Vietnam has much to do with the luck associated with these numbers in their respective cultures. Numbers chosen for price can have similar influence. Large ticket items (e.g., real estate sales) can be affected by something as seemingly innocuous as the numerical composition of a building's address; petitions to change them are received regularly. Even the supposedly high-tech and unsuperstitious United States has numerous buildings in which the "unlucky" number 13 is skipped as a floor designation.

LESSON: Think long and hard about the local implications of your brand name.

DATES

Lunar and seasonal considerations have religious underpinnings in all societies, with greater than average influence in Asia—China and Southeast Asia having the highest. Dates for signing contracts, holding negotiations, and opening businesses are as much dictated by the lunar calendar as they are by business necessity. Shintoism in Japan has a similar influence. Year designations (year of the rat, year of the ox, etc.) hold particular significance for business, as do the addition of certain words in company names (gold, luck, tiger, harmony). Sub-Saharan African cultures place a great deal of emphasis on animal references in brands or company names (Elephant Beer, Golden Lion Corporation), as these words have ceremonial significance. The world's auto industry has done the same for many years (Jaguar, Cougar, Viper, Lynx), although the religious connection is long suppressed. International marketeers may find that their joint venture partner will be very insistent on choosing just the right name and opening date for a project.

Wise marketeers may also decide to enlist the aid of local priests, monks, and holymen for the purposes of "blessing" their new operation or product line. A hallowing by a group of lion dancers, a *feng shui* practitioner, a rabbi, the local mullah, a respected bonze, or the regional monsignor may be the best piece of promotion available. This bit of public relations will not only keep your product or service in good stead with the local consumers (many of whom may avoid an unconsecrated business) but also hedge your bet for success.

LESSON: International businesspeople need all the help they can get.

Marketeers should be careful not to let their own religious beliefs overly influence their actions or marketing decisions. This is true even when working within the same general religious idiom as the targeted local market. Catholics in Colombo are far more devout than the average Catholic in Boston, and Jakarta's Islam is far more secular than that of Kabul. Religion is a very personal and emotionally laden thought process; treat it with trepidation.

WARNING: If your product has any potential religious ramifications, and few products don't, make sure that you've thoroughly researched your target market ahead of time from a spiritual aspect. Failure to do so may keep you out of a market for a very long time to come—perhaps permanently.

Family: Hierarchies and Decision Makers

Family units are the basis of a culture, and much valuable marketing information can be drawn from observing their hierarchies. Marketeers should see which face the family presents in public and which it preserves for "internal" purposes, as these will determine the buying patterns within a community for each type of product.

PATRIARCHAL SOCIETIES

Some cultures have uniformly male-dominated households. Men (usually fathers, but sometimes elder siblings in the absence of a father) will make virtually all purchasing decisions beyond basic household foodstuffs. They control all of the money, regardless of who earns it. Marriage is usually ironclad in such societies, with little divorce. Children remain at home well into their twenties, or longer if they are single females, but households rarely extend beyond two generations. They're usually agrarian-based cultures with primogeniture (eldest son is given the lion's share of the property). Although these cultures are globally dispersed, they're most common in Central and South America. Marketing in such cultures tends to have a universally male theme.

MATRIARCHAL SOCIETIES

On the opposite side of the coin are the female-dominated societies, like those of sub-Saharan Africa, where inheritance is matrilinear and women hold the greatest power in both village life and individual households. Matrimony can be readily dissolved (usually by the wife) and fidelity is on a case-by-case basis. Most of the entrepreneurship and finance is controlled by women, although this isn't reflected at the national level of politics, where the "warrior" aspect of male culture tends to hold sway. The segmentation is fairly clear, depending on what product a marketeer is promoting. Consumer goods should be directed at women; big ticket items (cars, maybe the occasional tank) will be male-oriented.

THE EXTENDED FAMILY

In between these extremes of dominance is a large spectrum of compromise. Much of Asia uses a family system of "extension." Up to four generations may live in the same household, and elders remain influential well past their earning years. In public, men take the lead and wives have little say. Companies are male controlled and very few females reach the boardroom. In the home, however, the situation is very much reversed, with wives making all decisions with regard to the household and children. Men earn the money and women control its dispersal—big ticket or small ticket, consumer goods or long-term securities investments. Divorce is growing in Asia but is still an uncommon practice. The family is a tight economic unit that extends well beyond the front door, as many of Asia's largest companies are family owned; it's not unusual to find several layers of management sharing the same family name. Because bloodlines are such an important factor in these cultures, initial failure or success will follow a marketeer for a long time and over a wide area. Having the right "connections" is very important here, and those connections revolve around families.

FAMILY-OWNED BUSINESSES

Europe has a traditional, family-oriented society (mother, father, children), though not nearly as traditional as Asia; many companies remain under private family ownership. Divorce is quite common, however, and some prominent nations (France and Germany, most notably) are facing flat or negative population growth as the size of families declines. A few women hold prominent positions in government and business. Most of Europe's traditional families are dual-income, allowing for increased purchasing power and "discretionary income" usage. There's an upswing in single-parent families and its concomitant drop in the purchasing of nonessentials. Marketeers will find that European cultures tend toward consumerism but with a Old World regard for quality.

WHOSE FAMILY VALUES?

At the top of the consumer heap sits the economic giant, the United States, whose cultural icons are globally pervasive. Most other societies look to the United States not only as a commercial role model but also as a harbinger of future problems—with emphatic fears on the family front. Its hallmarks: a high (and rising) divorce rate, single-parent homes becoming a social norm, poverty-ridden teenage mothers forcing up welfare roles, and violent young males who've had little (if any) contact with their fathers. And all of this is occurring as the economy booms, personal spending skyrockets, and unemployment lessens. Plainly, consumerism is best served by a society wherein freedom to do as one pleases is considered a cultural imperative. Marketeers will find a ready audience for virtually any product in the wealthy, I-need-it-right-now American culture.

Nations on the commercial rise find the U.S. template troubling. Even stodgy Japan has seen a close connection between its own economic prowess and declining family values. Asian leaders are fond of citing "Asian values" (Confucian, mostly) as an antidote, while Europe's governments rely mostly on centuries of being at the cultural center to protect them. Sociological considerations aside, marketeers should be forewarned that the recent emerging market attitude of "investment, not investors" is the first volley in the war against economic colonization. If your product smacks of cultural influence (videos, books, clothing), be prepared for some social backlash usually delivered under the banner of protecting the family. More of this will be considered during the discussion of xenophobia, where people, rather than products, are eschewed.

Climate: Don't Carry Coals to Calcutta

It's no secret that climate influences the tone of a nation's culture. Hot, humid climates tend to produce gregarious, outgoing people just as cold, pristine climes result in introspective, self-sufficient populations. Temperate zones are conducive to year-round labor and less subsistence-type living, with the result being high productivity and a general sense of well-being. Even within a single country, such as China, where extremes of weather and geography can be found in microcosm, the results are the same. Wealth, productivity and stability aren't evenly dispersed, but instead follow climatic and resource (e.g., water) lines dictated by nature.

Marketeers often follow these same geographic patterns as they attempt to have a nation adopt their products. Finding a locale that can afford a product is just as important as finding a group that has a use for it. Sometimes it is a matter of introducing a product to one portion of a population with the knowledge that it will spread throughout a culture in due course. This is called "coastline" marketing (although an actual physical coast is unnecessary) and relies on the fact that some segments of a population adopt products sooner than others.

Large urban populations have a tendency to consider and adopt goods or services far more readily than their less urban, and less urbane, countrymen. Such cities have become major centers usually due to their geographic location (coastline or waterway concentration is a norm when such geography has dictated trade routes), and they have attracted risk-takers in droves over decades and centuries. Because cities are viewed as centers of culture as well as commerce, suburban and country folk tend to adopt the lifestyles of their urban counterparts, but there are some signs of the reverse. Television and telecommunication in the form of the Internet have shortened this urban-to-rural flow from months to days and extended it far beyond national borders. The latest baggy logo-parkas of chilly New York's street youth can be found in balmy Missouri within a week and in muggy Manila by the end of the month. Meanwhile, another product, the British four-wheel-drive Range Rover, made the move from English country moors to London to the sands of Africa and on to the hilly streets of San Francisco at a somewhat slower speed.

LESSON: Unless a product has a specific agrarian use, goods and services will probably find a quicker reception in urban areas. Only the very wealthy tend to look on bucolic life with any sense of longing—mostly because they're generations away from the mandatory physical labor it requires.

Xenophobia: The Trojan Horse Effect

Earlier there was discussion of how cultures often wish to protect themselves from products they deem culturally subversive. The French RU-486 abortion pill was thought to be culturally dangerous to the United States, just as the English language laden Internet continues to be controversial in France. There's a rising chorus of cultures that wants access to the globe's goods and services while shunning the marketeers who accompany them. Most of this stems from the fact that marketeers also bring along ideas and lifestyles that, in the target market's view, may "contaminate" local values. When marketeers set up representative offices or settle in to oversee joint ventures, the possibilities of cultural crossover grow exponentially.

FOREIGN INFLUENCE

Developing economies suffer the greatest effect of this xenophobia as they become torn between advancing into the future (largely dictated by foreign technology,) and leaving behind a past that formed their present. They also feel financially and educationally outmatched by the industrial and technical powers that roam the commercial seas. These developing countries make a point of assuring that locals maintain control over any inroads made by foreigners by legislating ownership percentages. Countries like Vietnam make it virtually impossible for foreigners to own land thus physically and symbolically excluding them from becoming part of the country. Others, as is the case with China, prevent foreigners from ever attaining citizenship for the same reasons. To right the wrongs of past foreign exploitation, Malaysia and Indonesia have instituted *pri bumi* and *bumi putra* legislation that calls for "native born" citizens to be part of all major commercial undertakings. Naturalized citizens are considered on a par with foreigners, even when their families have been members of the community for decades.

Many South American countries, Brazil for one, have made similar steps to ensure that native tribal subcultures receive mandates to be part of any exploitation of the resources contained in their traditional landholdings. In many of the more volatile central African states, tribal affiliations determine commercial and political rights, when the government changes hands so do all of the contractual agreements. The new leaders want to ensure that "their people" get a suitable piece of the pie. In all of these cases, the motivation is to make sure that the citizenry (at least a designated cultural elite) remains in control of the great modern cultural engine: commerce. Nowadays, a culture that is out of money is extinct.

FIRST WORLD PROBLEMS

Xenophobic feelings aren't exclusive to undeveloped economies and obscure native tribes. The purchase of many British properties and companies by newly enriched Arab sheiks caused more than just eyebrow raising, just as Ford Corporation's buyout of Mazda sent shock waves throughout Japanese society. United States' paranoia about Japanese real estate peaked during the Japanese buying sprees in the Hawaiian market; this resulted in legislation that restricted the purchase of golf courses, out of fear that the new landlords would bar locals. (When the Japanese bought New York's Rockefeller Center, it was viewed as a grave insult. This imagined transgression was salved some years later when the bankrupt Japanese owner had to put the building back on the auction block.) Canada's relationship with the United States is heavily tinged with a fear of simply becoming known as the "fifty-first state," and the Canadians react by regulating the amount of American music and TV shows to be broadcast. Virtually any major deal in France, from trucking to aerospace, that gives foreigners a decided advantage is roundly (and sometimes violently) protested, even when the venture and its jobs will remain *in situ*. Plainly, the developed world isn't just concerned about the "hollowing out" of its industrial base but of its cultural base as well.

WARNING: Marketeers should take measures to assure that their dealings have a minimum of cultural impact on their target market. Whether it's a simple trade or a substantial investment, keeping a "low profile" is recommended. Soliciting the direct and indirect aid of local government officials and business leaders prior to market entry is essential. Cultural imperialism is a very real and expansive concern in the global marketplace. It has sunk just as many deals as bad financing.

Cultural Adaptation: Understanding Isn't Agreement

Not every potential market is looking for reasons to reject products and producers. Much of the cultural interplay is unconscious and is virtually invisible until conflicts arise. It's not unusual for the conflict to be caused by the marketeer rather than the targeted culture.

Both sides of a deal will need to be aware of each other's cultural baggage. However, when it comes to cultural differences and international business, there's no such thing as "meeting the customer halfway." It's more like 95 percent of the way. Successful marketeers play by other people's rules, eat other people's food, speak other people's languages, and meet other people's standards of quality. Very few companies are alone in an entire marketplace, and competition can be fierce. If one company doesn't cater to the demands of international customers, there's another that's ready, willing, and able to answer the call. Remember: Only customers can afford to be intolerant.

International marketing can be very demanding on many levels, not the least of which involves cultural interplay. You'll be called upon to participate in unusual activities, eat strange foods, sleep in uncomfortable rooms, endure awkward social situations, and witness business practices that are a great departure from your home culture. Many activities may be in direct conflict with your religious or philosophical beliefs. Professional marketeers must continually remind themselves of the first rule of cultural tolerance: understanding isn't agreement.

Guidelines for Cultural Analysis: A Checklist

Not everyone is cut out to work in the arena of international business, and a lack of marketing skills will be very costly. Regardless of how much commercial law governs a deal or how tight the contract is, international business is still a relationship between and among people. Often, those people have conflicting philosophies and will never completely share a perspective. The following is a simple checklist that the reader should review in order to determine whether or not international marketing is a viable career choice. If you answer "yes" to all of the questions, you're over the first and most basic hurdle of business—the capability of understanding your customer. If you answer "no" to more than a few of the questions, a change of heart or change of career may be in order.

	YES	NO
1. Do I find other cultures interesting?	❑	❑
2. Do I believe all societies have positive and negative aspects?	❑	❑
3. Do I believe all nations have the potential for economic success?	❑	❑
4. Am I comfortable meeting people who speak a language other than my own?	❑	❑
5. Am I willing to take the time to learn another language?	❑	❑
6. Am I comfortable with people of different races?	❑	❑
7. Am I comfortable with people whose educational level is different than mine?	❑	❑
8. Am I comfortable with people of different economic levels?	❑	❑
9. Am I well schooled in the history of my own society?	❑	❑
10. Am I well schooled in world history?	❑	❑
11. Do I attach great value to my own culture?	❑	❑
12. Can I look at issues from several perspectives?	❑	❑
13. Do I believe that any two people will have some common ground?	❑	❑
14. Am I considered an "understanding person" by my peers?	❑	❑
15. Am I capable of subjugating my own beliefs in order to achieve greater goals?	❑	❑

Profile of an International Marketeer

There is, of course, more to choosing a career in international marketing than just the ability to understand other cultures. Some of the requirements are physical, but most are intellectual talents that can be developed and used (in most cases) to overcome any of the physical problems, should they be present. The following is a profile containing the twelve attributes that characterize the type of person most suitable for this dynamic and demanding career.

ORGANIZED

Marketing can be an extremely complex issue on the domestic front and doubly so at the international level. It must be meticulously planned and meticulously executed. The stakes are very high and competition is fast and furious. Thorough organization at the macro- and micro-levels will make the difference between a long-term success and a short-term failure. Beyond just the planning of the marketing scheme, one must add in the demands presented by international travel. Flight schedules, hotel stays, and negotiation agendas can take a disastrous toll on the best laid marketing plans. Many domestic marketing personnel find out quickly that international work is far more demanding than the domestic variety. People who are incapable of looking at the "big picture" while juggling all of the concomitant details should remain on the home front.

ENERGETIC

International business places extraordinary time demands on its participants. Because so much can happen in a relatively short period of time, marketeers should be prepared and able to work long hours for many days running. While this pace isn't constant, when it does occur everyone involved must be ready to give their undivided attention. Business meetings may be scheduled after a restful weekend or the morning after a fifteen-hour, multi-time-zone flight. Global work also requires that you work to a customer's schedule on the other side of the world—which may find you on the telephone or at the shipping pier at four in the morning. Travel and jet lag are very real adversaries. Many deals have been lost or poorly negotiated by tired, worn-out marketeers, and some foreign companies will use your fatigue to their advantage. If you require eight hours of sleep every night and a forty-hour workweek, international marketing is best left to others.

DURABLE

Physically and emotionally frail types will be devoured by the rigors of global business. Long hours, strange food, water of dubious quality, extreme climates, and poor accommodations are common problems. Change is tough on the human body, and just as many people get sick traveling from the emerging markets to the developed world as the reverse. The ability to avoid physical problems, as well as to endure them when they do occur, is a necessary attribute of the marketeer. When opportunities arise they must be seized, and that can't be done from a hospital bed or a hotel bathroom. Staying in good health is part of a marketeer's job description.

Travel can take an emotional toll on the ill prepared. Smaller companies may be sending just one person overseas to make their proposal, and that solo marketeer may find himself feeling quite isolated. Loneliness, homesickness, and sometimes actual fear (many emerging markets are as dangerous as they are potentially lucrative) can greatly influence one's judgment and actions, in spite of solid advanced planning. There have been numerous cases of marketeers rushing their research or closing deals early just so they can get home or at least out of the target country. Marketeers (and to some degree, their loved ones) must steel themselves against these emotional influences.

NOTE: Business moves at its own pace, be prepared to see every deal through to the end.

CALM

Marketeers will be part of the planning, as well as the negotiation and execution, of the deal. Marketing isn't only a "paper skill," it's a people skill also. While negotiating is a topic unto itself (see *A Short Course in International Negotiating*, World Trade Press, 2009), the reader should note here that maintaining a cool, calm demeanor is necessary when dealing with tough or indecisive customers. Additionally, international travel will present you with numerous opportunities to lose your temper with bungling customs personnel, snail paced immigration officials, and other officious government types. A wrong word, or for that matter any sign of impatience, may scuttle your entire business trip. It may even result in some legal problems for your host. It should also be noted that some cultures view emotional outbursts as a sign of mental problems rather than as an expression of resentment or arrogance. Regardless of what culture you may be operating in, cooler heads usually carry the day.

GREGARIOUS

People everywhere prefer to do business with someone they like, and repeat business can turn solely on this issue. Friendly, outgoing marketeers make business contacts more easily and they're more capable of the interaction necessary for cutting deals. Though stern measures may occasionally be called for around the conference table, the old adage that "you catch more flies with honey than with vinegar" is still very true.

International marketing makes social demands of its participants. Many long lasting and profitable deals have been sealed over the dinner table or at the golf course. The vast majority of top businesspeople worldwide put as much stock in the character of their counterparts as they do in their balance sheets. Getting to know people and the ability to let others know you is an important business skill for the domestic as well as the global market. Regardless of contract law, trust among individuals is still the underpinning of commerce, and a gregarious nature permits that confidence to grow.

OPTIMISTIC

Many things can and do go wrong with an international deal, as well as with the travel necessary to make it work. The last thing any company needs is a pessimist in the marketing department. Even when planning is ideal and travel is effortless, enthusiasm and a strong belief in ultimate success must buoy the weary marketeer. Customers will hardly consider buying a product about which the seller has little fervor. A positive outlook tends to breed the same in those that come in contact with it; the opposite is true as well.

NOTE: Complainers, whiners, and doom-and-gloom practitioners make very poor marketeers (or anything else for that matter), so leave such negative attitudes behind if you plan on pursuing a career in international business.

EDUCATED

If ever there was a venue that could be aptly described as in a state of flux, it's the global marketplace. Marketeers must become informed and stay informed. Even once the initial research is complete on a target market the information gathering is far from over. Companies that do the best in international business continuously "take the pulse" of the marketplace. Everytime someone in the global marketplace loses, someone else wins, with little doubt as to which of the two sides had the best information.

While academic degrees are very useful for marketeers, they're no guarantee of success. Commerce isn't an academic exercise, but it can be the harshest of realities. Many an MBA have met their match in an experienced marketeer who had no formal education beyond grammar school. The camel traders of the world are just as savvy in their marketplace as the best traders on Wall Street or in Hong Kong. Experience is always the best teacher.

Never, under any circumstances, should marketeers fool themselves into believing that they're "experts" on a particular market. The ground is shifting constantly and far too quickly for anyone to know everything, even in the supposedly stable markets of the West. The best anyone can hope for is to know the most at any given time.

WARNING: Global market information is very time sensitive. News that's more than a week old is doubtful, and when it's more than a month old, consider it useless. Marketeers should guard their lines of communication and information sources as closely as they do their passports. They can't go very far without them.

AGILE

A sharp and decisive mind is essential during the implementation of a marketing scheme. While the use of consensus may be of high importance during the planning phase, implementation is best done by the nimble. Negotiations, sales presentations, and deal closing require that thought processes, information sorting, and decision making be put in high gear as marketeers respond to the demands of buyers. Pausing for lengthy deliberation only gives the customer time to consider the competition.

The ability to "think on your feet" will serve you equally well at the conference table and during social interludes. The right word here, the generous gesture there, or the judicious timing of a business proposal may all work to advance your plans and stave off failure.

NOTE: There are few more formidable combinations in commerce than the coupling of good information and a quick mind, but one without the other is of little use.

PERSPECTIVE

The travails and intensity of international marketing often cloud the real issues. As there's little doubt that stress takes both a physical and mental toll, the ability to maintain perspective is a desirable virtue in a marketeer. Keeping priorities straight and the marketing plan on track isn't always an easy process, especially when success seems distant. Even without the wisdom that comes with experience, marketeers new to the global scene have to be able to see the whole picture from all perspectives.

Keeping a clear head and an even clearer eye will allow you to take in all of the available information (your own and that of the target) without becoming emotionally involved with the outcome. This can be very difficult when a marketeer is also the owner of the company or the inventor of the product. Being too closely tied to the product reduces your ability to see things from the consumer's point of view ("How could they not want this?") and resistance is taken as a personal affront. Maintain a professional perspective about both the product and the marketing process. It may be what you do for a living, but it's not your life.

NOTE: Being enthusiastic about a product and having a personal attachment to it are two very different things.

VERSATILE

A marketing effort may require the assembly of a large team, with each member assigned to perform very specific tasks. Such an assemblage may be then broken into planning and implementation subgroups. This is usually the mark of a large company with sufficient finances to support a large effort. Smaller companies may use only a group of three or four; traders and entrepreneurs are more likely to handle the entire process as a solo act. From large to small to solo, the need is the same: versatility.

Professional marketeers should be skilled in all aspects of the marketing effort so that they can operate and provide input for any level of the scheme. Information shouldn't be "hoarded," nor should the ability to analyze it be a talent reserved for only a few specialists. Overseas travel can present teams with problems that may require the substitution of regular members; versatility permits this. Solo acts, by their nature, must be able to handle any and all aspects of the marketing process from initial research through implementation.

Although specific national markets and geographic regions may interest a company, marketing department, or trader, there's great danger in too much specialization. The connectivity among nations and regions is now so great that a new joint venture set up by a French company in Cambodia may suddenly find itself providing goods and services to a Venezuelan end-user. All markets are worthy of a marketeer's attention but no market should be focused on to the total exclusion of others. It's been many decades since any market could operate in isolation; failure to see this will greatly limit your effectiveness.

NOTE: Versatility combined with perspective will keep you in the world marketplace for a long time.

FARSIGHTED

Even the most meticulously planned marketing scheme can result in failure when conditions beyond a company's control take effect. However, such failure is only short-term. Success can be equally fleeting if implementers lack followthrough. Adopt a long-term approach—view failure as merely a lost battle and success as a truce in need of constant management.

NOTE: Commerce is eternal. It's just a matter of how long you will be part of it.

ACCOMMODATING

Domestic customers need to be wooed but international customers need to be seduced. An international marketeer will be viewed both as an unknown quantity and as a foreigner. This will make the job of selling much more difficult, but being accommodating—in the word's original sense—will offset this difficulty.

Accommodating derives from the Latin infinitive *commodare* meaning "to make fit "or "to measure," and that's exactly what marketeers must do to succeed. After taking the measure of their targeted market segment, the product (no matter how successful it may have been elsewhere) must now be tailored to fit the new customer. Rarely does a new market buy something "ready made" or "off the rack." It may be size, color, quantity, or delivery time, but the product will require alteration. Heading overseas without a specifically tailored plan or with one that's identical to your domestic effort will rarely, if ever, meet with success.

WARNING: You must treat every new market as if you were starting from zero. If you don't, that's where you'll end up.

NOTE: A detailed outline for the information needed to conduct a cultural analysis is included at the end of Chapter 8 on the research process.

CHAPTER 7

Developing Products for the Foreign Market

LET EVERY MAN MIND HIS OWN BUSINESS.
— CERVANTES

EVERY NATION (and its various market segments) has its own way of viewing the goods and services offered to it by international marketeers. Even in domestic markets, a product could do very well in one region and get a middling reception by another less than 100 miles away. When marketing entails a movement across national borders, the differences will be more dramatic (even when the nations share a language, climate, or geography). A good example of this disparity can be seen in national cuisine. Why are the Belgians beer drinkers and the French wine fanatics? Why does China have a long history of complex cooking while Russia makes do with much plainer fare? While neighbors Argentina and Chile both have lengthy coastlines, large fishing fleets, and thriving cattle industries, why is it that the former's menus concentrate on beef while the latter favors seafood and chicken? If these examples of cuisine are any indication, crossing a border with a product is almost like cooking from scratch.

Carrying an Established Product Across Borders

There are many reasons to consider breaking out of your domestic market and selling across borders. The following section discusses many of the possible motivations.

SATURATION

Finding that the home market has peaked and is now saturated with your product is the most common reason for focusing a marketing effort overseas. Although true saturation is rarely achieved, it's sometimes easier to penetrate foreign markets than new domestic ones, especially if you operate in a large country. Moscow businesses find it easier, and more lucrative, to sell products in eastern Europe than they do in far-flung Vladivostok.

DECLINING INTEREST

Every product has a life span in a particular market before it's overtaken by new or improved products, which are often developed internally (e.g., Windows superseded by Vista). The original product, whose development costs have long since been recouped, may still be useful in markets untouched by the original product line. Much of the West's technology was given just such a new "product cycle" in the emerging markets, some of which are decades behind in technical matters. When you're used to plowing your field behind a water buffalo, a 1980s-vintage tractor is a welcome addition, even when it arrives in 2010.

FOREIGN DEMAND

It's not a rarity for a company that's doing quite well in their domestic market, with rocketing sales, to receive an unsolicited demand from a foreign buyer. This happens repeatedly in technology and consumer goods but also increasingly so in many capital-intensive businesses (such as auto production or hotel construction). If you have a very high quality product or are an industry leader, the foreign market may come looking for you.

SHARE ENLARGEMENT

Many companies move into foreign markets simply because they can. Flush with cash or energized with curiosity, they wish to increase their sales by increasing their exposure. High-end consumer goods or specialist services (e.g., yachts or investment banking) often go hunting overseas, not out of need but simple drive.

COMPETITION

Once one company markets abroad, even just to test the waters, the competition is quick to follow. Often, it's a move made with great reluctance and out of fear that allowing a competitor to reap riches in foreign lands may have future domestic ramifications. It's fast becoming a reality that if you're not an international player, you're not a player at all—big business means global business. Rushing onto the international stage, maybe even feeling pushed, can be costly if planning is sacrificed for speed. A prime example is the failed attempt by Apple Computer to duplicate its domestic success to overseas markets with personal computers, particularly in Asia. The young company self-inflicted serious brand-name damage in the 1990s because its products demanded a price that was not seen as adding significant benefit. Only the move into the realm of music (iPod) saved its reputation outside of the American market.

NOTE: It's better to arrive a little late, but prepared, than to leave early without a map.

EXCHANGE VALUE

The value of national currencies can fluctuate wildly, often with deleterious effects on domestic companies. The effect is even worse when the company must buy foreign materials for production. When production costs rise and domestic buying power declines, the marketeer may have no choice but to look offshore for customers. High-ticket items are the most affected, though consumer goods occasionally are as well.

On occasion, a company may find that foreign markets are ready, willing, and able to pay a higher price for a product. Barring the intervention of customs officials, products normally earmarked for domestic production are diverted overseas. If domestic consumption remains stable, then local prices will rise to buy up the now-diminished supply. The producer now has the best of both worlds if the wrath of the local government can be avoided. Commodities such as beef and coffee are often subject to such surges in foreign demand.

PREPRODUCTION PENETRATION

Prior to setting up full-scale offshore production, a company will sell to the targeted market as a way of testing demand, observing price elasticity, or educating the population about a product. The last reason keeps the price of the "learning curve" low, in advance of producing inside of the new market. The computer hardware business has done this repeatedly in emerging markets around the globe. Knowing full well that most of their foreign production will be exported out of the producing country, hardware manufacturers often "dumped" cheap computers into the target market as a means of spurring interest and building future demand. (Singapore and Malaysia, once only makers of computer hardware, are now a major users.)

GOVERNMENT REQUEST

Many developing countries finance their growth through exports, since domestic buying power is limited. Even some economic giants, Japan being the most famous practitioner, greatly restrict imports and encourage exports to finance growth. In both cases, domestic producers are protected from foreign (and often more efficient) producers, while hard currency pours back through the busy port system. In extreme cases, export quotas may be rigidly set and marketeers are sent abroad with do-or-die marketing plans. Some countries purposely weaken their currency so as to encourage foreign companies to buy their products (e.g., the United States is often accused of using this tactic by Japan, and vice versa).

NOTE: When governments start to see rising trade deficits or droopy foreign currency reserves, overseas marketing may no longer be an option but a mandate.

When to Make New Products

As stated in Chapter 6, even a proven product may have to be altered slightly to succeed in a foreign market. Sometimes, however, research or unsolicited demand requires that a company devise a whole new product line for overseas consumption. While a lucrative opportunity may be presenting itself, a marketeer should be careful to view the long-term potential and future problems that may result. Here are ten basic questions that should be posed before taking on the task of creating a new product line for a foreign market.

1. Will the new product cause brand-name confusion in the target market?
2. Will the new product cause brand-name confusion in the domestic market?
3. Is the company financially able to enter a new product development phase?
4. Will the new development divert resources away from domestic activity?
5. Will the new product line adversely affect domestic marketing efforts?
6. Will the current employee base be capable of developing and handling the new product line?
7. Does the company management team fully and enthusiastically endorse the product development?
8. Will the new product and company brand name have legal protection overseas?

9. Does the new market have the potential to accept the company's current product line along with the new developments?
10. Has a marketing plan been thoroughly researched and formulated for the new market?

The vast majority of companies attempt to remarket their current product line overseas prior to offering completely new developments. Obviously, going into an unknown market with an unproven product is the apex of risk, but it can pay off if demand is high and brand recognition isn't too rigid. For example, when U.S. pizza giant Domino's Pizza entered the Taiwanese market, its standard line of pizzas wasn't well received, although quite successful elsewhere. Local buyers wanted seafood-based products in their stead. Because the company had no real brand recognition established on the island, it could easily break free of the pepperoni-mushroom-cheese image it promulgated elsewhere. The result: Domino's stores have a big presence in Taiwan, making the company the pizza industry leader on the island, with sales upwards of US$50 million annually. The biggest selling item: the Seafood Pizza with squid, shrimp, crab, and peas.

The Product Cycle: Expanding the Average Lifespan

The product cycle is more easily defined than it is predictable. It's the sum total of the stages in the marketing existence (or "life") of a product. The stages are: development, introduction, growth, maturity, and decline. Products don't stay in the market forever; the wastebasket of history is chockablock with instant failures and multidecade market leaders alike. The length of the cycle is indefinite, as growth may be steep or gradual and maturity a sharp peak or a long plateau that might be followed by a precipitous decline or a barely perceptible crawl toward the final sale.

There's not a single rise or single fall but a series of each throughout the cycle that can be controlled, to some extent, by observant management. Sometimes the speed of growth is far in excess of forecast and can overwhelm an inexperienced or undisciplined marketeer. That same marketeer will be unable to halt the spiraling decline of a poorly adapted product in an unforgiving marketplace. Marketing personnel at all levels of experience must be prepared to accept the fact that while commerce may be eternal, their products are decidedly mortal.

Much like human beings, those products that are actively cared for and subjected to the right preventive measures have a statistically longer lifespan than those left exposed to the unchecked vagaries of the marketplace. Also like humans, products are subject to anomalies that defy explanation by the keenest observer or the planning of the most astute marketeer. The meteoric and global success of the Tamagotchi virtual pet and the resounding mediocrity of Java programming are two cases in point. The first is a widely owned piece of useless gadgetry, and the second, a revolutionary piece of software technology unable to live up to its promise.

Resistance to Old Products: Both Sides of the "Cutting Edge"

The life cycle of a product depends on the market segment. When an established product is introduced or adapted for a new foreign market, care should be taken to understand how it will be perceived there. The perceived newness of the product line, rather than its actual age or applicability, will determine its success. Consider the selling of technology in emerging markets. Much of the developing world is severely lacking in the telecommunications infrastructure needed for modern business. Vietnam in the early 1990s had a teledensity of one telephone for every one hundred people in a nation of seventy-two million. The telephone system was a mish-mash of French colonial, 1970s Warsaw Pact, and mid-1950s U.S. technologies cobbled together to no one's satisfaction. Payphones were nonexistent, as the country had no coinage. This was going to severely limit the country's growth, and any improvements would be major ones.

RELATIVE AGE

Telephone companies from Britain, Canada, Germany, France, Australia, Japan, Italy, Sweden, and the United States all saw Vietnam as a chance to extend the life cycle of products now being replaced in their home markets by fiber optics, cellular, and fixed-wireless technologies. Surely warehouses bulging with 1980s' switches, handsets, and PBX panels would draw a handsome (though now discounted) price to fill Vietnam's we-can-use-anything needs. Unfortunately for these telecom companies, it never happened. What would have been a marked improvement for Vietnam was viewed by its government as an insulting "colonial" gesture. Vietnam was not about to accept technological cast-offs, no matter how "cutting edge" those cast-offs would be for the local market. Like China, Vietnam wanted to skip over decades and even centuries of development and head straight for the 21st century. By skillfully pitting the British, French, Japanese, and Australians against each other in a fight for market share, the Hanoi government held out for and received the real "cutting edge" technology at considerable discount.

TOO MUCH, TOO LATE

But not all life cycle problems involve whiz-bang technology, nor do they always result in the customer thinking they're getting out-of-date products. Sometimes an old and established product can appear too revolutionary for a new market. Such was the case when Campbell Soup attempted to move its time-tested product into Brazil. After investing U.S.$6 million and conducting a marketing effort that won two national awards, the company found that its canned, ready-made soups offended the Brazilian housewives' concept of their duty to cook for the family. Rather than being seen as a time-saving measure, canned soup was seen as a piece of unwanted modernity and a threat to family life.

Much preferred by Brazil's mothers were the dehydrated products of a competitor, Knorr. Rather than a completed soup, the dried concentrate served as a base upon which cooks could add their own ingredients. Knorr was modern but not perceived as being too modern, like Campbell—which lost U.S.$1.2 million and eventually shut down its soup operation. Most of the blame for this fiasco was laid at the feet of the company's marketing staff, which had confined its research to the climatically mild city of Curitaba, neglecting the more traditional, sub-tropical zones of this vast country.

BONA FIDE EFFORTS

Several lessons can be drawn from these examples. In the case of the Vietnamese telecom system, never assume that a new market will accept old products simply because they're better than what's currently being used. Offering only your second-rate products first is hardly a way to build a customer base. It's much better to price the older product line so as to make it more attractive than the new one. Let the customer believe that they're getting a bargain and making the choice for themselves. Remember, most consumers make decisions with their wallets, their hearts and their brains—in that order.

Another lesson to be taken from the Vietnam example is that foreign markets may be new to your product line but they're experienced bargainers nonetheless. Furthermore, poor people are better at bargaining than rich ones because they have to bargain for everything to make ends meet. If you approach a market with the idea that you can outwit it rather than service it, your stay will be brief. Acting in good faith is good business sense and, to my knowledge, no one has ever refused to do business with an honest person.

KNOW YOUR TERRITORY

The Brazilian example points up two deficiencies in Campbell's approach: Poor cultural understanding and lack of comprehensive research. Large companies have long since gotten out of the habit of assuming that everyone in the world wants their products. However, it's unlikely that Campbell sought local input or utilized Brazilian management in starting up its operation. They assumed that Brazilian mothers would appreciate the value of the soup's convenience, just as U.S. mothers had for decades. Many U.S. women were more worried about corporate advancement than family-style cooking; meanwhile, Brazilian mothers were still housebound and devoted to raising children. Even a modicum of cultural insight would have revealed this discrepancy.

What research was conducted was hardly sufficient for a market of Brazil's size. A nation with 8.5 million square kilometers of geography and 190 million people deserves decidedly more than the study of a single, secondary city. Few national markets can be understood by looking at a single city. France isn't Paris, China isn't Shanghai, Egypt isn't Cairo, and Canada isn't Montreal. Although Singapore is Singapore. Though research will be taken up in detail in Chapter 8, it should be clear that when attempting to move any product—whether old or new—across borders, comprehensive research will determine success.

Meeting the New Demands for Quality: What is the "ISO"?

One of the many areas where cultures collide is on the topic of quality. What is top quality for one nation can be shoddy goods for the next. The use of terms such as "high grade," "precision," and "top quality" leave much room for interpretation by seller and buyer alike. Increased competition in international markets has led to increased demands for quality and a yardstick to judge it by that would be universally recognized.

Formed just after WWII under the auspices of the United Nations, the International Organization for Standardization (a.k.a. ISO, it's not an abbreviation but from the Greek word for *equal*) was designed to be just such a tool. Originally used to control industrial products, the Switzerland-based organization now provides guidelines for goods and services of all types. From foodstuffs to ships, bolts to books, wrenches to walnuts the ISO sets the process standards for its voluntary membership. These members control more than 95 percent of the world's output and many refuse to do business with companies that don't meet ISO standards, whether they're members or not.

Marketeers must maintain quality to stay in the marketplace, and many have turned to ISO ratings in order to avoid arbitrary, fluctuating, or self-serving standards set by ever-demanding clients. Attaining an ISO rating is not easy and those that do proudly display it as part of their promotional effort. It isn't unusual to be asked to present ISO certification (a.k.a. registration) in order to even be allowed to bid on some international projects.

ISO ratings don't guarantee the actual product but document the processes and systems by which those products (goods and services of all types) are developed. The idea is that high-quality processes result in high-quality products. The ISO9000 certification and its subdivisions (9001, 9002, 9003, 9001–1, 9004–1) are the common certifications, with ISO9001 being requested most often. ISO14000 standards are utilized by companies whose goods or services have environmental impact, these are often used as a trade barrier against countries and companies unable to meet "green" requirements. All ISO standards are voluntary, but member countries are permitted to insist on compliance for imported goods or services. The ISO14000 standards cover packaging and shipping as well as the actual product and usage, and they're increasing yearly.

Of course, marketeers will have their own quality standards, which may meet or exceed those of the ISO variety. But even in the latter case, it's advisable to seek ISO certification because of its international recognition. Because most large companies have already sought such certification, the author has included the names of two texts in the "Resources" chapter at the end of this book that are specifically geared to small companies seeking ISO9000 and ISO14000 certification. Readers are advised to consider ISO participation, as commercial competition may hinge not just on quality but which company can certify that quality.

Financing & Product Development: How Much Speed Can You Afford?

Products, regardless of quality, are expensive to develop. A marketeer may have a very savvy concept and a well-thought-out plan, but money will be required if a new product, or a revamped one, is going to succeed in the marketplace. Lack of development-phase financing is probably the leading cause of a product never becoming available to consumers. Some products may require enormous amounts of capital investment just to develop a prototype, to which expensive alterations will then be made before attaining a "marketable" end-product. High-tech hardware, heavy industry (e.g., steel, automotive), and transportation all fit this category. Other industries (e.g., some processed foods, software, and financial services) may have very fairly low development costs, but costs nonetheless.

Development costs also include the marketing research phase, which many times is the greatest portion of the expenditure.

Here is a brief listing of ways in which marketeers, especially novices, can obtain financing for product research and development. (Some of these sources can be used for financing international transactions as well. See Chapter 9):

JOINT VENTURE

Small companies, entrepreneurs in particular, have found that partnering with a larger company for a project provides both needed capital and managerial depth. This type of partnering can be of set length and easy to dissolve, as it will only cover very specific projects and not other parts of a company's operation. The partner may be located in the marketeer's domestic market, from the targeted nation, or even from a third country. If a domestic market partner is utilized, consideration should be given to the recognition their brand name has in the international economy. There's no harm in riding the coattails of an established firm. The same is true if a partner is to be located in the target market. Here, there's an additional consideration of political connections that may become the determining factor in success or failure. Choosing a partner from a third country should be based almost entirely on their experience in either the target market or international business in general. By no means should another novice entrepreneur be chosen, regardless of their funding.

VENTURE CAPITAL (VC)

Development money is the specialty of venture capitalists and high risk is their stock-in-trade. Though they're most famous for technology projects, their influence is felt in all sectors. Unlike joint venturing, these capitalists take a large (often upward of 40 percent) and long-term equity stake in a company in return for providing financing and direct managerial input. Their plan is to guide the entrepreneur through the early stages of success and then take the company "public" at which time they sell their original stake at many times the price of their original investment. Many big companies, including Intel and Microsoft, had their humble beginnings financed by venture capital. This American invention has spread around the globe as a financial tool for all sorts of products. Some VC companies subspecialize in various forms, from early, high-risk "seed money" through the subsequent and progressively less risky injections of money known as "rounds" that are needed as business prospects increase. Entrepreneur/marketeers who are prepared to give up a portion of their company would be wise to consider this path.

INVESTMENT BANKS

Another American invention, but this one from the 19th century, is the investment bank. Not to be confused with your check-cashing, Christmas Club, commercial-type institution, I-banks (as they're known) raise funds by acting as the intermediary for selling a company's securities (usually debt-creating bonds) to pools of investors in order to finance businesses. I-banks don't take an active role in the operation of the marketeer's business, but they often oversee the reselling of the original bonds as well as profiting from the initial sale. Many I-banks are famous and enormous institutions (e.g., Goldman Sachs), but the process is also open to smaller operators around the world. The selling of bonds is considerably cheaper than VC but it does create debt, which is paid regardless of the success of the marketeer's plan.

COMMERCIAL BANKS

Commercial banks are notoriously risk-adverse and demand collateral for most loans. This keeps their risk low and a borrower's interest rate down. This type of financing, which may be used in conjunction with joint venturing, is really only open to marketeers if they wish to incur debt.

INTERNATIONAL AGENCIES

If a marketeer's product has the potential to serve infrastructural, educational or humanitarian purposes, financing for its development can be sought through agencies set up to promote international economic progress (see Chapter 3). Agencies such as the International Monetary Fund (World Bank) and the Asian Development Bank can also provide financing for projects that will significantly increase employment in developing markets. Interest rates are very low and payment schedules generous.

CORPORATE EQUITY

For marketeers that already operate established companies, the issuance of corporate stock may serve to finance the development of a new product or the extensive revamping of the current line. Incorporating in the target market is also a consideration. Rules of incorporation and stock issuance vary greatly from nation to nation, and many countries have strict laws regarding a company's responsibility to shareholders. The corporation may be held privately or publicly, depending on the local law and degree of oversight desired by the marketeer. While this is a common means of raising capital, the reader is advised that it can become a legal quagmire if not properly structured.

PRIVATE FINANCE

Contrary to popular postulate, rich people don't sit around their mansions counting their money all day. They invest it. Many of these folks are entrepreneurs who like to plow their money into other people's projects and thereby do well by doing good. These "angels" (as they're called) keep a significant part of their investment portfolio available for "staking" the projects of other entrepreneurs and marketeers in fields usually related to the donor's original success. Angels can be found in a marketeer's domestic market, the target market, or virtually anywhere on the globe. The Internet is brimming with sites that specialize in putting private investors together with promising marketeers.

AN INVESTMENT WARNING: As is true with any attempt to seek outside investment, take care with the selection of your future partners or creditors. Bad political choices can be just as devastating to a project as choosing someone who fails to produce the promised financing. Measures should be taken to determine just how the investor's riches were earned. Marketeers may also find that certain types of projects will attract direct government intervention and the "appointing" of qualified investors.

Research: Insight Over Intuition

Product development and the financing that makes it possible require a great deal of research into the vast number of possibilities and configurations that present themselves. The move into an overseas market will be expensive from several perspectives: Time, money and energy. It's not an intuitive process. Rushing into a market simply because a "feeling about it" presages success will rarely (if ever) bring about the desired result.

It's very difficult for a company to be objective about its product and especially so when the product has been a money-maker in the domestic market. However, marketeers can't afford to be subjective in a global commercial environment, where brand and company loyalty is fast becoming ruled by a what-have-you-done-lately attitude. A consumer's emotional attachment to goods and services is short-lived and so should be a marketeer's. A company must ask itself, "Does a product have what it takes to please the target market or not?" Research, when properly done, will give a marketeer the needed insight.

CHAPTER 8

Market Research

THE ROOTS OF EDUCATION ARE BITTER, BUT THE FRUIT IS SWEET. — ARISTOTLE

PROPER RESEARCH in a new market always brings about a surprising result—you find out how little you really knew before you started. Even the globe's tiniest markets are complex commercial carpets with thousands of tasseled ends. Methodical research allows the marketeer to understand how each carpet is woven and what binds that weave together. No two carpets are exactly alike, and each contains a variety of subpatterns that can be revealed as the market is continuously segmented and products refined.

Research has its roots in education, but it's not an academic exercise for those involved in international business. It's a very real, vital, and costly process without which business decisions must be made on conjecture alone. Derived from the Anglo-French *sercher* by way of the late Latin *circare* (to go around), research demands that the practitioner gain a total perspective before drawing a conclusion. Marketeers who fail to conduct a thorough survey of a nation's commercial carpet before stepping onto it run the risk of having the rug pulled out from under them.

Defining Research Objectives: Plan Your Work

Marketing research is often associated with lengthy questionnaires and complex formulas more akin to calculus than customers. For multi-billion dollar or trillion yen companies, such elaboration is standard and affordable. Small- and medium-size companies have trimmer budgets and marketing departments with fewer personnel to be assigned calculus problems. Be assured that regardless of the size of a company or its yearly gross sales, the process for doing market research is the same.

ESTABLISHING OBJECTIVES

The first part of the research process is to establish objectives, which aren't to be confused with outcomes. Objectives should be about gathering information, outcomes will be the result of analysis. Marketeers must start off the research process by avoiding the possibility of self-fulfilling prophesies—you can't be subjective about objectives. A proper initial objective would be: Determine the level of demand for Product X in the Hulinese market. An improper overall objective for entering a new market would be: Determine the best distributor for Product X in the Hulinese market. The former assumes nothing, while the latter presupposes demand. The basic questions must be answered first if the research is to have value, as there are no "givens" when entering a new market.

An objective is a precise statement of the research's purpose. In its fullest form, it will have three vital components.

- RESEARCH QUESTION The first is the research question that asks what information will be specifically required for the research. Since the ultimate goal of research is to aid decision makers, achieving an answer to this question is the measurement of thorough research. In the example above, the research question leading to the objective statement would have been "What is the level of demand for Product X in the Hulinese market *at this time*?" A follow-up question might be "Can demand be created through promotions?" "If so, what type of promotion would be suitable in the Hulinese market?"
- RESEARCH PROPOSITION The second component is the research proposition, in which the marketeer anticipates possible answers to the research questions posed. These hypothetical answers can be as general as "Demand will be high in the Hulinese market" to the more specific "Hulinese acceptance of the product will be the result of a strong local economy and increased consumer purchasing power coupled with a growing awareness of international brands." It should be obvious that the more detailed the proposal, the more specificities the research will have to cover. Additionally, because this is meant to be an aid to decision makers, negative proposals should also be offered. Marketeers must always be prepared to accept less-than-stellar results when viewing new territories, with the knowledge that neither good nor bad results are permanent.

NOTE: If the first time you looked at the downside of a marketing scheme was after the research had been completed, you wasted a good deal of time and money.

- RESEARCH LIMITS The third component that must be put in place to formulate an objective is a determination of the research limits. Some of the limitations will be set by the propositions, some by the budgetary restrictions placed upon the research process, and still others will be the result of the availability of the desired information. In the first and second cases, limits should be in direct proportion to the size of the potential investment. A simple trade for a container load of foodstuffs will require a few days worth of investigation, whereas investment in a multibillion Deutsche-mark seafood packaging plant may require enormous expenditures and years of time to get the proper answers. Marketeers are advised never to skimp on the research budget, as money well spent at this stage can save potential losses or ensure future profits. Even if you decide to use outside contractors to secure information, make sure you secure the best that money (and your budget) can buy.

AVAILABILITY OF INFORMATION

The major limiting factor is the availability of information. Western marketeers, especially the U.S. variety, are often shocked at the secrecy many cultures maintain regarding consumer activity and commercial statistics. This is widespread in, but not limited to, the emerging markets. Asian markets are particularly sensitive about having their economic futures reduced to a series of statistics open to interpretation by what they view as hostile foreign forces. China has jailed journalists for the reporting of national commercial statistics in advance of the formal governmental announcement, and Vietnam has declared its commercial statistics to be state secrets. Sub-Saharan African markets, where accurate accounting can lead to mortal accountability, have a different spin on information protection. Few, if any, statistics are kept and new regimes are quick to rework what information is available to justify new policies. South America, where varying degrees of openness exist, prefers a very judicious approach to foreign information gathering.

Countries that are having economic problems, even developed nations, can suddenly and decisively drop a curtain around the type of information market researchers need. All nations want to paint the rosiest picture possible about the value of their country in the global marketplace and individual companies within those nations will be doing the same. These very real stumbling blocks reinforce the value of deliberate research and the need for setting suitable objectives. As much research as possible should be conducted on-the-ground in the targeted country.

WARNING: Research is a very serious and necessary part of any overseas marketing effort. A common mistake made by small companies and entrepreneurs is to combine their in-country commercial research with vacation time in an effort to "kill two birds with one stone." The standard result of this unsuitable mixture of business and pleasure is inadequate research and an unrelaxing vacation. Besides the effect on research, it may also damage your future business relationships in the target country. The same types of countries that clamp down on commercial information are also the ones that frown on visitors conducting business activities while traveling on tourist visas. Fines, expulsion, and "blackballing" can result—for individuals or entire companies. Vacations are fine for soaking up casual cultural ambience, but hard-core marketing research demands full-time attention.

Designing Your Research Process: Work Your Plan

Once the objective (or objectives) for research is set, a marketeer needs to plan the method by which each will be obtained. The objective serves as the driving why of the research process, and now the marketeer/researcher will need to determine the what, where, when, and how necessary for completion. Devising a blueprint for conducting research will enable the marketeer to attain the original goal and avoid the myriad diversions that will present themselves during information gathering. The research plan also assures that everything has been taken into account before the real investigative work begins.

WHAT

Under ideal circumstances, all information could be laid before a researcher and quickly sorted into nice, neat, relevant piles. The reality is that information is scattered, sometimes hidden, often completely unavailable, located in far-flung corners of the earth, written in other languages and many times hopelessly out of date. Access to it may be restricted by governmental, proprietary, budgetary and temporal constraints. A detailed list is presented in chart form at the end of this chapter of the areas that need to be covered when planning research, but marketeers are advised at this point to plan the content of this process from a very realistic viewpoint. The research should be divided into two main sections:

Cultural information and commercial information. Researchers may find a good deal of overlap but both areas should receive equal emphasis and planning. Research depth and content usually hinge on the financial constraints inherent in the following three categories.

WHERE

Cultural research should always be conducted inside the target nation by the marketeer or trusted staff. Do not, under any circumstances, use second-hand cultural information. Reading tour-guide books and national histories should be preparation for a research trip, not a substitute. Even when consultants or research contractors (see Sources for International Commercial Research, below) are used, cultural information should be secured by the marketeer for everything but simple trade projects. Commercial research may be partially conducted in the marketeer's domestic market if the target nation has a history of economic openness. The Internet and governmental databases are good sources of statistical information, but surveys and product testing must be conducted within the target market for obvious reasons. Wherever possible, use your own personnel. Keep a keen eye on expenses but don't pinch *pesetas*—good research costs money.

WHEN

Global business moves quickly, but research and access to information sources can be time consuming. These should be conducted as soon as possible and within the shortest period deemed prudent. A research project that takes a year to complete may contain information that's quite out of date at the time of the final report. It can be very expensive to travel on short notice, but ideally good planning will have preceded any necessary research trips. Research and planning should trigger sudden moves made by a skilled marketeer, not the other way around.

HOW

A company may choose from a variety of means for conducting research. It may gather its own information or use that produced by government agencies or consulting companies. It may conduct face-to-face surveys among consumers or observe their behavior from a distance. It may use raw statistical data to build elaborate mathematical models of how a market will perform, or rely on experiential evidence and cultural history. Successful international products have been launched by all of these methods, by companies from large to small. Methodology provides usable information that in its turn provides insight—and the international market favors insight over intuition.

Sources for International Commercial Research

Since information will serve as the marketeer's education about the marketplace, research should have a logical structure to its plan. Much in the way scholastic education proceeds, the marketeer must move from general study to specifics, as the target goes from a distant overview to pinpoint inspection. From an informational standpoint, this is a movement from indirect sources to those derived directly from the targeted market. These are called primary and secondary sources by many researchers (commercial and academic), but for marketing purposes, that type of nomenclature tends to confuse the order in which the information gathering takes place. Marketeers should move from the more general (indirect) to the specific (direct) sources, in that order. Indirect sources allow the researcher to determine which direct sources will be of the greatest benefit.

INDIRECT SOURCES

- GOVERNMENTS Governmental agencies are the first source that small- and medium-size companies turn to when seeking international marketing information. Each nation (and sometimes their major cities) has a governmental department devoted to promoting trade. They compile statistics and formulate profiles on all of their current and potential trading partners but are greatly restricted by budget and the talent of their operatives. Politics also comes into play and data tends to be more comprehensive between nations that are on good terms.

  Marketeers in the research mode may seek out data from their own government or from the target market's agencies. Most of the larger industrial and technological powers make their data available to all researchers so marketeers from smaller nations may consider using them in lieu of their own government agencies.

WARNING: All governments are in the habit of promoting their own trade, often to the detriment of their neighbors and competitors. Government statistics shouldn't be accepted as infallible pronouncements. If important data (governmental or private) can't be corroborated by at least one other source, disregard it.

- TRADE ORGANIZATIONS Private agencies and trade associations abound in international business (e.g., Chambers of Commerce) and often their sole purpose is to gather trade statistics and analysis. While they may duplicate some of the biases of governmental groups, trade associations can be a source of quality information about potential competitors, as well as about the market in general. Rarely will such groups provide information to nonmembers without a fee. If this is the case, check the quality of a small amount of information before making a final decision to sign on for what may prove to be a good deal of self-promotion or very shallow fact finding.
- LOCAL PARTNERS AND AGENTS When utilizing a joint venture, a strategic partnership, or even a distribution agent, don't overlook their ability to provide insights into the new market, even when their business experience may be minimal. As mentioned earlier, these partners may not be of your own choosing but they're partners nonetheless, and the best should be made of a less-than-ideal situation. Besides being able to provide commercial statistics and competition profiles, local partners can provide roadmaps for the political and licensing landscapes; in fact, this may prove to be their greatest contribution. Some markets are quite clannish, literally, so some care ought to be taken regarding a local partner's recommendations and situational analysis. The partner may be under great pressure (governmental or familial) to influence the direction of your venture.
- CONSULTANTS Market research consultancy firms are burgeoning throughout the developed and undeveloped world at an unchecked rate. The reason is quite simple: Even small companies expanding overseas have recognized the need for

professionally assembled information. But few of these small companies, even some large ones, see the need to maintain a full-time staff for what's viewed as either a one-time effort or, at best, a part-time vocation. Enter the consultant to fill in the gaps. Most consultancy firms or single operators will not only gather the information but also formulate a marketing plan—usually for a very stiff price. Quality varies immensely, as there's no licensing requirement for calling yourself a "marketing consultant," and few practitioners put much stock in academic certification.

Marketeers that decide to utilize a consultancy firm for research should insist on being able to contact that firm's former clients. If the firm won't provide any names (usually claiming client confidentiality), drop them from consideration. When a list is provided, find out how in-depth the research was and if it's related to the market you're targeting. Most firms will only give you the names of satisfied customers so you may want to do some background checking of your own if the fees stand to be large (Internet forums are a useful tool for this exercise).

WARNING: While most consultancies are reputable, the least reputable ones tend to go after contracts with smaller companies, knowing that the demands will be less stringent. Consultants may be using readily available resources that you could access yourself at far less expense. Don't sign any contracts until they've proven themselves with a small assignment. Many consultants are guilty of "boiler plating," which is the reselling of standard information to multiple clients as if it were recently (and expensively) unearthed. (The "find and replace" capabilities of word processing software have taken this practice to new heights, or lows, as the case may be.) Insist upon detailed billing statements, along with daily activity records, and avoid signing a consultancy's "standard contract" unless you can amend it to your benefit. Providing your own contract is the best method.

- CONTRACTORS Marketeers with sufficient resources may decide to keep the information gathering under closer scrutiny by hiring contractors, as opposed to consultancy firms. The contractor acts as a temporary employee and is more subject to the direction of the company's management. This maintains control over the process without making a long-term hiring commitment. Contractors should be given detailed instructions and their interaction with the manager/marketeer should be as frequent as possible. Since marketing research isn't dissimilar to academic research, a good source of eager and reasonably priced contractors is available on every university campus. Marketeers may also uncover other talents (e.g., linguistic, accounting, engineering) in these researchers that can be of longer term use to the company. Your company may be small now, but that can change quickly, and the need for a full-time marketing department may present itself sooner than you thought.

NOTE: Since these contractors can be hired in either the domestic or target market, take care to abide by the applicable laws for their hiring, remuneration, and termination. In some countries, there's no such thing as a "temporary" employee.

- DATABASES AND THE INTERNET Computer databases and the Internet have very rarely lived up to the hype that has preceded every new advance; still, they can be very useful tools for marketing researchers. CD-ROM and database technology has allowed libraries and data companies to store enormous amounts of information in an easy-access format, with quick search capabilities. Information that once took months to collate can now be assembled in a matter of minutes. Free or near-free access, on disk or on-line, to national demographics, industry statistics, cultural profiles, company quarterly reports, business forums and even on-line trade shows makes database searches a great starting point for any researcher. Email is also an economical way for marketeers to make initial contact with potential partners and customers.

NOTE: Very few companies, other than Internet service providers, have actually made money while transacting business over the Internet. Once contact is made, a more personal follow-up will be required. Computers are tools and all tools have limitations.

- MEDIA Publications, from books to magazines to newsletters to newspapers, are awash with useful business and cultural information. Astute marketeers will read as many sources as possible to overcome the various biases inherent in news publishing. Most publications maintain archives, while libraries assemble their own in microfiche for ready access to historical data. Some publications and publishers that specialize in business (e.g., *the Economist*, *the Wall Street Journal*, World Trade Press) have also established an Internet presence.

WARNING: There can be a great deal of overlap among government and media sources. In countries with totalitarian governments, they're one in the same. Determining the "source of the source" will help marketeers analyze the information gathered.

DIRECT SOURCES

- DIPLOMATIC If your country permits you to do business with the target market, then the chances are good that your government maintains a diplomatic office there staffed with a number of commercial attachés. Their job is to provide information drawn directly from the target market for use in promoting import/ export projects. They're also a good source of information regarding the true nature of local investment policies. In countries where "connections" are needed to do business, diplomatic staff can set the marketeer on the right path toward the right people.

NOTE: During the Cold War, the title of "commercial attaché" was a common designation among the major powers for intelligence agents. While that practice has greatly subsided, such personnel may be considered suspect by the target market government. If there's any diplomatic rancor between your government and that of the target market, keep your contact with such attachés discreet. It's no surprise that many of the world's former security intelligence personnel have switched their attention to commercial research. Conflict has gone from the war room to the boardroom.

- INDIGENOUS STAFF When the budget permits, a company may wish to tap into a storehouse of market information by employing personnel recruited directly from the target market. Management personnel, in particular, are quality sources of cultural, linguistic, commercial, and legal information that would take months, even years, to acquire. This type of information shouldn't be confused with that obtained from local partners who may be very self-serving (especially when the partner was not of a marketeer's choosing). Indigenous personnel are employees of the marketeer's company—not the joint venture—and may be hired as immigrants to the marketeer's country or in the targeted local market itself. Their loyalty should be firmly established, especially when hired locally, as industrial espionage is a growing concern for all international companies. Even when they're not hired from the ranks of management, these employees are excellent sources of the cultural information necessary for working in the new marketplace.

RESEARCH BY WANDERING AROUND (RBWA)

By far and away, the best information that can be acquired by a researcher is that which is obtained in-person and in-country. Also known as "on the ground" research, RBWA is the only way to actually observe the consumer and the marketplace in action. While much commercial information can be reduced to a series of statistics in a database, cultural nuance and consumer behavior is best assessed in the environment where it's applied.

The wandering part of this terminology is meant to suggest the expansive nature of the research, not aimlessness. RWBA, like all good research, should start with the general and move to the specific. It's a common mistake in international business to move in the other direction.

NOTE: A good example of this is the continued failure of foreign companies in China that have confused the thriving coastal cities with the nature of the market as a whole. If you want to market your product exclusively in Shanghai, fine, but if it requires "Chinese" acceptance, get thee to the countryside.

Extensive RWBA can be an expensive proposition, as it uses up both a marketeer's time and money. The return-on-investment, however, is quite sizeable. No one in the history of international business has ever regretted attaining the insights that come from extensive travel in a foreign market. Those that have come to regret a lack of RWBA are generally explayers in the global marketplace.

Because of the expense, RWBA should be well planned and timed for maximum effect (e.g., don't plan a research trip to Rio that coincides with Carnival or try to schedule meetings a week before Christmas in Edinburgh). Larger companies may send teams to spread out over assigned areas but they, like smaller operators, should allow several weeks (three minimum) to get the job done properly. A few days simply will not do; two months is ideal, even when spread over a year's time. It's important for any company, large or small, to take an organized approach to RWBA in order to avoid failing to produce results or turning research into an unscheduled vacation.

Collecting Information: Statistical, Qualitative and Observational Methods

There are three types of information that researchers must secure in order to be able to apply the word "thorough" to their information gathering process. They're known as the statistical, qualitative, and observational methods. All marketing research contains these three elements. They don't necessarily receive equal emphasis as much depends on the goods or services under consideration.

STATISTICAL METHOD

The statistical method (for the purposes of this book) will refer to the data that researchers obtain from any of the indirect sources delineated above. These can be of a demographic, climatic, economic, political, and geographic nature. While much of this can be accessed from databases and archives, it's to be stressed that even this type of information is highly susceptible to bias in its scope and reportage. All statistical information should be corroborated and never taken at face value.

NOTE: Benjamin Disraeli once said: "There are lies, damned lies, and then there are statistics."

QUALITATIVE METHODS

Qualitative information is that which is derived from surveys and interviews conducted directly in the targeted market. Some of this information may be acquired from the actual consumer base or from the diplomatic and indigenous staff mentioned above. When consumers are surveyed, this should be done in a formal manner with standardized questions and interview situations.

WARNING: Marketeers in the research mode are advised to check with the local authorities before conducting surveys or interviews. Many emerging markets, and even some developed ones, have governments that are very sensitive to political or economic inquiries made by foreigners. Don't be surprised if a person is assigned to "assist" you with your interviews.

OBSERVATIONAL METHODS

Observational information gathering takes place during the all important RBWA period. The information can be acquired randomly or according to a set plan. The latter method is the most advisable, but the marketeer/researcher should be prepared to take notes on the marketplace wherever and whenever valuable information presents itself. Unlike conducting surveys, observation requires some subtlety and researchers must not give the appearance that they're gathering information, or the subjects will tend to act in an uncharacteristic manner.

NOTE: Another reason to be discreet with your observations is to avoid the attention of local authorities. Foreigners who jot down copious notes or speak into cassette recorders may be perceived as something other than harmless commercial researchers.

Effective Competition Studies: Keeping a Clear Head

All businesses have competition of some kind. Even when products aren't in direct competition, they always compete for the spending patterns of the consumer. Competition can be located in the target market, in the marketeer's domestic market or in another foreign economy. Information should be gathered on all forms of competition during the research phase of market planning. Market segmentation, total demand, and market share must be considered simultaneously if the marketeer is to obtain a clear picture of the foreign marketplace. Oftentimes the local government, its state-owned companies, or businesses conducted as fronts for officials will be the major (or sole) competitors. This may make research somewhat more difficult, but not impossible.

When conducting competitor research, it's essential to remain objective about a rival's capabilities—actual or potential. This is particularly difficult for entrepreneur marketeers who conduct their own research. It's also difficult for subordinate managers who, placed in the role of researchers, don't want to be the ones to present their home office with bad news. In either case, appearing to be a "defeatist" shouldn't be the issue. If a competitor has a better product, a lower price or even a government sponsored "lock" on the market, that information must be passed along. Withholding the information or "sugar coating" it will only serve to create an incorrect analysis of market conditions. Researchers, whether they're a solo act or part of a massive team from an international commercial giant, must be honest about the realities of the marketplace; let the analysts deal with the fallout.

The Value of Objectivity: Sometimes the Answer is "Not Now"

All information gathered by researchers, not just that concerning competitors, must be sought out and looked at objectively before inclusion in the final report. Much of what's collected will reflect the biases of the provider to some extent, and these must either be filtered out or offset by other viewpoints. No opinion is absolute and no fact tells the entire story. The assembling of cultural information is far more prone to subjectivity, although commercial information can be equally tainted when big money is at stake.

Emotions can run high when attempting to enter a new market; researchers must maintain a cool heart when making decisions about information. Much of the emotion stems from a marketeer's fear of missing a great opportunity in a foreign economy. It's important to realize that some opportunities are best forgone, at least for the time being. Marketeers and their researchers need to understand that while the answer provided by market information is never "no," it can be "not now." Only objective information and dispassionate analysis will give the marketeer a true reading of a target's potential and the timing necessary to tap it.

Interpretation of Research: Good Idea, Good Product, Good Timing

In many ways, the gathering of information can be far easier than deciding what to do with it. This is where good interpretation and analytical skills come into play. It's important not to confuse the two, which are very different.

INTERPRETATION OF RESEARCH FINDINGS

Interpretation of factual material is the rendering of information into a form that can be understood and digested by the end-user (the marketeer). Much like the job of a translator of languages, a good interpreter knows that communication, even between two markets, is full of nuance. Parsing information can be properly done by consultant, staff, or contract researchers only when they have a clear idea of the end-user's goal. Though disregarding useless information is as important as highlighting the productive, interpreters must wait until set portions of the research are complete to make these distinctions. Even when marketeers act as their own interpreters, they must take great care to select material after all parts of the research plan have been satisfied.

WARNING: Don't attempt to interpret information as the research is in progress. Seemingly useless information uncovered early on may not have any bearing until it's associated with data acquired later in the process. Research interpretation is really a process of setting up connections.

ANALYSIS OF RESEARCH FINDINGS

Analysis follows on the heels of interpretation and is the process whereby translated information is applied to the problem at hand. Having good information and knowing what to do with it can be very separate things. Evidence of this can be seen everyday in the world's stock markets. A buyer and a seller may look at the same information about a stock and yet one sees an opportunity to enter the marketplace while the other believes it's the best time to get out. One of them is right, one is wrong. Both may also be right for entirely different reasons. The one with the proper analysis wins, while the other loses. The same is true in international marketing. Comprehensive research and quality interpretation can provide the marketeer with a detailed map, but only proper analysis will determine if it's a propitious time to start the trip to market.

It's said that good analytical skills can't be learned, and that experience may serve to hone talent already present. Successful marketeers have the inherent analytical skills necessary to make profitable decisions and they never, ever, rely on luck. Marketeers may hire others to collect information and even interpret it, but analysis must eventually be done by the marketeer. As is true with information gathering and interpretation, egos must be put on hold during the analytical phase. The only emotion that should affect the process is an enthusiasm for getting the job done right. Personal attachments to products, packaging, and advertising will only cloud the analysis. Marketing research is first and foremost a discipline, not an intuitive process.

Guidelines for Cultural Research: Past, Present and Future

Cultural information will provide the marketeer with the knowledge about how people in the target market live and their views of the marketplace. Besides providing a basis for product development or redesign, cultural information will also give insights into how business is conducted and the population's sentiments about foreign products. The following is a list of topics that need to be covered to obtain a thorough profile of a culture:

HISTORICAL
- Political
- Historical ruling factions
- Foreign invasion or colonization
- Wars and international disputes
- Economic progress
- Legal development
- Religious groups
- Ethnic groups
- Linguistic roots

GEOGRAPHICAL
- Continental location
- Boundary demarcation
- Weather patterns
- Natural resources
- Topography
- Population dispersal
- Population projections

FAMILIAL
- Basic family unit
- Role of extended families
- Birth and death rates
- Marriage and divorce rates
- Parental roles
- Male/female roles
- Effect of kinship groups
- Role of age
- Role of government in families

POLITICAL/GOVERNMENTAL
- Current national structure
- Departments/ministries
- Budget as percentage of GDP
- Major political parties
- Local governments
- Voting restrictions
- Stability assessment
- Internal security
- Taxation policy
- Trade policies
- Role of military in politics
- Role of government in business
- Risk assessment
- International relations and treaties

EDUCATIONAL
- Primary and secondary
- Tertiary levels available
- Literacy rates
  - by gender
  - by locale
  - by ethnic group
  - by economic class
- Role of government in education
- Private industry support
- Areas of emphasis (e.g., engineering)
- Role of overseas education
- Language education
- Technological instruction
- Educational forecasts

LEGAL
- Strength of judiciary
- Basis for legal code
- Police (national and local)
- Role of bribery
- Protection for foreign nationals
- Patent, trademark, and copyright laws
- International agreements (e.g., WTO)
- Ethnic participation
- Expropriation laws
- Profit repatriation laws

PHILOSOPHICAL
- Cultural philosophies
- Religious groups
- Secular and ecclesiastical influence
- Symbology and icons
- Religion and government
- Inter-religious conflicts
- Role of cults

ARTISTIC

- Ethnic folklore
- Foreign influences
- Level of development
- Music
- Drama
- Visuals
- Government support
- Private support
- Role in daily life

LINGUISTIC

- National language(s)
- Dialects
- Ethnic influences
- Foreign languages spoken

RECREATION

- National sport
- Leisure activities
- Attitudes toward leisure
- Income devoted to recreation
- National holidays
- Festivals

CULINARY

- Cuisine style and background
- Nutrition levels
- Foreign influence
- National dishes
- Class distinctions
- Ethnic distinctions
- Sanitation concerns
- Dining protocol
- Alcohol consumption
- Gender roles

HOUSING

- Rural versus urban dwellings
- Population densities
- Cost of housing
- Taxation
- Rate of ownership
- Non-citizen ownership rights
- Sanitary conditions
- Size of average household
- Inheritance policies
- Treatment of poor
- Employer role
- Government role
- Housing projections

WORK

- Labor relations
- Average wage
  - National
  - Rural
  - Urban
- Workweek
- Income taxes
- Percent of industrial versus agricultural
- Training programs
- Mandated benefits
- Holidays and vacation policies
- Payment methods
- Industrial forecasts

HEALTH

- Average lifespan
- Doctors per capita
- Major health concerns
- Government coverage
- Hospitals per capita
- Health care for foreigners
- Health and lifespan projections

Commercial Research: A Decision-Making Checklist

In many ways, economic research is more straightforward and easily accessed than cultural information, as much of it is readily available in databases. There can be little doubt that all of the topics covered under cultural research have a great effect on the economy (and vice versa). It's virtually impossible to do a thorough job of researching one without becoming involved with the other. The guidelines have been separated to show the differences in concentration, not to clarify any exclusivity. The following is a list of topics that require research when attempting to get an accurate picture of a nation's commercial sector.

DEVELOPMENT

- Historical economic growth patterns
- Changes in economic philosophy
- Gross domestic product (GDP)
  - Total
  - Per capita and per family
- Growth rate
- International standing

POPULATION

- Total
- Distribution
- Geographic
- Ethnic
- Racial
- Religious
- Age
- Growth rate
- Gender percentages
- Rural/urban densities
- Immigration rates and policies

WEALTH

- Income distribution by:
  - Class
  - Ethnicity
  - Racial group
  - Religion
  - Gender
  - Geographic region

AGRICULTURAL

- Major crops
- Distribution of crops
- Total foodstuffs consumed
- Climatic factors
- Percentage of total workforce
- Ratio of imports to exports
- Contribution to the economy
- Growth projections

INDUSTRIAL

- Major industries
- Major categories
- Resources available
- Percentage of total workforce
- Ratio of imports to exports
- Contribution to the economy
- Growth projections
- International rating

TECHNOLOGICAL

- Major companies
- Major categories
- Resources available
- Percentage of total workforce
- Ratio of imports to exports
- Contribution to the economy
- Growth projections
- Level of development
- Research and development funding

INFRASTRUCTURE

- Transportation
  - Roadways
  - Waterways
  - Seaports
  - Airports
  - Rail System
- Energy
  - Petroleum/natural gas sector
  - Import/export ratios
  - Gasoline sources
  - Local refineries
  - Electrical power plants
  - Power consumption

- Household
- Industrial
- Growth projections

Communications
- Television
  - Sets per capita
  - Number of private stations
  - Number of public stations
  - Satellite capability
  - Foreign involvement
- Radio
  - Sets per capita
  - Number of private stations
  - Number of public stations
  - Foreign involvement
- Telephone
  - Teledensity
  - Government ownership percent
  - Foreign ownership percent
  - Cellular capability
  - International long-distance
- Internet access
  - Service providers
  - End users
  - Restrictions on use
- Postal System
  - Public versus private
  - Foreign carriers
  - Postal rates
- Newspapers/Magazines/Publishing
  - Total nationwide
  - Major publications
  - Censorship concerns

GOVERNMENT

- Budget as percentage of GDP
- Total national debt
- Budget deficit
- Inflation rates
- Balance of payments
- Currency
  - Rate(s) of exchange
  - Pegging
  - Stability
  - Foreign currency reserves
- Role in domestic commerce
- Internal tariffs
- State-owned enterprises
- Role in foreign trade
- Import/export controls
- Tariffs
- Quotas
- Customs process
- Licensing process
- Embargo restrictions
- Foreign aid
- Public and private sources
- Usage rates
- International bond rating
- Economic policy
- Foreign investment policy
- Property ownership rights
- Business ownership rights
- Entry/exit visa policies
- Permanent resident policies
- Taxation rates
  - Personal
  - Corporate
- Foreign-owned businesses
- Expatriate workers
- Profit repatriation laws
- Expropriation and domestication risks

LABOR

- National productivity
- Applicable sector productivity
- Hiring practices
- Training needs
- Minimum wage requirements
- Mandatory benefits
- Work week length
- Overtime requirements
- Religious restrictions
- Dismissal policies
- Union activity and strength
- Local management percentage requirements
- Linguistic concerns
- Local labor attitudes

ADVERTISING AND PROMOTION

- Government oversight
- Cultural concerns
- Available advertising modes
- Pricing
- Reach and impact projections
- Local familiarity
- Available promotion formats
- Use of local agencies
- Logo and brand recognition

DISTRIBUTION

- Potential for foreign involvement
- Availability of locally run distribution

- Services offered
- Product experience
- Financial status
- Extent of retail operations
- Quality of agents
- Quality of retail outlets
- Ability to store and transport goods
- Credit requirements
- Quality control systems
    - Local
    - Self-administered

ENVIRONMENTAL

- Pollution concerns
- Industrial guidelines
- Government controls
- Environmental treaties

Competition Profiles: When to Compare Apples to Oranges

Competitors in the target market may not always be immediately visible. It's even possible that they'll only spring into view when they find out you're researching their domestic market. Any product (goods or services) that can be duplicated will be duplicated. The ease of duplication and the laxity of legal protection will determine the speed at which the duplication takes place. Competition can't ever be completely eliminated, but it can always be forecasted by analyzing astute research. Competition profiles will help the marketeer determine what competitors are already in the marketplace and the potential for other rivals in the near or distant future. The following is a list of the types of information that should be kept on file (and regularly updated) regarding competitors:

- Competitor name
- Country of origin
- Presence in target market
- Presence in neighboring markets
- International presence
    - Total number of operations
    - Estimated revenues
- Domestic presence
    - Total number of operations
    - Estimated revenues
- Directly competitive products
- Pricing
- Features
- Packaging
- Indirectly competitive products
- Advertising
- Promotional efforts
- Local distribution channels
- International distribution channels
- Governmental connections
- Strategic partnerships
- Joint ventures
- Importer relationships
- Estimate of current market share
- Potential for future competition

NOTE: Bear in mind that if you've found a new market interesting, someone else has probably found it equally enticing and is researching it as well.

CHAPTER 9

Preparing for Market Entry

SEIZE OPPORTUNITY BY THE BEARD, FOR IT IS BALD BEHIND. — BULGARIAN PROVERB

MARKETS ARE NEVER completely open or completely closed. Every market presents would-be entrants with an enormous number of possible doors through which to pass. Some of the doors are unlocked and as clear as glass, while others may be as solid as steel, equally opaque, and tightly bolted. Ease of entry doesn't guarantee profitability and often, the gatekeeper government is keeping its most lucrative markets well-secured for itself and local business. Other times, doors are left open and unguarded in an attempt to lure unsuspecting investors or traders to a pitiable and profitless fate. Lucrative doors may suddenly swing wide for just a moment, while others must be cajoled for years, even chivied, into opening. Many portals need only to have the name of the right person dropped on their threshold to gain entry. In all cases, a marketeer's ability to properly analyze the information available will determine which door to approach and what product to present when the door opens.

Segmentation: How to Subdivide Opportunity

The procedure whereby marketeers determine how large or how small of a group to approach with their products is called market segmentation. Opportunities for segmentation in international marketing may seem endless. The world can be treated as a single marketplace, or it may be seen as composed of billions of single-member markets in the form of individual human beings. Any groupings in between these two extremes can be considered a market segment. The degree of segmentation is determined by the appeal of a product to a general market and by the ease with which that product can be adapted to increasingly specific markets. For this reason, most companies start off with as broad an appeal as possible, then sharpen their focus as more insights are gained.

Initially targeting an entire country can be risky, especially when the geography is expansive and the population diverse. Marketeers must determine how consumers in any particular group respond to the marketing mix—that is, the product, its price, promotional efforts, and the means of distribution. Information gathered during research will be used to make this initial determination, which over time will be increasingly refined. This doesn't necessarily mean that a company will change its focus from the market segment it originally targeted. Even when the segment remains the same (e.g., Hulinese executives between the ages of thirty-five and fifty with large disposable incomes), in time it will be further dissected into smaller and smaller niche groups as consumer tastes are perceived more precisely, or as they change.

Differentiation: Engaging the Competition

Differentiation is the conscious effort by a company to distinguish itself from its competition. Even when a segment has been selected, it must be understood that a competitor has already made the same selection or will shortly. This is where differentiation comes into play as a means of reaching the consumer. Every consumer has a reason for buying a particular product—necessity, convenience, status, impulse, emotion, color preference, or a host of other motivations. Starting at the macrolevel of marketing, marketeers will have only a general understanding of such motivations upon entering a new national market. Time and familiarity will bring about microlevel marketing approaches as consumer buying patterns (and their underlying motivations) make themselves evident. Continued differentiation from competitors can lead to an expanded market, a further segmentation of a current market, or both.

The athletic footwear industry is a fine example of ongoing marketing that utilizes segmentation and differentiation to expand and subdivide. Initially just purveyors of running shoes, they've progressively marketed designs for *specific* sports and even cross-training footwear for those that can't make up their minds about which sport to play. The manufacturers have refined the segmentation, all the while seeking to differentiate themselves in the consumer's mind by seeking the endorsements of famous athletes and the addition of technological gimmicks (e.g., airpumps, quasi-scientific designs). The original target group, athletes, has been "niched" into its various fields of sport, while the shoes themselves have left the athletic context and entered the realm of fashion. Only by paying attention to what consumers want (since, in this case, very few actually use the product for the design purpose) could the manufacturers move with equal success through the macro- and microlevels. Some shoe companies, like Nike, have logos that have become cultural icons, as their focus moved from shoes to clothing to luggage and eventually to their own retail outlets.

Positioning

Positioning is the means by which a marketeer establishes the product as a distinct image or brand in the consumer's mind. Simply put, it's the management of perception and it goes beyond consumers' general beliefs about a product. Products are seen as part of a larger category, but a marketeer seeks to hold a separate and singular position in the consumer's mind (e.g., before positioning: Heineken is just beer, after positioning: Heineken is that imported Dutch beer in the green bottle that costs a little more but shows sophistication). There are six main steps that you can use (as did Heineken on its way to becoming a world leader) to prepare a positioning strategy.

SEGMENT THE MARKET

Deciding which group to go after in the foreign market is usually based on similarities found with successful marketing efforts at home. The wants and needs of consumers in this new market must be researched (surveyed) to not only fine tune the targeting but also to determine whether or not the original product will require modification.

LIST COMPETITORS

Competitors may be very evident or you may have to do some searching. Even if your product is the market prototype, likely competitors can be profiled from related industries. For details, see Competition Profiles in Chapter 8.

DETERMINE HOW COMPETITORS ARE POSITIONED

You must determine where the competition stands, as your position will only have meaning relative to theirs. If they're a local company, then chances are good that they're already well-established in the marketplace (even if it's just a related field) and consumer perceptions of them are readily available. If your competition is another foreign company, information may not be as forthcoming.

IDENTIFY OPEN POSITIONS

Since no market is completely closed, suitable openings are to be assessed. Competition may be met "head to head," as is the case with pan-Asian transporters like Cathay Pacific and Singapore Airlines. Each attempts to out-service the other in the exact same segment of luxury travel over almost duplicate routes. Both realize there are other segments (business commuter routes) and other positions (economy flights), but each refuses to relinquish the luxury field to the other. Airlines have made fortunes by exploiting various positions (fast, sophisticated, economical, luxurious, comfortable, professional, sexy, etc.) and each consciously chose the image to be implanted in the consumer's mind. Openings may be found in that "mind" or, as is more often the case, openings can be expanded and exploited. Either way, they must be identified.

DETERMINE HOW CONSUMERS MAKE DECISIONS

Once a position has been identified, marketeers must now find out how consumers reach decisions to act on that positioning at the purchase point. For instance, in the preceding example, do consumers choose Singapore Airlines for luxury, convenient scheduling, newness of its aircraft, multiclass ticketing, or the perceived sexuality of the "Singapore Girl" prominently featured in the advertisement? Whatever the answer is (and it may be all five of them at different times), new competition should position itself accordingly. Finding out how consumers think can only be determined by direct contact.

DIFFERENTIATE YOUR PRODUCT

The final stage of positioning strategy will be to differentiate your product so as to maximize its appeal. This should only be done after consulting directly with consumers; do not attempt to guess how they think. You may decide to position yourself as a higher quality alternative to a competitor or as a more economical one. It's even possible to succeed as a duplicator of goods and services already present in the marketplace. Product "clones" often surpass the original in some markets (computers, beverages, clothing).

Public Relations: Image is Everything

Public relations (PR) is any of the activities a company performs in order to maintain its image while promoting goodwill toward its products and personnel. Positioning is part of this image maintenance, and images in today's information society require constant protection. Marketeers realize that a company's image can, oftentimes must, be changed in the consumer's mind but that too much change or too drastic a change may result in damage. When an image is altered it should be done so deliberately and by degrees. Unfortunately, the image of a company isn't entirely under its own control. The media can be a very powerful tool both for building an image and destroying it. Good relations with the media in all of its forms (print, radio, television, Internet services) are the goal of a public relations effort (decades ago, PR stood for *press relations*, but the subsequent non-print media emphasis inspired the name change).

International companies have enormous PR concerns, as they must contend with a wide variety of overseas media cultures as well as with their own domestic news outlets. Abroad, virtually everything a foreign company does, both prior to and after entering a new country, will be scrutinized; the larger the company, the greater the scrutiny. Back at home, their actions and associations overseas will be used as a measuring stick for acceptability in the local marketplace. Two very good examples of this double-edged sword can be seen in the recent problems created for Swiss banks and companies doing business in Myanmar (Burma). Swiss banks had a century-old image of discretion and legitimacy that suddenly came to an end as news of their involvement (at first denied) in Nazi financial deals from more than 50 years prior gained attention. Major companies of all stripes in Britain and the United States were quick to distance themselves by withdrawing funds from Swiss financial institutions. In Myanmar, where human rights concerns have made headlines, numerous foreign firms from around the globe have ceased investment activity to avoid a consumer backlash in their domestic markets. In both instances, companies found that their image, so deftly cared for, was now out of their control and they could only *respond* to consumer perceptions, not *manipulate* them.

Good public relations are essential, even when the brand name is well known and well-thought-of before a product enters the target market, and that PR effort must start prior to actual entry. When a company already has an international presence, its reputation for fair dealing and for sensitivity to local cultures may already be locked into the local psyche, long before market entry is even considered. The use of goodwill gestures (e.g,. art patronage, education programs, sports team sponsorship) is a common way for foreign companies of all sizes to ingratiate themselves. Creating employment opportunities for local personnel (at both the managerial and staff levels) is another way for foreign firms to counteract the impression that they're goal is simply to profit from the new market.

NOTE: PR, like product positioning, requires that the practitioners have a firm understanding of local culture and methodology. When a small company is trying to establish a foothold, they may be judged by the actions of the personnel sent out to research that market. Arrogant attitudes, missed meetings, professional slights, and lack of preparation all add up to bad PR before the product ever reaches the market. PR isn't just for the big players, and it doesn't always appear in the newspapers.

Problems to Avoid in New Markets

There are some pitfalls to avoid when attempting to segment the market and differentiate the product. Most problems occur when assumptions are made. The following assumptions are some of the most common.

PRODUCT IS PRODUCT

There's always a service component for goods sold, and services sold usually include the use of some physical goods. However, goods and services can't be marketed in the same way. Although there's a section of this chapter devoted to this difference, it should be noted now that consumers have a less demanding view of service when goods are the focus of the sale. Consumers buying a service, in turn, have a less stringent requirement of the goods that are often needed to perform that service. Marketeers should understand this when selling goods or services as their main product.

BIGGER IS BETTER

When segmenting, start with a size that your company can handle even when the potential for sales may be countrywide. Putting your company in a position in which it can't handle solicited demand is a surefire way to attract competition. When dealing with differentiation, major differences may not be what the consumer is looking for at the point of purchase. Adding table service in a fast-food restaurant, for example, tends to confuse rather than please. Differentiation can be any size, from subtle to blatantly obvious, as long as it's in keeping with consumer expectations.

ALL CHANGE IS GOOD

Consumers aren't stupid. They want *improved* products, not merely *changed* ones. If you're going to alter your product to differentiate it in the marketplace, make sure that the changes are of benefit (real or perceived) to the consumer. Most of the time, changes can be simple and not necessarily costly. They're always costly if made without seeking the direct input of consumers.

NOBODY CAN RESIST A BARGAIN

When the phrase "priced themselves out of the market" is used to describe a company's product line, it usually refers to overpricing. However, many companies, from airlines to fast-food restaurants, have actually underpriced themselves into failure. This can occur even when large discounts keep the product potentially profitable. This results because customers tend to believe that low prices equate with low quality. When this occurs, people become highly suspicious rather than appreciative of cheaply priced products. This is especially apparent in goods that are physically consumed (food, beverages, medicine) or services that apply to security or health (e.g., how many people would trust a doctor who worked for minimum wage?). Discounting can also lead consumers to believe that they were gouged for past purchases, the logic being that if a company can afford to offer a 50 percent discount today, then yesterday's price was overstated by 100 percent. If price reductions are to be the point of differentiation, take care not to "cheapen" the consumer's opinion of your product.

PEOPLE LOVE LUXURY

Most people do prefer luxury, but very few are willing or able to pay for it. If your products are luxury oriented and presumably demand high prices to cover high cost, care must be taken to direct them at consumers who can afford (or at least will not resent) paying for them. Airlines recognized some time ago that "first class" has limited appeal and went on to subdivide luxury into affordable bites; various forms of "business class" are now standard. Hotels have taken a similar route with "concierge club" and a wide variety of suite-style lodgings. It should be noted that consumers always expect more than they pay for but rarely accept less. Creating an atmosphere or appearance of luxury is problematic if the product doesn't live up to the created expectation. Keep in mind that luxury isn't a universal concept; one person's pampering may be another's standard mode of living.

PEOPLE BUY WHAT'S GOOD FOR THEM

If this were true, the use of motorcycle helmets and seatbelts would never have to have been made a legal requirement. Likewise, the widespread popularity of cigarettes, alcohol, fatty foods, and even heroin all speak of humanity's desire to forsake health for pleasure. Making improvements to a product to advance its health or safety aspects may actually *decrease* sales, as happened in the auto industry prior to safety regulation. It was also the case with "low alcohol" beers, which had a decidedly brief appearance in the 1980s. Other times, as was the case with "light" beer, the health aspects were underplayed and other more attractive attributes touted (less filling) to make consumers believe the change (mostly lower alcohol content) was adding to enjoyment. Marlboro cigarettes for their part marketed "regular" and "light" versions, so that consumers could choose their own level of nicotine and tar reduction. In recent years, they've even added "medium" as a new niche.

EVERYBODY WANTS CUTTING-EDGE PRODUCTS

Marketing texts designate the people who buy new products, regardless of dependability, as being early adopters. Having the "latest thing" is more important to these people than if the product actually works or is useful. The computer industry regularly depends on these types to pay for the privilege of field-testing new products. Sometimes this is a function of brand loyalty (as is the case with Apple products like the Newton PDA), or it may be due to the desirability of a technical advance (as occurs every time the size of cellular phones decreases). High-tech industries may be rife with early adopters, but few other sectors are so lucky. Most industries (banking, textiles, construction) change incrementally; major technical advances (ATMs, polycarbonates, modular homes) may take years to reach widespread usage after their original introduction. In other sectors (such as medicine and food processing), it may take decades, excluding governmental approval, to gain enough public trust for technical advances (laser surgery, freeze drying) to find general acceptance. Even more "creative" industries (fashion, music) regularly suffer the consequences of assuming that most people like to be avant-garde.

CONSUMERS WILL KNOW OUR PRODUCT IS BETTER

Just as it's unwise to make your differentiation too dramatic, it is equally foolish to make it too subtle. If the differentiation is small, and sometimes it may be, it must be brought to the consumer's attention via advertising or packaging. Long-distance telephone companies worldwide regularly do battle over a few pennies difference in by-the-minute rates. Wisely, they always couch the amount of money saved in terms of monthly or yearly totals. Otherwise, the consumer would have little impetus to change carriers.

THE COMPETITION MAKES A BETTER PRODUCT

Somebody has to make the best product on the market, and it isn't always your company. But this is no reason to throw in the towel. There are two approaches a company can take when facing a better-positioned competitor. The first is to exploit the rest of the market not occupied by the competitor. Industry leaders are often loathe to take on the lower end of the market sector, for fear of decreasing the value of their brand name, but carving a niche in an area not used to much attention can be very lucrative. Japan's conquest of the U.S. auto market resulted from exploiting the low-cost, compact market neglected by Detroit companies that had made their name with gas-guzzling, four-door sedans. Remember, there may always be room at the top, but there's more in the middle. The second approach is to build on your competitor's success by making improvements to their product line. This was the method taken by computer-clone manufacturers who broke IBM's stranglehold on the market. By taking advantage of the groundwork laid by "Big Blue," companies like Compaq and Dell have seen their fortunes rise. In turn, their progress has been exploited by Acer and Gateway.

EVERYBODY WILL WANT OUR PRODUCT

On rare occasion, consumers will accept a product "as is," with zero alteration to the form in which the company originally intended it. Inexplicably, some companies resist the changes regularly requested by the marketplace in an effort to bend consumers to their will. This we-know-best attitude is oft repeated in the television industry, where "knock offs" of successful programs are shoved down viewers' throats long after consumer tastes have changed. Swimming against the tide of clearly stated consumer desires is not the way to differentiate yourself in the marketplace.

NOTE: You don't have to pander to every consumer whim, but you'll have to address enough of them to keep consumers interested.

PEOPLE ARE DIFFERENT, BUT NOT THAT DIFFERENT

MTV (Music Television) is one of the great international marketing successes in recent years. From humble New York City beginnings in the early 1980s, MTV went on to become a global arbiter of music, fashion, and even morality. So powerful is its influence that it's regularly denounced by parents, religious leaders and governments worldwide (much to the glee of its marketing department). Such planetary success can be attributed to their realization that the only thing their viewers really have in common is that they watch television. Beyond that commonality, MTV has become as diverse as prudence and finances will allow.

Multilingual, multicultural, multiracial, multigenerational, multinational, multicontinental, multimedia and multifaceted are the hallmarks of this entertainment giant that has outniched competitors right off the map. Differentiation isn't just a marketing tool for MTV, it's a mission statement.

NOTE: Product preferences are as different as they are permitted to be and there's profit, big profit, in giving consumers that permission. If you can afford to microsegment, do it.

OUR BRAND NAME CAN SELL ANYTHING

Brand names can indeed be very strong (their development will be discussed in detail later in this chapter). In many ways, brands are what companies use to stake their claim in a market segment. A marketeer must take care to protect the image that's bound up with the brand, while maintaining a differentiation from competitors. There's little value and potentially great harm in confusing the consumer with a product line that's too diverse. Using the previous example, MTV can diversify almost indefinitely in the entertainment industry, and they've already begun with expansion into movies and casinos. However, if they suddenly attempted to market a line of securities brokerage houses, success would be very improbable. The key word in the previous sentence is suddenly. Over time, consumers can be convinced that a company (and its brand name) stand for much more than their original product. Long-term planning and segmentation will help a marketeer protect the brand while diversifying.

NOTE: MTV Securities may not be so far-fetched. In 1997, brokers Fahnestock & Co. sold over US$50 million worth of "futures" in rock star David Bowie's recording royalties. Similar offerings regarding artistic copyrights are now referred to a "Bowie Bonds."

THIS MARKET IS STABLE

Markets do stabilize, but not forever. Marketeers must be ever watchful, not just for a market to open but for them to expand and contract as well. Inside each market, new segments can present themselves through technical developments (e.g., laptop computers gave birth to a plethora of new specialized accessories) or legislation (e.g., in Thailand, sales of motorcycle helmets soared as soon as they became mandatory equipment) or environmental conditions (e.g., respirator masks are de rigueur throughout Southeast Asia during Indonesia's regular forest-fire season). The dwindling or eradication of opportunities must be considered as well.

WARNING: No opportunity or its demise should ever be "sudden" for the professional marketeer. In this case, "sudden" is a euphemism for "not paying attention." There are no surprises in marketing, only missed observations. Never be so busy that you can't pay attention, or you won't be busy for very long.

THIS MARKET IS PLAYED OUT

Markets are never played out; it's only the products offered to them that have an expiration date. Failed marketeers who blame the marketplace for their woes are only revealing their own inadequacy. As in the case of stability, awareness is the key to staying in the eternally evolving international markets. Goods and services can outlive their usefulness (e.g., mimeograph machines, mimeograph repairs), and a marketeer must be prepared for the rejection that will eventually take place. Preparing new product-lines (e.g., photocopiers, computer repair) and reorganizing market segments will keep you moving at the same pace as the global economy.

WARNING: In the world's current commercial atmosphere, to stop changing is to die.

Matching Goods to Market: Make It and They Will Buy

Up to this point, the term *product* has been used to describe both goods and services, with the implication that there's little difference in the marketing strategies necessary to bring either to the marketplace. The selling of goods will, by necessity, include some form of a service component, but the very fact that goods are physical in nature makes their relationship with the consumer different from the more intangible services. Goods (a.k.a. merchandise) may include commodities (grains, livestock, petroleum, minerals, currencies, securities), manufactures (machinery, textiles), or property (real estate). These three subgroups cover every form of physical merchandise available in the marketplace. (Although property isn't considered movable like other merchandise, its title—the rights to the real estate—can be traded internationally.)

PACKAGING OF GOODS: LITTLE THINGS MEAN A LOT

Packaging is the design and production of the appearance of, the features of, or the container for merchandise. It's the physical manifestation of the positioning that the company has chosen for each individual marketplace. Packaging, in all of its forms, is what piques the interest of consumers at the point of sale. Goods at the retail level are, for the most part, experienced visually. The cover of a book, the wrapper of a candy bar, the tea tin, the toy box, the shape of a personal computer cabinet or a milk carton all beckon the customer to buy. These are examples of primary packaging—the product's immediate container. Secondary packaging are the containers used to hold the primary packaging. Tertiary packaging are those containers used to ship or store the product. Packages are used to market (not just contain) the product at the point of purchase through six standard means.

- ENCOURAGE LARGER SINGLE PURCHASES Jumbo cans of beer, five-kilo bags of onions, and cartons of eggs get the consumer to buy in larger quantities than they can immediately use. Larger single-packaging can also invite greater use, as consumers feel the need to match consumption to availability. Fast-food giant Burger King uses this concept with its ever larger versions (usually by layer) of the already substantial Whopper. Like Australia's Fosters beer company, Burger King has found that larger packages breed larger appetites.
- FACILITATE USAGE Some packaging eases usage and thereby increases consumption. Frozen four-course dinners, twist-off bottle caps, tea bags, or personal computers with built-in speakers all make products easier to use and their purchase more attractive. Sometimes the ease may come in the form of storage, as in the case of Sweden's Tetra Pak International whose "asceptic"

packaging for juices and milk allows storage for up to five months. This can be key to businesses with irregular or infrequent delivery dates.

- CONSOLIDATION Cellular phones with paging features, TVs with built-in DVD players or photocopiers with printer/fax capability all allow several products to be packaged as a single unit. Sometimes the consolidation is so successful that consumers lose sight of the fact that multiple products are at work. Personal computers with factory-installed modems or sound systems are a good example of how consolidation can blur the line between separate products, even when each product is made by a different, often individually famous, company.
- PROMOTIONS Packaging can promote a product by identifying and establishing a brand at a visual level. The shape of a Volkswagen Beetle or of a Coca Cola bottle can trigger immediate recognition by consumers. Likewise, other packaging elements can bring continuity to a brand as its products change or as new products are brought to market (e.g., the Mercedes hood ornament, the Louis Vuitton logo). Beyond use as a brand platform, packaging can differentiate the product from competitors through size, shape, quantity, or color.
- INTRODUCTIONS Packaging can be used as a signal to consumers that a product has been updated or that an entirely new product is being offered. Changes in design and color, even the inclusion of the famous marketing phrase "new and improved," all attract consumers to the purchase. Sometimes the packaging is the only real "new" part of the product line (e.g., new auto models built on old frames and drive trains). But for many consumers, "new" means "better," even when no substantive change has occurred.
- EASE OF DISTRIBUTION Every market has a distinctive form of distribution that each marketeer will have to deal with—even when they operate their own distribution channels in the target country. The size, weight, shape, and recyclability of packaging will affect its acceptability to the distribution channel and to end-users. Because of this, packaging and the expense of redesign will have to be considered when planning for a new market. Labeling is often the main focus of packaging redesign, as government regulation is increasingly stringent. The EU's requirement that all weights and measures be listed in metric <u>only</u> will have an enormous effect on companies wishing to package for the United States and European market, as two separate packaging designs will now be required. Language and ingredient/component requirements can also make packaging design difficult and expensive. When consumers buy in small quantities (the Japanese) as opposed to bulk (North Americans), the size of packaging for storage may have to be redesigned. While tertiary (and most secondary) packaging has been standardized internationally, primary packaging is still the subject of cultural nuance.

NOTE: Sometimes the proper packaging and the willingness to conform to local distribution requirements will give the marketeer the upper hand over less cooperative competitors. Being prepared with new packaging will definitely give you a time advantage. Getting to the consumer first is always best.

The Pricing Process: Relativity of Value

Price is the value of what a consumer exchanges in return for products. It may take the form of monetary exchange, bartered services, or other goods. The price must be set so that both the consumer and the marketeer "profits" by the exchange if only at the perceptual level. The price (at least the starting price) is set by the marketeer, and consumers the world over consider price a major factor in purchasing decisions, whether they're buying vegetables at the local store, diamond rings, office furniture, or factory machinery. The key to controlling the pricing process is a firm understanding of how the targeted consumer perceives the value of goods.

NOTE: Much of this section on pricing can be applied to services, as well as to goods. Special concerns regarding the pricing of services will be taken up later.

Consumers must believe (and it's only a belief) that the price is less than or equal to the value they derive from the goods being sold. Marketeers can create this belief in the consumer's mind through adjustments to the quality of the goods themselves (raise or lower quality to match consumer buying capabilities), the atmosphere in which they're sold (raise or lower consumer expectations by manipulating ambiance), or by promotions (discounting).

Pricing will be driven by three main forces: cost, demand and competition. Each of these forces can, in its turn, be the main focus of a company's pricing strategy.

COST-ORIENTED PRICING

The cost of producing something represents the lowest possible price that a marketeer can charge for goods without incurring a loss. However, cost isn't as simple as it seems and its full extent can be hidden. Understanding cost is primarily an accounting process. These accounting concepts will be presented in a simplified form so as to assist in explaining pricing strategies only.

Fixed costs are those expenditures that don't change, regardless of how much is produced. These include such items as rent, management salaries, depreciation, and property taxes. While these costs remain static for extended periods of time, the fixed cost per unit will decline as production increases. Variable costs are expenditures that change according to the quantity of a company's output. These might include employee wages, materials, transportation, and packaging. The variable cost per unit may actually decrease when production expands—as efficiency increases and the savings that come with mass raw material purchasing become evident. Total costs are the sum of all fixed costs and variable costs. Marginal cost is the added cost that occurs when a single unit of production is added to current levels; it only affects variable costs and is used to determine the effectiveness of expanding production and its ultimate effect on pricing. Six cost-oriented pricing schemes are described below.

- COMPONENT COST This strategy takes a single component of cost (usually the major variable component, such as labor or materials) and expands it by a standard percentage to arrive at a market price. (e.g., unit material cost x 300 percent = sale price). That percentage, added by the original producer, is called a markon (as opposed to the markup added by middlemen) and is a very common, if simplistic, pricing scheme. It disregards consumer demand and doesn't take into account total cost per unit or competitor pricing.

- COST PLUS This strategy adds a profit percentage to the total cost per unit. This is more efficient than the component cost method as now all costs are considered, but there's still no accounting for demand. The cost plus strategy also relies on costs remaining relatively stable, making large fluctuations difficult to absorb. At the primary producer level, this pricing represents a markon. Middlemen using this strategy to set their sale prices are adding a markup.
- AVERAGE RETURN In this method, a company adds a fixed amount of profit (rather than a percentage) to its total cost. This amount is then divided by the total number of units to be produced in order to derive the price. The average return scheme relies on the selling of its entire production run in order to realize profits. But as many companies that have used this method have discovered, it's impossible to raise prices to recoup profit if demand is lower than projected, and discounting further erodes what little profit has been secured by earlier sales transactions.

$$\text{average return} = \frac{\text{total cost of projected unit} + \text{desired profit}}{\text{number of units to be produced}}$$

- BREAKEVEN Volume sales can be used to secure profit by figuring the level of unit sales at which revenue (money coming in) equals total costs (money going out). This is the breakeven point. Beyond this point, additional sales represent profit; below this point, all sales will incur a loss. The breakeven point will vary for different prices; projected sales volumes and variations on competitor prices or sales forecasts can be experimented with to arrive at the most favorable price. Like average return, this method assumes that whatever quantity will be produced will be sold and that variable costs will remain stable during the production period.

$$\text{breakeven point} = \frac{\text{total fixed costs}}{\text{price per unit} - \text{variable cost per unit}}$$

NOTE: Even when this method isn't the scheme ultimately used, it's an effective means of determining where your company stands (and has potential) in a new marketplace.

- MARGIN Breaking into a new market may require drastic measures to gain market share or recognition. Pricing below total cost—margin pricing—is a method utilized by large and small companies alike. It can be used to quickly grab a piece of a burgeoning market or to drive competitors out. When the former is the goal, a company hopes that long-term efficiencies and gradual prices increases will make up for early losses. When the latter is the goal, a company plans on becoming the market leader (if not its sole supplier) and making up losses with long-term volume. This tactic is called "dumping" when it's utilized by large international manufacturers; in some economies, it's an illegal procedure.
- ECONOMIES OF SCALE Characteristically, as a company's amount of market share increases (along with its production levels), there's an accompanying increase in the efficiency and a decrease in cost. These economies of scale are brought about by the discounts on volume material purchases and by increased worker productivity. For manufacturing processes, there is typically a 15 percent decrease in per unit costs for every 100 percent increase in production levels.

Companies fight for market share as a pricing strategy because the money saved by increased production can be passed along as price reductions, which further increase market share. This is rarely considered for start-up companies, but it's a regular ploy of established ones entering a new market with less efficient competitors.

DEMAND-ORIENTED PRICING

Cost may set the base for pricing but demand sets the high end, as consumers often place value on goods far in excess of the costs required to produce them. Gems and precious metals are examples of goods whose prices are set almost entirely by arbitrary demand. Demand can fluctuate wildly, and forecasts of consumer demand are taken on faith (rather than fact) and always as short-term considerations. Demand, price and supply are closely related and require continual monitoring. In the classic economic principle of supply and demand, as price increases on a steady supply, demand drops. If demand rises and supply is limited, prices increase. If supply increases and demand remains fixed, prices drop. Marketeers can manipulate demand to a degree by promotion and they have an obvious control over supply, but it's far easier to tinker with pricing, especially when goods must be produced in advance. Different goods react in differing fashion to price manipulation, a phenomenon known as price elasticity of demand. The four main categories of this price-demand relationship are discussed below.

- ELASTIC DEMAND When price is changed by a percentage, demand changes by a greater percentage. Normally, demand will drop dramatically as price increases and rise sharply as price decreases. However, consumers sometimes interpret price as a quality indicator, in which case demand will actually rise with price increases (wine, housing) or drop with price decreases (convenience foods, clothing) without any pressure from the supply area.
- INELASTIC DEMAND When price is changed by a percentage, demand changes by a lesser percentage. Prices of goods considered to be necessities (medicine) or near necessities (sugar) can absorb very large price increases without affecting demand. Similarly, goods can have a sharp price decrease and demand will change only slightly as there is a limit to consumption (e.g., milk).
- UNITARY DEMAND (A.K.A. UNITARY FALLOFF) When price is changed by a percentage, demand changes by an equal percentage. Like elastic and inelastic, these two percentages run in opposite directions, but it may not always be so for some luxury goods or those goods subject to short supply and high demand.
- CROSS DEMAND When goods are used in conjunction with other products, their price will fluctuate with that of the other product. For example, as the price of DVD players began to decrease, usage increased and the demand for movies in DVD format increased.

NOTE: Fans of popular music readily adopted CD and mp3 players, while classical music and jazz fans stayed with record albums claiming higher fidelity. Only recently have recording artists of all types returned to producing music on record albums (along with digital format), with a commensurate rise in the price of vintage turntables and amplifiers. Price, supply, and demand continue to orchestrate the market.

Determining the price elasticity of demand can be reduced to a formula, but it also requires the marketeer to understand how consumers in the target market make decisions. Because of the difficulty met by small companies when gathering survey information prior to entering a foreign market, elasticity shouldn't be used for setting initial pricing, only for subsequent changes. A simplified version of the formula is stated below.

$$E = \frac{\text{percentage change in quantity sold}}{\text{percentage change in unit price}}$$

E equals the coefficient of elasticity. If E is greater than one, demand is elastic. If E is less than one, demand is inelastic. Unitary demand exists when E = 1.

COMPETITIVE-ORIENTED PRICING

Cost and demand may set the extremes of pricing but a marketeer rarely has a market to himself—at least not for very long. Prices are a matter of recovering cost, meeting demand, and—most importantly—responding to the prices of the competition. Some industries (such as auto manufacturing) respond directly to the pricing initiatives of competitors. Others (global beer manufacturers) respond to a competitor's price change by increasing their advertising in order to maintain a customer base. Still other industries (fast-food operations) respond to competitive pricing by offering consumers a package of goods at discount, in a mix that disguises the marginal profits of the individual goods. A recent trend in pricing is to lower the upfront cost of the product and make up for the reduced price by raising the price on supplies needed to maintain the original purpose. Ink and toner cartridges for computer printers and photocopying machines are prime examples of this trend.

The key to competitive pricing is to keep the consumer from seeing that there's a direct link between your price setting and that of the competition. When consumers are aware of this link, they begin to play one company off of another (as regularly occurs when shopping for automobiles). A company that chooses to "hold the line" when a competitor lowers prices must work doubly hard to convince consumers that the product is worth the now-higher price. This can be very difficult if the product was previously positioned head-to-head with the competitor's. Similarly, discounting and mix-packaging can very often cheapen the consumer's opinion of the value of your product, especially when the price changes are dramatic. When price changes are seasonal (holiday sales, for example), price increases can be viewed as "gouging." Many countries in the developing world institute rigid pricing guidelines or "caps" during holiday seasons to protect against inflation and an angry population. Even in technological societies, companies may be subject to investigation and prosecution if their competitive pricing of certain vital commodities (fossil fuel, electrical power) gets too extreme or if it seems they're taking advantage of a spike (sudden increase) in demand.

Product Life Cycle: Pricing and Time

All products have a marketplace life span that goes through the phases of development, introduction, growth, maturity, decline and on to eventual withdrawal (see Chapter 7). During this cycle, a product may enter a market at a very low price and increase that price until it reaches "maturity of demand" and then decline in price as interest wanes. Many products, especially technological ones, have required extensive research and development costs prior to market entry. The introductory price for these goods may be very high but will actually decline as demand increases and research and development costs are recovered (as was the case with cellular phones and digital calculators). When goods merely imitate goods already present in the new market, a special introductory price is offered to get consumers to try out the imitator.

LIMITED DEMAND

During the decline phase of the product cycle, competitors start to leave the marketplace altogether. A company may find itself the sole supplier of a commodity that's still required by a small group of consumers but that's needed in amounts too small to warrant competition. This situation can greatly extend an otherwise doomed product. For example, large computer companies regularly sell off the rights to retail the replacement parts for computer models that are no longer available for retail sale, usually to original suppliers of those parts. Consumers still using the out-of-date models are now dependent on these suppliers to maintain a product that has, from the original seller's viewpoint, run the length of its cycle. This secondary market has become a very lucrative niche, as the price of limited supplies can be increased. Being a sole supplier with a limited market comes with the proviso that prices should be set just high enough to prevent the consumer from switching to a new product line altogether.

PLANNING THE CYCLE

Companies with a great deal of experience in a particular market can plan their product cycle along with their pricing scheme. Consumer behavior is a known quantity and elasticity has already been tested. The result can be a set of goods that have a "planned obsolescence" (consumer electronics) or even "disposability" (throw-away instamatic cameras). These experienced marketeers don't leave the life span up to the consumer but take it upon themselves to limit it. They price (and manufacture) these short-term goods with disposability in mind—not too costly, not too sturdy.

At the other end of the spectrum are producers that wish to offer a product whose main feature is durable luxury, as exemplified by quality timepiece manufacturers. Here, the consumer base is wealthy but few in number. The resulting price is usually quite high and doesn't necessarily reflect just the costs of materials and labor. Since the few consumers targeted will probably buy just a single unit in their lifetime, each sale must provide a huge margin. This type of pricing has a certain snob appeal, since a cheap digital watch will tell time just as well as an expensive Patek Philippe. High-end pricing for easily substituted goods like watches, clothing, or food relies on the consumer's willingness to equate price with quality. From the producer's point of view: Why should they sell a hundred items at a low price when they could sell a single quality item at a hundred times that price? Unlike the hope-filled little boy who, when asked why the lemonade he was trying to sell cost a thousand dollars a glass, responded with "I only need to sell one," a company with a high-pricing strategy requires a keen understanding of consumer behavior.

LONGEVITY AND PRICE

Even when entering a new foreign market, some consideration must be given to the relationship between longevity and price. A good deal of understanding about consumer behavior in the target market will be derived from the research process. If competitors already exist in the new market, then their pricing can be used as a guideline for establishing the introductory price. Most companies chose to underprice their rivals in order to establish a foothold. When Pepsi Cola entered the Vietnamese market in 1994 (against local producers as well as longtime rival Coca Cola), they discovered that the best introductory price (at least for a few days) was "free" if they wanted consumers to give them a try. Not every company can afford to give away its goods just to gain market entry, but it stands to reason that the stronger the competition and the greater the absence of consumer awareness, the lower the introductory price.

Warranty and Service Considerations: Customer Needs

Goods always have some component of their transaction that relates to service, even if it's only that of the retail sales personnel's labor. Nowadays, consumers demand more and more follow-up service on purchases. For centuries, when something was purchased it became the responsibility of the buyer—hence the ancient warning *caveat emptor* (let the buyer beware). Even a hundred years ago, if a farmer bought a plow, he was expected to maintain it himself and if it broke, it behooved him to know how to fix it. Modern-day economies have relieved the consumer of this burden and shifted it onto the shoulders of marketeers. Most countries have various forms of legislated warranties that require producers to "back" the quality of their goods for prescribed periods of time after the sale takes place. These mandated warranties vary widely in scope and duration from country to country, or even from province to province. Marketeers need to fully understand their legal obligations to consumers before entering any marketplace. The consequences can be dire for noncompliance and some nations actually prosecute the cases as criminal (rather than civil) violations, especially when consumers stand the risk of injury from poor quality products.

VALUE OF SERVICE

But not all warranties are mandated. Savvy marketeers have learned to distinguish themselves—not only by the quality and price of their goods but by their ability to guarantee them for lengthy periods of time. Along with these guarantees comes a host of consumer services in the form of repairs, maintenance, training, and upgrades. For some "high ticket" (expensive) items like automobiles, computers, or washing machines, after-sale service and the length of the guarantee are major selling points. Companies often compete based solely on their ability to service the product better than a rival, but each industry has its own take on the topic. For example, Fujitsu PC Corporation uses an advertisement to boast about how their computer service people answer the telephone in two minutes, rather than the industry average of thirteen, but the ad contains scant information about the computer itself.

Whereas automobile manufacturers have consistently widened the scope and length of their warranties and service, computer companies have done the opposite. The former found that consumers were keeping their cars longer than expected (especially during periods of economic downturn) and therefore wanted the greater product life span inherent with maintenance. However, computer buyers (laptop users, in particular) found they had little use for a three-year warranty, as they were buying new machines every eighteen to twenty-four months. Computer companies dropped the warranties to one-year, and now some even charge consumers to use their telephone "help" lines for service. Understandably, as these two opposite approaches to service were being formulated, the price of automobiles rose and that of computers dropped.

NOTE: When consumers pay more for something, they expect more service and tighter guarantees. Expectations of "more" become skewed over cultural lines. For example, Westerners are often cited for being demanding and intolerant of counterparts or sellers while working in Asia. This stems from Westerners having higher expectations of service. Asian businesspeople seem unusually passive to Western counterparts, but much of this is the result of Asians having different expectations beyond product delivery. In either situation, the buyer rules. The marketeer bears the burden of knowing what the consumer culture "expects" of service. The seller's opinions are of no importance.

Matching Services to Market: Selling Intangibles

"Services" are the work done by a company that benefits another company or a consumer. They're often referred to as "intangibles" because there's often little or no physical component to the process. Services include education, banking, hospitality, airline travel, accounting, consulting, brokering, software, insurance, health care, communications, and a host of other "acts" performed by one group of people for another. While there may be a physical item as part of a service (banks have money, restaurants have food, schools have books) a company is denoted as a service because the greatest part of what it sells is the labor of its staff. Services are a fast growing sector in developed economies; international trade in services for all nations has topped US$700 billion per year. Far from connoting servitude, becoming a "service society" is now indicative of having attained the most advanced form of economy beyond industrial and technological. It's a standard economic observation that the majority of what wealthy people purchase isn't goods but services. Services in this case are, literally, for those consumers who have every*thing* that they or their companies need.

Commercial and Consumer Services: Different Attitudes

Services are divided into two main groups: commercial services, which are marketed to other businesses, and consumer services, which are directed at individual buyers. Each group has needs and attitudes very different from the other. Two service industries—banking and hotels—provide contrasting approaches to dealing with this divergence on an international basis.

A bank will offer its commercial and consumer patrons similar services but in a very different manner. Merchant and corporate customers demand immediate service and preferential treatment. Beyond deposit, withdrawal, and checking, these commercial customers want payroll accounting, low-rate business loans, investment advice, foreign exchange transactions, correspondent bank connections and letters of credit. And they want (and receive) enormous discounts on these services, based on how much they keep on deposit.

Individual consumers receive basic checking and savings account services, along with bank card privileges (Visa/Mastercard). They place few demands on the bank and accept without question (for the most part) whatever rates the bank offers. Most consumers put little more thought into which bank they choose than determining which has a branch closest to their home. Few major banks have found value in offering consumer services, due to the extensive administrative work required to handle these relatively small accounts. Many nations *force* banks to maintain consumer services in order to retain their licensing. Banks have responded by entry into more lucrative areas (such as insurance and securities brokering) to make up for losses incurred while handling small consumer accounts, which they consider a nuisance, at best.

Hotels take the opposite view of consumer/commercial differences. They see even corporate customers as individuals and market their services accordingly. Large hotel facilities have "business class" or "concierge level" floors set aside for business travelers, although they're available to tourists as well. Corporate accounts allow for the discount purchases of blocks of room-nights spread over a year's time. These are often sold to airlines for housing their flight crews or to repeat corporate accounts. And like the airlines, hotels offer their noncorporate guests the opportunity for similar discounts with "frequent guest" promotions. International hotel companies like Marriott have created "extended stay hotels" for business travelers on long assignments while, at the same time, maintaining resorts for leisure travelers. Rather than shunning one segment in favor of another, hotels have focused on the needs of each and attempted to exploit them to the fullest extent possible.

No one can deny that banking is a profitable business or ignore the importance of the hotel industry to international trade. Each of their service marketing strategies has been successful. Every marketeer who works in a service industry must make the decision to focus on commercial service, consumer service or both. Marketeers will find that, for the most part, commercial customers are far more demanding and have greater "clout" because their purchasing power is so large. There's a natural tendency to work harder to maintain the business of a large account. (If a bank teller or a hotel clerk loses a single consumer account due to rudeness, there will be little consequence. However, if the account in question is the Philips Electronics corporate account, be assured there will be much greater concern.) This isn't to say that consumers can't be demanding or have considerable purchasing power, only that the scale is smaller.

Pricing: How Much is Service Worth?

Much of the earlier discussion about pricing goods can be applied to services. However, the *pricing* of services creates problems for marketeers. Since there's no size, shape, or weight to a service, it's difficult for consumers to value it relative even to other services with which they may be familiar. Unless a service is presented by a known brand name, consumers tend to equate price with quality. This sense of "you get what you pay for" has been the standard pricing scheme for many services from lawyers to leisure.

This consumer perception is often called the Disneyland Effect—people spend so much to arrive at and enter into the theme park that they're reluctant to admit that, in the end, they aren't satisfied with the result. Even after standing in long lines for virtually everything, people go away happy. ("It cost so much, I must have had fun.") Similarly, consultants charge huge fees in the belief that customers will find their work more satisfactory if it comes at a premium price. And it works. Consumers know that high-quality goods demand a high price so, in reverse logic, they assume that high-priced services provide top quality.

VALUING SERVICES

Values for services are really a matter of personal values, and those values are easily manipulated. Consider the following examples:

- A New York exporter pays a lawyer $100 per hour to look over a trade document but pays only minimum wages to the immigrant *au pair* who takes care of her child.
- A global manufacturer pays a British business consultant £500 per day plus expenses but grumbles about the 15 percent service charge a Hong Kong hotel applies to a banquet check for a deal-closing celebration.
- A subsidiary of a Canadian financial planning company operating in France charges clients for brief telephone consultations but regularly makes bootleg copies of its office application software to avoid paying for additional licenses.

MARKET PRICES

Services are like goods in that the value placed on them seems culturally arbitrary but different from goods in that there's no "market rate" for services (as is the case for commodities). A service company can set its own pricing in isolation (e.g., a consultancy) or position itself relative to competitors (e.g., a fast-food restaurant). Big global players have traditionally marketed their services on a market-by-market basis in which prices are customized to each target's perception of the service, to its local costs, and to its ability to pay. A service may cost ten times as much in one market as it does in another, even though the true cost of providing that service to each set of consumers may differ only slightly. In the past, this could be done because, generally, services weren't easily transferred from low-priced markets to high-priced ones. However, this has changed enormously in the last few decades as information flows have accelerated. Some services are increasingly transferable (finance, telecom), and consumers are now more aware of what other markets are paying. This has resulted in demands for more equitable pricing.

UNIFORM PRICING

Much of the difficulty of having a uniform pricing policy, in which prices in each market are matched to the exchange rate without regard for other factors, stems from the tariffs, taxes, and other local costs that plague international companies. Consumers only see the products or goods, not their underlying costs. This can be very telling on something as intangible as a service. Market-by-market pricing is still the best approach especially when the marketeer works in an economically diverse landscape. Services are better understood and more highly valued in technological societies than in agricultural based emerging markets. If the service is provided for the same price in both marketplace extremes, it can run into problems. If it's priced for technological markets, the service will be beyond the reach of emerging market consumers. If the service has its pricing geared for emerging markets, the low rate will be taken by technological markets as a sign of poor quality.

NOTE: The pricing of services requires extra attention during the research process. Researchers must determine the local market's familiarity with the service to be sold, as well as local attitudes toward services in general. While many markets are familiar with globally branded commodities, it's less common that foreign markets recognize service providers by name.

Financing Strategies: Buy Today, Pay Tomorrow—Perhaps

Having a great product that's in high demand and marketable at a profitable price is absolutely no guarantee of success. Consumers everywhere are prone to wanting products they can't afford to pay cash for—at least their own cash. Marketeers must be concerned about the way that purchases of goods and services will be financed and the mode of compensation. Being paid in local currency isn't the only option and, in some cases, it may not be an option at all.

FINDING FINANCING

Finance literally means the "end of debt," which implies that a debt was created. For the purposes of this discussion, finance will represent the use of a third party to pay a seller for a transaction on behalf of the buyer. Marketeers who wish to work in the global arena are increasingly required to understand finance and the various financial avenues available. It's not unusual for a seller to be expected to line up the financing for the buyer as part of his responsibility for having a successful transaction. Buyer access to financing may be severely limited due to location or education. In emerging markets, sizable transactions will most likely require the seller to bring the financial package to the table. Many of the following sources of financing can also be used for product development prior to entering a marketplace.

- COMMERCIAL BANKS Both domestic and foreign commercial banks are willing to finance international transactions, but only when there's minimal risk and the contract is short-term. This lack of risk is reflected in a relatively low interest rate. Large commercial banks (e.g., Citicorp, Sumitomo) have suffered severely in each of the last three decades for lending to high-risk projects that have gone bust. Such banks can be very wary of international deals. They're best approached for financing only if the deal is rock-solid and the buyer dependable.

- INVESTMENT BANKS (I-BANKS) Traditionally, investment bankers sold securities on behalf of a company taking per-trade fees or differentials for their services. Newer forms of investment banking firms raise money for projects from any and all of the sources listed in this section. Primarily connected with technology projects or the building of manufacturing plants, investment bankers can be well worth their fees for large, difficult projects.
- EXPORT-IMPORT BANKS (EXIM BANKS) This is a general term for banking services set up by national governments to promote the export or import of goods and services deemed profitable for the country. They work with short-term (less than 180 days), medium-term (180 days to 5 years) and long-term financing (5 to 10 years). Short-term usually provides low-cost insurance for a transaction so that the exporter can more readily acquire a commercial loan. Medium-term offers a combination of insurance and discount lending for transactions. Long-term financing extends direct credit to the foreign buyer or a guarantee (rather than partial payment insurance) for a private loan. Both medium- and long-term financing will require down payments by the buyer.
- DEVELOPMENT BANKS These are international bodies set up to promote development in parts of the world considered lacking. They offer low interest loans for worthy projects, and in the last decade they've even "bailed out" entire economies that were floundering. The more specialized the bank (e.g., The Bank of Central African States), the more likely that it will finance trade transactions. Some development banks can be found at the provincial and city level.
- FORFAITING (FINANCING WITHOUT RECOURSE) In this process, a seller takes the debt incurred by the buyer (a receivable) and sells it at a discount to a company willing to collect the debt over an extended period. Sellers figure the discount cost into the selling price and collect their money immediately, even when the transaction or project has long-term financing. Forfait companies specialize in debt collection and are betting they can collect the debt within a set period of time. They may even resell the debt in a secondary market in the form of a promissory note or bill of exchange.

WARNING: As mentioned earlier, countries following orthodox Islamic law will not become involved in "usurious" transactions, that is, those in which moneylenders take interest for their participation. Forfaiting under these circumstances is out of the question. Some cultures that rely on the personal relationship rather than the commercial contract may also take affront at finding their debt being sold off to a third party and then into the open market. If forfaiting is used, make sure the buyer is aware of the ramifications.

- PRIVATE INVESTORS (ANGELS) Many private citizens, especially expatriates or former citizens of the target market, are willing to finance international projects. This is exemplified by the massive amount of foreign investment that flooded into China in the 1980s that was orchestrated by groups of so-called Overseas Chinese. Wealthy individuals or groups of individuals inside the target market may also be likely candidates.

- VENTURE CAPITALISTS (VC) This funding is, by its very nature, reserved for high-risk projects. Venture capitalists see potential where commercial banks fear to tread. VC companies command direct involvement with the project (40 percent or more equity stakes) and they're active at the managerial level. The seller may bring the VC to the table, but the buyer will have to live with them for a long time. VC companies have the long-term goal of selling off equity interest once the project becomes profitable. Although they rarely get involved in trade deals, venture capitalists can bring a wealth of business acumen to a project.
- INTERNAL FINANCING Larger companies and small companies with large cash reserves may choose to finance the sale themselves. Build-Operate-Transfer projects (BOTs) often take this form, in which the seller literally pays for the sale and the buyer repays the seller over time. This is common for infrastructure ventures in developing countries. On a smaller scale, exporters may finance initial forays into a new market as a way to "get their foot in the door" and make a good impression. When this becomes a common practice, some companies actually form separate subsidiaries designed solely for the purpose of financing new projects in new markets.

NOTE: Buyers in markets new to international trade can be reluctant to pay even short-term interest to a seller. Rolling the interest directly into the sale price causes even more problems. Forming a separate financing subsidiary tends to ameliorate the buyer's opinion of internal financing.

- ENGINEERED FINANCE Sellers with far-flung offices and global experience can call upon financing from around the globe. These sellers offer buyers the opportunity to arrange financing in whatever country provides the most beneficial terms. As a marketeer's company grows and successes mount, financial relationships in one market can be utilized in another, possibly even years after the original project. As is true of other parts of commerce, maintaining networks of contacts is the key to long-term success.

Transaction Settlement

CURRENCY

In international commerce, not all national currencies are of equal value. The stable value of a currency (known as its degree of "hardness") makes it more desirable for being converted into other currencies. Some currencies, like the *renmibi* of China, are completely inconvertible, and because these currencies are less desirable for transactions they are described as being "soft." The U.S. dollar, on the other hand, is considered to be one of the hardest of currencies along with the Japanese yen and the EU's euro. Their values change but do so over long periods of time, as opposed to the volatility of soft currencies. Sellers prefer contracts in which they're paid in a hard currency assuming a stable value; buyers prefer to commit to paying in soft ones assuming a drop in value.

Nations with high inflation problems and soft currencies will oftentimes place severe restrictions on how foreign companies will be paid for their products. War-torn central African nations forbid the carrying of foreign currencies within their borders, thus making payment for foreign shipments difficult and subject to direct government approval, even for small transactions. Countries (like Vietnam and China) that are attempting to build large hard currency reserves go so far as to put restrictions on how much their business-people can spend while traveling overseas since these expenses must be paid in something other than their domestic currency. During periods of crisis (such as the summer of 1997 currency devaluations in Asia), some countries will actually cease currency exchanges of all kinds in an attempt to protect their economy. Experienced sellers must attempt to ensure transactions against this type of interference when dealing in risky markets. See also *A Short Course in International Payments*, also by World Trade Press.

NOTE: A great deal can happen between when a contract is signed and when payment is made. Marketeers must be aware of the prevailing value of the currency specified in a transaction, as well as of the political and economic milieu in which the transaction takes place.

COUNTERTRADE

As many Thai companies found out in 1997, foreign-denominated debt can ruin a firm if the local currency drops in value. Another aspect to keep in mind is that marketeers are buyers of raw materials as well as sellers of product. Currency valuation may work in your favor during the sale but against you when it's time to purchase raw materials or labor. Marketeers working in the fluctuating landscape of global business will find that there are times when buyers will simply be unable to achieve financing in a currency that's suitable. When this occurs—and it does occur in an estimated 10 percent to 15 percent of all international trade—buyers may offer goods or services in return. This process of exchanging one product for another is known as countertrade.

BARTER

Barter—the equal and full exchange of goods between two companies—is one form of countertrade. No currency is used for the transaction and there may be more than just the two original companies involved, as each part of the transaction attempts to get a useful product in return. For example, Company A sells sugar to Company B, which can only pay with wheat. Since Company A doesn't need wheat, Company B sells it to Company C, which can only pay with alcohol, a product unneeded by Company B but useful to Company A. Company C, in turn, delivers alcohol to Company A in an amount of equal value to the original sugar. This type of bartering can have as many segments as efficiency will permit. It should be noted that even when no currency exchanges hands, customs offices will still be levying tariffs. And they rarely barter.

MIXED COMPENSATION

Mixed compensation is another form of countertrade, wherein goods or services are exchanged for a mixture of other goods and services as well as currency. The importer may, for example, pay for goods with 40 percent cash, 25 percent commodities and 35 percent services. In another scenario involving A, B and C from above, Company A sends sugar to B, which sells wheat to C. Company C sends 30 percent of the original A–B trade to Company A in cash and 70 percent in alcohol. Sometimes an importer and an exporter from the same country will transact business with a foreign company that exports as well as imports. Different products (but of equal value) are sent to and received from the foreign country, and money is exchanged only between the original importer and exporter.

OFFSETS

An offset or buy-back agreement is a special arrangement between the seller and the buyer. It involves the seller making a commitment to purchase from the buyer, at a future date, products that have been made possible by the original sale. This type of arrangement is usually reserved for very large purchases or those that effect an economy at the national level. It generally requires the cooperation of governments as numerous companies or industries may be involved. As one example, a large auto manufacturer is allowed to sell automobiles in a foreign market only if the manufacturer agrees to import parts from the target market. In another example, a chemical producer will be permitted to sell the manufacturing processes for a new polyethylene plant in a foreign market only if it agrees to import raw petrochemicals from that same market.

NOTE: Often, groups of smaller marketeers will band together in an effort to set up their own buy-back agreements. This takes a great deal of internal as well as intergovernmental cooperation.

Brand Selection and Equity: Building on Success

A brand is the distinctive name or design (logo, package, trademark, etc.) that becomes a recognized marketplace image, a way for buyers to distinguish a product from its competitors. The establishment of a strong, positive brand image can actually enhance the value of a company and is considered at this point to be brand equity. As with price, marketeers must give consideration to how a particular brand name will be received in each different market. After all is said and done, brands are images, and images can be controlled to a great degree by skilled management and a firm understanding of what motivates the consumer. Like all images, they're much more easily destroyed than created.

BIG COMPANY, BIG NAME

Some companies have established international brand names (e.g., Toyota, McDonald's, Shell Oil, Nestlé) that are recognized virtually anywhere on the globe. Names as famous as these are often part of a market's language even before the products cross the borders. However, most marketeers aren't equipped with such reputations in advance of their arrival and must literally "start from scratch" when entering a new market. This situation has both positive and negative aspects.

On a positive note, the target markets have no preconceived notion about what the company represents. Famous companies often have to overcome not fame but notoriety (deserved or not). Toyota and McDonald's, for example, not only bear the standard for their products but are also often seen as representatives and promulgators of domineering foreign cultures. Shell Oil and Nestlé are often taken to task for the environmental (oil drilling) and medical (baby formula) impact that their products have had, respectively, on a global scale. It's not unusual for a project to come up against enormous local protest, even when the brand name company is a small investor or supplier for a venture. Beyond the possibility of notoriety is the problem of wealth. New markets assume that wealthy corporations will just throw money around (legally and illegally), and local partners can become indignant about the stringent financial controls that are part and parcel of international business.

LITTLE COMPANY, BIG PROBLEMS

Of course, the negative aspects of being an unknown company can be even more troublesome. Business and government leaders in the target market may be reluctant to meet with an obscure foreign marketeer. When meetings do occur, the marketeer has to spend extra time explaining the company's background and reliability. Distributors and consumers will have to be equally persuaded and may see little value in carrying or using an unrecognized brand. But this must be looked upon as a challenge, just as it was in the domestic market.

The creation of brand awareness in a foreign market faces the same obstacles as those found in the domestic market, but with the added problems of language and cultural differences. Awareness moves from recognition to recall to preference. This can be managed in a new market through a variety of promotional and design methods.

DISTINCTIVE NAME

Choosing a name to use in a foreign market can be a delicate issue. A literal translation of the domestic market name may create humor where none is intended, or possibly offense. It may even serve to confuse consumers about the product line. Similarly, retaining the domestic name without translation may cause problems as well, as it may sound like an unattractive word in the target market's language (e.g., Sunbeam's Mist Stick hair curler went to the German market untranslated. Then it was discovered that "mist" is German for manure).

Companies that have a widespread international presence may choose to simply abbreviate or use the initials of their domestic name (e.g., ING Bank). The name should be chosen based upon the image desired, consumer cultural perceptions, and the marketeer's product line.

ATTRACTIVE SYMBOL OR LOGO

This topic can be as sensitive a subject as the brand name, and symbols often create more powerful reactions in consumers. For instance, a Japanese manufacturing company may use flowers as part of its logo, as these symbolize perfection and symmetry in their domestic culture. Those same flower symbols in the U.S. market connote feminine images not generally associated with factories and machinery. Another Japanese company, Subaru, uses its namesake constellation, Pleiades, as its company logo. However, this symbolism has virtually no significance outside of Japan. In both examples, the names and logos were chosen long before the companies went international. Nowadays, companies shy away from logos that are too easily identified with a single culture and have moved toward more generic images. Microsoft Windows, for instance, uses an easily recognized windowframe pattern, while Lucent Technologies uses a simple red circle. Even when your logo has an apparently neutral image, test it out in the foreign market before committing it to exposure.

SLOGAN

Slogans or promotional jingles should be customized to each market. Poetry and music are very highly linked to culture. Beyond just making the slogan attractive to the local audience, it must also have meaning. Even something as simple as the old slogan for Ivory Soap, "So Pure It Floats," can fall flat in cultures like Japan, where washing is done *prior* to getting into the bathing tub. A bar of soap that floats is of little value. Conversely, the Japanese recognized the American obsession with individuality (and imperfect grammar) and marketed Toyota with its "You want it, you got it—Toyota!" slogan. Burger King taps the same sensibility with its "Have it your way!" jingle. Jingles and slogans tend to stay in the consumer consciousness for extended periods. Consumers can repeat radio and TV jingles decades after they've stopped being broadcast. While their content may vary from culture to culture, their effectiveness doesn't.

GOODWILL CREATION

This topic was discussed earlier in the section on public relations regarding a company's need to maintain its stature in the community. However, goodwill efforts are also an efficient means of gaining brand awareness when entering a new market.

Donations to cultural events, art projects, or health facilities can be very effective for marketeers if the logo or company name is visibly affixed to program materials, bulletin boards, signage, and other promotional collateral associated with the event or project. This isn't to be confused with advertising, although the lines between the two can be quite blurred. In order for a goodwill effort to be effective, the target public must believe that the company is offering their money, product, or labor as a donation to the particular cause.

WARNING: Displays of the company logo or name should be kept to a discreet, but visible, minimum and should never overshadow the main event or cause. Grabbing too much of the spotlight can easily backfire.

EVENT ASSOCIATION

This type of association goes more to the heart of blatant advertising than goodwill. Here, a company seeks to establish a close and long-term relationship in the consumer's mind between a favorable event and the product. It's most often utilized with championship sports events and major rock music tours, and it's best exemplified on the grand scale by the number of companies that wish to become the "official ——— of the Olympic Games." The hope is that good feelings engendered by the event will somehow be transferred to the product. This works just as well at the local level and is an effective way for foreign companies to gain acceptance in new markets.

ENDORSEMENTS

A company may choose to labor for some time to achieve recognition in a new market, or it may simply seek endorsements from respected members of the target community. Endorsements can take the form of a quote or advertised use of the product. Marketeers will usually supply the product for free to the endorser in return for such an endorsement.

NOTE: While this is a great way to quicken the pace of brand acceptance, marketeers must be careful to select only those endorsers that can bring them the most benefit and the least harm. Having your logo proudly displayed by a local celebrity is great, unless they're being led away in handcuffs for some malfeasance.

BRAND EXTENSION

Brand extension is the process of applying an established name to new product lines. This is a risky concept even in one's own domestic market, and no less so when entering foreign terrain. However, risk has the potential for greater success and the marketeer may want to consider attaching their brand name to a product line already accepted in the new market.

The idea is much like an endorsement, except that the marketeer is now the endorser and will take full responsibility for the product, rather than just being associated with it. Extending the brand name to new products may improve exposure; however, marketeers must select their lines carefully so as not confuse consumers. While consumers accept some extensions (Nike seamlessly moved from shoes to clothing), it will not accept others (McDonald's has continually failed to gain favor in most markets for its barbecue sandwich).

CO-BRANDING

This awareness-creating technique involves the direct linkage of brand names from separate companies. A widespread example of this is the display of the "Intel Inside" logo on the cabinet of most personal computers. Both the computer manufacturer and Intel gain by this exposure if the computer performs well. Of course, even if a component of the machine not under direct control of Intel (such as the monitor) malfunctions, then both companies will suffer. This points up the necessity of choosing your co-branding partners with care.

NOTE: A foreign company entering a new market may link itself with a successful local company or an already established foreign firm. In emerging or unstable markets, local partners may be the best choice, at least initially, as such a collaboration can be very useful for gaining political as well as economic protection.

REPETITION

Creating brand recognition and recall is often a matter of simple repetition. Consumers at all levels prefer to purchase products with which they're familiar, even if that familiarity is with the brand name only. Merchandise such as cigarettes, beer, fast food, athletic equipment, toys, and recorded music rely on repetition, due to the vast amount of competition in these areas as well as the frequent usage rate. The logic here is that since consumers are buying these products on a regular basis, they must be continually "reminded" which product to prefer.

Repetition can be done on the grand scale as it is by Umbro sportswear, during internationally televised soccer events, with their logo displayed on the clothing of every player and prominent on field signage. Or it can be done cheaply as Marlboro cigarettes did in Vietnam—by putting small but colorful logo stickers on Ho Chi Minh City's numerous *xyclo* pedicabs, without mention of what the product was. The effect is the same. Repetition causes a subconscious recognition and eventual recall of the brand name that can be triggered at the point of purchase. This is perhaps the oldest form of creating brand awareness, and it can be one of the most economical. Companies of all sizes should consider its use as part of an overall plan.

PROVISO: Some national governments (and almost all localities) have restrictions on advertisements from cultural, language, and artistic perspectives. Before a full-scale repetition scheme is put into action, check with the proper authorities about local standards and linguistic content.

PACKAGING

When it comes to merchandise, the inclusion of a prominently displayed brand name or logo in the packaging can stimulate the consumer to make the purchase. This is why supermarket shelves have all of the products' labels turned to face outward toward the passing shoppers. Food producers even vie for prominent shelf space to assist in triggering the purchase. At this level, the package is the last chance a marketeer has to reach the consumer. On a larger scale, the automobile industry has combined the packaging with the repetition process and made every one of their products a rolling brand-awareness mechanism. Some logo hood ornaments (such as those of Rolls-Royce, Mercedes Benz, and BMW) have become cultural icons of their own and indicators of status.

Gaining Market Share: Slicing the Big Pie

Market share (a.k.a. brand share) is the number of product units a company sells in a particular market as a percentage of the total number of units of that product type sold in that market. It may also be calculated on the basis of revenue generated by sales, rather than units sold. However, market share is calculated based on the segment that the marketeer has chosen to target, and those segments may be of virtually any size. Market share and its expansion is at the root of all marketing efforts.

Marketeers may choose a target and slowly develop their share of it over a long period of time or they may choose to simply "seize" market share by purchasing a company already active in the target market. The latter process is very common in capital-intensive sectors (heavy manufacturing, hotels). Whatever strategy a marketeer chooses between these extremes, the same variables must be considered for entering any foreign market. Each will be discussed from the viewpoint of companies marketing goods or services.

EXPORTING

Exporting of products (discussed in some detail in Chapter 2) is the most common way for a company to attempt entry into a foreign market. Merchandise manufacturers use exporting as a way to test consumer interest with minimal risk. Service providers often find that exporting their product is the only way that foreign governments will permit its use. Some services (software, publications) find that they've become "exporters against their will" through copyright violation. Such companies are then forced to formally export to the new market just to prevent further monetary losses and the erosion of quality control.

LICENSING

Licensing is the procedure wherein a company assigns the right to a brand, a trademark, a copyright, or the patent for a product or a process to another company for a fee. The fee may be a one-time-only charge, a per-unit produced fee, or a percentage-of-total-sales agreement. Licensing agreements usually cover specified periods of time and allow a company to have equity in the foreign market as they control the licensee's ability to produce. Rather than wait for market share to develop, the licensing company allows the licensee to take the majority of the risk for a product's success or failure. Beer manufacturers such as Anheuser-Busch and Heineken are prime examples of companies that license their process to local manufacturers rather than go to the expense of building their own breweries. On the service front, book publishers such as Macmillan, McGraw-Hill, and World Trade Press license out the translation and publication of books to foreign publishing houses on a regular basis. In both goods and services, if a market proves to be potentially expansive, marketeers can consider setting up their own production in the foreign country once the licensing agreement expires, subject to local governmental regulation. Of course, a marketeer must choose their licensee wisely, regardless of the levels of long-term risk. Local governments may require that the technology or process be transferred to the licensee at the end of the agreement, further complicating full-scale market entry. Keep in mind that trademark and patent protection varies a great deal from market to market.

FRANCHISING

Franchising is a more extensive form of licensing wherein a company in a target market agrees to purchase or license the brand name, products, logo, method of operation, promotional plans, and sometimes even building design from the marketeer. Besides larger fees, this gives the marketeer (the franchisor) greater control over quality and local market positioning. The targeted foreign company (the franchisee) gains procedural and management expertise, as well as an established brand name. In the service field, hotel operator Holiday Inn (owned by Britain's IHG) is a world leader in franchising, providing both operational procedures and room design to franchisees. In commodities, BP (British Petroleum) franchises their filling stations and refining expertise around the globe in an effort to keep up with the ever-expanding automotive market. Some franchisors, like KFC, provide what are called turnkey operations—the entire building, operating manuals, management training, and production supplies are purchased as part of the franchise agreement.

NOTE: Most franchise contracts include clauses that permit the franchisor to revoke the agreement or take over the venture if the franchisee doesn't maintain the quality standards required or causes the brand name to fall into disrepute. Marketeers may find it difficult to enforce such agreements in foreign markets that lack legal protection for noncitizens.

REPRESENTATIVE OFFICE

A representative office is an overseas "branch" that's opened to either investigate market potential, solicit business for the home market, or oversee a licensing/franchising agreement. Since these offices rarely generate revenue of their own, their costs of operation can be difficult to justify. However, these "rep offices" serve also as superb centers from which to conduct marketing surveys and as springboards for larger market entry plans. This applies to both goods and services producers. Some countries mandate that foreign firms open "rep offices" that are partially staffed by locals if the firms wish to conduct any business in the new market. This brings in hard currency to the local economy in the form of rent and local employment—both of which create the all important "goodwill."

WARNING: Many marketeers have sought to evade the office-rental price gouging of the emerging markets by using their hotel room as a "rep office" for extended periods. While this makes short-term practical sense from the marketeer's point of view, local governments (and their landlord constituents) frown on this practice and long-term public relations can be damaged.

CONTRACT PRODUCTION

Under "contract production," a foreign marketeer arranges for local production, after which the products are turned over to the marketeer for distribution and sale both locally and internationally. The marketeer only commits to the number of units produced over a specific time and forgoes the expense of building a facility or hiring employees, although some facility upgrades and training may be necessary. Computer hardware manufacturers such as Compaq and Texas Instruments regularly contract out production in low-cost Southeast Asia. In services, international banks have made Ireland a focal point for contracting out some of banking's credit card reconciliation operations. Though contract production may first appear as a cost-cutting measure, manufacturers and service providers alike know that as incomes grow in the "contracted" market, so too will the need for goods and services. It's a long-term strategy that may take a generation before true market entry occurs.

ASSEMBLY

An assembly strategy requires that a portion of a manufacturing process be located inside the target market. Usually, this portion takes the form of the "final assembly" but utilizes imported parts. This strategy allows the marketeer to take advantage of skilled but low-cost labor while providing the target market with the beginnings of a technology transfer, as well as "value added" finished-product exports. Countries trying to attract this type of investment will often establish export processing zones (EPZs) or special economic zones. These government-sponsored areas permit foreign companies to have tariff-free production if the end-product is exported.

LOCAL PRODUCTION

Establishing a local production plant in a foreign country is very expensive but it may be the best way to achieve market share goals. This is true for several reasons:

- Some governments will not permit foreign companies to sell finished, value-added products within their borders unless that company makes the firm commitment to employ locals. These countries will also require the marketeer to transfer technology.

- Local production may be the only way to access the market without paying prohibitively high importation tariffs. Denmark's toy producer Lego found this to be the case in Brazil, even though there was no sizable Brazilian toy industry for the government to protect.
- It's not unusual for a successful export marketeer to suddenly find that its success has caused local producers in the target market to seek high tariff protection. As exporting becomes untenable, local production becomes the only way to protect what market share gains have been made.

NOTE: Even when local production is instituted, governments may also add in a "local content requirement" to ensure that the production plant doesn't become simply an assembly plant.

- Service businesses must often go where their customers are, since a good deal of personal contact may be required to perform the service. The customers may be local to the foreign market or they may be other foreign marketeers establishing a beachhead. Companies not set up for franchising (Deloitte-Touche, British Airways, Credit Lyonnaise) must provide their services in person and therefore must set up local "production" in the form of accountancy offices, airport service desks, and banks, respectively.

FINAL NOTE ON MARKET ENTRY: A marketeer should remain aware that while the international markets may appear infinite in size, individual nations may be far less expansive. Local competitors can easily decide to have their government intercede on their behalf to protect or recover market share. Good political connections are as valuable as good commercial ones.

CHAPTER 10

Developing Distribution

HERE MUST ALL DISTRUST BEHIND THEE LEAVE.

— DANTE

DISTRIBUTION IS THE PROCESS of getting the product to the customer at the right place and the right time. This seems to be a simple requirement, but it's one that has caused the failure of innumerable companies over the centuries, despite the fact that many of these companies have had well-made and well-priced products. The main cause of failure isn't the unavailablity of distribution channels but the lack of consideration given to distribution during the early stages of market planning. This chapter will examine all of the variables that need to be part of distribution planning.

Controlling the Channels: Getting to the Customer

A distribution channel is the route a product takes when moving from the producer to the consumer. Channels may be simple with few intermediaries or they may be composed of complex networks with numerous layers of middlemen. Marketeers must contend with their domestic market distribution to get supplies as well as with international distribution networks to get their product or service to the foreign market. Once this is done, local distribution inside the target market will have to be considered. Plainly, the greater control a marketeer has over these three distribution channels, the greater the likelihood of success. The amount of control will be determined by the following factors.

COST

Initially, there's the cost of setting up the channel, which involves the management labor to locate and negotiate distribution deals—a process that can be as lengthy and expensive as finding the consumers for the product. Secondly, maintenance costs on the channel include the cost of internal sales staff, middlemen, and promotional efforts. The final costs to be considered are those associated with transportation, storage, and administration. All costs determined at this level will eventually be passed along to the consumer; therefore, marketeers seek to reduce these expenditures whenever possible.

CAPITAL DEPTH

The choice and control of a channel will depend greatly on a marketeer's ability to capitalize the process. Some parts of the distribution chain may pay for the product as it moves through the channel, in which case the marketeer must only finance the production. This is true, for instance, of an import distributor that buys a product from an marketeer/exporter for eventual resale to local retailers, who've bought it outright for sale to consumers. Each member of the chain receives payment as the channel lengthens and each has very short-term exposure. At other times, the distribution chain can be just as lengthy, but no single member (including the producer) receives payment until after the sale to the end-user. This is the case when agents are utilized who only represent (rather than purchase) the products for resale. Even if the agent has better connections than the import distributor and proves to be a better marketing choice, a marketeer with little capital may not be able to wait for the extended payment process.

PRODUCT LINE

The type of product under consideration will, of course, greatly influence the method of distribution. Broad product lines attract distributors, whereas single items are more the territory of specialist agents. Perishables will, by necessity, require short distribution chains and quick handling. Some consumer products (personal care goods) may need more personal selling while high-tech gear may move from producer to end-user directly, with only a shipper as intermediary. The per-unit size and price will also have an impact on the availability and choice of members of the chain.

CONTROL REQUIREMENT

Total control of the distribution channels may not always be necessary, desirable, or even attainable. Each marketeer must determine how much control is needed and how much they'll accept. With direct sales a company controls promotion, quality, and price, but the expense of doing so may be large if it entails the use of separate retail outlets (as is the case with designer clothing stores as opposed to department store retailing). Other times, a company may find that its product requires little care once it has reached its final form. The distributors are willing to buy the product "up front," rather than after the sale to the end-user (as is the case with companies producing recorded music for worldwide distribution).

RANGE

The success of a product in the marketplace will depend greatly on the size of the area over which it's distributed—also known as its range. Not all products require the same amount of range. Legal services, for instance, may only need to be marketed in urban areas, while a commodity like eggs will need distribution over a much larger area. When seeking an external distributor, agent, or broker, the following should be considered:

- Current office location (will show the effort's focal point)
- Previous sales by geographic locale (demonstrates the effect of the effort)
- Other accounts (helps determine familiarity with the product type)

COMPATIBILITY

Regardless of how stringent a contract is, distribution will not be successful if the producer and the members of the chain don't work together in an efficient manner. Incompatibility may spring from differing goals, business practices, or cultures. All of these must be made consistent before any attempt at distribution is made. In the cases of goals and practices, a marketeer must have them clearly delineated before expecting to find compatible chain members. Large companies produce guidelines for external members of the distribution chain and make adherence a contractual matter. Smaller companies (with less marketplace power) may not be able to get chain members to sign off on guidelines, but a clear statement of requirements can only help the situation. Other companies (whose products require follow-up service) may choose to work within the confines of "authorized dealerships" to maintain standards. Cultural compatibility can never be the subject of contract or authorization; it must be a matter of tolerance among the chain members. Consideration should be given, in descending order, from those that deal most closely with the end-user down to the producer level. Marketeers that work for companies that place executives at the top of the organizational pyramid may find this difficult to swallow initially, but such cultural considerations are at the heart of international (maybe more aptly named "intercultural") business.

Distribution Strategies: Matching Resources to the Marketplace

DISTRIBUTION DENSITY

Distribution density refers to the number of sales outlets required to provide adequate range for a product. Density requirements are a direct function of the end-user's purchasing habits. Changes in density needs will ripple through to change other components of the distribution chain. The key to proper density is consumer habit research. A fine example of density and its effect on distribution can be found in the computer industry. For many years consumers went to computer sales outlets scattered around the globe to look at, compare, and test personal computers prior to purchase. They shopped for computers much in the same way that they shopped for stereo equipment or televisions. Not surprisingly, outlets for these two types of electronic consumer goods were also some of the early distributors of computer hardware. Over time, however, consumers became more skilled at computer usage and more knowledgeable about the technology, to the point where they no longer required the assistance of sales personnel or hands-on comparison shopping.

INFORMED CONSUMERS

This change in consumer skills has altered their buying habits. The latest growth in PC sales is in Internet direct sales with companies like Gateway and Dell, which service customers from remote low-cost locations. Consumers can now review hardware options on-line, order custom-built hardware and have it shipped directly to their home or office within a matter of days. No retail outlet, no salespeople, no local warehousing—a shrinking distribution chain. For Gateway, distribution density is an assembly plant in South Dakota and cyberspace. (In an extreme example of this new process, crew members of the Mir Spacecraft ordered computers from Gateway via radio, although the delivery details weren't immediately made clear.)

While some distribution chains contract, others expand, as is the case with Starbucks Coffee. This one-time coffee roasting company has now taken their "coffee bar" and retailing concepts worldwide, with thousands of outlets worldwide. Because the service (coffee brewing) that accompanies the goods (coffee) must be delivered daily (sometimes more often) and face-to-face, Starbucks had to continually open new outlets to reach new customers. Like the fast-food operations that have preceded it, Starbucks increased its density to acquire market share. However, by 2008 it had "saturated" the American market and began to close units and retool its operation. While some wholesale/retail operators may look to a future of catalog or on-line direct distribution, hospitality operators face ever-expanding density until they find themselves overbuilt.

Each marketeer will need to consider the density requirements of new markets and the expansion or contraction necessary to thrive there. Technical developments (Internet), distributor channel upgrades (international delivery services such as DHL) and competitive moves (Apple Computer challenges Dell Computer by threatening its "direct sales" market share) can all force a company's hand when reviewing the density of the distribution.

NOTE: Market share can often be won or lost based entirely on creating the proper distribution density, as product quality and price take a secondary role to access.

DISTRIBUTION LENGTH

Distribution length refers to the number of intermediaries needed to move a product through the marketplace. The expanding density mentioned above doesn't imply length, as density may utilize very few intermediaries (as is true in the case of Starbucks). A company may choose to shorten the length of their distribution by setting up a vertical marketing system in which all parts of the chain come under direct control of the producer. There are three types:

- CORPORATE The company owns all areas of the distribution channel, including shipping and retail outlets.
- CONTRACTUAL Distribution channel members are under long-term contract to the producer and must perform to exacting standards set by that producer.
- ADMINISTRATIVE The producer, through dominance in its market segment, oversees all areas of the distribution channel. Members willingly participate, due to the amount of business generated by the producer. (Some international companies, such as McDonald's, have taken this a step farther by controlling all areas of their business, including the supply lines, an approach known as vertical integration.)

TWO COMPANIES, ONE SYSTEM

Another way to control the length of the distribution chain is horizontal marketing, wherein two or more companies combine their marketing efforts and their distribution to the benefit of all participants. This is similar to cobranding, but the partnership is deepened to sharing costs and efficiencies of distribution. A prime example of this can be found in the designer eyewear industry. Clothing designer Giorgio Armani sells a line of prescription eyeglass frames through optometrists and sunglasses through his own retail outlets. Italian frame designer and manufacturer Luxotica also distributes through optometrists and retail outlets. Luxotica found that linking itself with designer names (Armani is one of many) and combining the two distribution networks has both expanded market share and reduced promotional cost. The "name" brands, in their turn, have opened market segments formerly closed to them before their marketing went "horizontal."

The addition of intermediaries or "lengthening" the chain can result in a loss of control, which may be damning to some products. It does, however, save the costs of purchasing shipping fleets, retail outlets, and local warehouses, as well as the training of a retail-level sales force. As a general rule, companies whose products require tight quality control have short distribution channels while those with products that are less sensitive can afford (but may not use) longer distribution chains.

NOTE: Marketeers may not be able to control as much of their distribution during the early stages of establishing market share as they would prefer. Local government edict may even prevent them from having a hand in any part of the distribution. Still, marketeers should always plan their distribution channels and seek any opportunity to make them more efficient.

LOGISTICS

Physical distribution (a.k.a. logistics) refers to the physical requirements necessary to move a product from producer to end-user. Logistics include export processing, freight forwarding, import processing, warehousing, fulfillment, and just-in-time delivery. On a global scale, logistics can become the most complex issue of market planning. Although logistics is most commonly associated with the movement of goods, services face similar problems. Logistics can impact heavily on a company's resources, both financial and administrative. Logistics can command more than 33 percent of revenues and generally exist outside of a company's "core business" (main focus). It's not unusual for a company to turn over the problems (and much of the expense) of logistics to external specialists. Efficient logistics is very often the determining factor in obtaining, maintaining, and expanding market share.

Managing Logistics: How to Get There from Here

The goal of a logistics management system is the efficient and dependable movement of products from producer to end-user. Logistics management is the primary service that all companies provide to consumers. As a marketeer plans the logistical aspects of the distribution process, the following topics must be considered.

TRANSPORTATION

The traditional modes of transportation have been by airplane, ship, railroad, or truck, but now the Internet also delivers product—digital product at least. In all areas of transport, there are three main areas to be reviewed during the planning phase.

- TRANSIT TIME The amount of time it takes the selected mode of transport to move from the shipping point to its intended destination. Sea, rail or trucking transport may be a matter of weeks, while air transit time can be measured in hours and the Internet in seconds. With the exception of the Internet, cost is a function of speed; the shorter the transit time, the higher the price.

- **LEAD TIME** The time that it takes between when a product is ordered and when it arrives. (Lead time shouldn't be confused with transit time, although the length of the transit will affect lead time.) Lead time includes all of the other factors that slow down delivery such as order handling, financial transfers, customs paperwork, and loading. A company that can afford a long lead time can usually take advantage of the cheaper and slower modes of transport.
- **BORDER COST** These are transport costs (in addition to those listed above) associated with each port of entry. For example, it may be cheaper to ship a product by sea to a country neighboring the target consumer and then truck it across the border, rather than to send it via a more direct route, due to differing customs and port charges. Countries regularly adjust their port charges and landing fees without notification, so logistics managers and marketing planners must stay well informed at all times.

INVENTORY

Control of inventory is essential to a distribution plan for two reasons: the reduction of the amount of capital devoted to stored materials and the reduction of storage space expense. Streamlining inventory has become the goal of almost every company, and much of the burden has shifted to suppliers, who in turn must seek to control their own levels. International companies tend to keep larger stocks on hand than domestic firms to allow for the problems that come with long-distance operations. However, even globally, the storage of only enough materials and finished products to cover a few days or weeks (sometimes hours) is a common practice—a concept known as just-in-time inventory or JIT. This system requires a great deal of cooperation from suppliers, and companies tend to reduce their number of suppliers so as to make the linkage worthwhile for all involved. Increases in efficiency are matched by increased savings of both labor and materials.

ORDERING

An inefficient process for handling orders can increase the lead time needed to receive a product just as easily as slow transit times can. Also, since the ordering process is typically handled internally, a marketeer must accept all responsibility for its smooth operation. Marketeers should strive to make ordering procedures as quick and as uncomplicated as possible. (A company that fills orders quickly can insist on prompt payment.) Fax and email ordering systems are fast becoming the standard in international business, as these communications media function regardless of time-zone differentials. Similarly, global pagers and satellite telephones can make even the remotest location and order taker accessible twenty-four-hours a day, every day.

NOTE: Customers must be informed of the technological limitations of all members of the distribution chain. The ordering process can only move as fast as its slowest participant. A Tokyo company may place an order with a producer in Montreal, but if the order must be routed through a subsidiary in the Andes with limited communication gear, the whole process may grind to a halt.

SUPPLY AND PRODUCT STORAGE

The four main considerations when planning storage facilities for an international operation are size, conditions, systems, and placement. Preproduction materials must be properly stored, either domestically or (more problematically) in overseas locations. While ample facilities may be available in the home market, the foreign market may not have the size or number of warehouses necessary. Even when there are dimensionally suitable facilities, the warehouse climate control may be inadequate. Handling systems such as elevators, forklifts, conveyor belts and so forth may also be far from ideal and perhaps even detrimental to the materials being stored. Another possible problem is storage facilities that aren't properly situated for the efficient movement of goods from ports or internal transport routes. Even when facilities are physically ideal, poor location or too few locations can greatly limit a company's ability to process orders, make products, and deliver them to the buyer.

It's not unusual for marketeers to wish to build their own facilities in a target market, especially when working in the less-developed economies. Even when the marketeer is economically willing and able to build storage facilities, local regulation may either hinder or halt the project. Local law may make it impossible for a foreigner to own land in the target market or to operate without taking on a local partner. In extreme cases, the foreign company may be banned from the entire distribution process.

NOTE: If your materials or products require special handling or large storage facilities, the warehousing process may become the determining factor for success. Consider it closely and consider it early.

Channel Options and Problems: Choosing the Right Methodology

When the distribution system is open to foreign players, there are a variety of methods for access. The greatest challenge in trying to distribute in a new market isn't always the location of the proper intermediaries but gaining their interest in carrying the new product line. Competitors may dissuade the local channel members from dealing with a foreign producer, or those members may be unconvinced of the foreign producer's viability.

The following are some common problems that marketeers may encounter and some options to consider when they find that the new market poses distribution entry problems.

MEMBER BLOCKAGE

When a market has a limited number of distribution choices, the members of that chain can exert a dictatorial force over what enters and what succeeds. Marketeers may find themselves confronted with one of these "middleman markets" where the consumer isn't given choices until the intermediaries have decided a "go or no go" on products. This position of power may be the result of a natural market dominance, legal edict, or a cultural tradition of strong linkage among local producers and intermediaries. Many of the complaints about market entry in Japan stem from this form of distributor blockage.

COMPETITOR BLOCKAGE

A more common form of blockage is when a powerful competitor persuades the local distribution network to spurn the advances of foreign producers. Local chain members may be threatened with financial ruin if they assist a foreign marketeer. Sometimes this type of coercion comes directly from the competitor or through political connections. Such "locked" markets exist all over the world. Even the vaunted Microsoft faces continual scrutiny from the U.S. government for its distribution tactics against domestic and foreign competition.

■ OPTIONS

- LEGAL ACTION It may be possible to seek legal recourse if distribution is blocked, but only in countries that are signatories to international commercial treaties. This action may be conducted in the local courts or in the international commercial courts of the World Trade Organization (WTO). Besides the enormous expense entailed, adverse publicity can result from trying to "sue" your way into a market. Local competitors and distributors are more likely to win local sympathy, so that even when the courts favor the marketeer, consumers may reject the product for emotional reasons.

NOTE: Many countries view foreign producers as the enemy, not the competition, and they have little shame about keeping their markets closed and their distribution locked.

- DIPLOMATIC ACTION This is the preferred way of attempting to pry open a locked market. It can only function if the marketeer and the target market have diplomatic relations and there's an embassy or consulate with a commercial component to serve the marketeer. Most of the negotiations are conducted out of public view; thus, the emotional levels are kept low. Much of the time foreign marketeers find that their motives have been greatly misunderstood. Diplomatic action allows all parties involved to clear the air. It can also lay the groundwork for other ventures in the new market.

- POLITICAL ACTION A producer may find it necessary to remind the target market of the interdependence of the global economy. By using the political structure of their home market, a producer can limit the target's exporting ability, either in a directly related sector or in another segment entirely. United States manufacturers of all sizes regularly lobby their government to restrict products from markets where these same manufacturers experience distributor or competitor blockage. Similarly, all of the trading blocs mentioned earlier in the text were partially devised to ensure this type of "fair" (if not free) trade.

NOTE: Smaller companies that lack the individual means to influence their own politicians into taking action may wish to join forces with co-ops or trade groups that are adept at exploiting the power of numerous small voices.

- FINANCIAL ACTION Blockage is always a matter of money, as some party or other is worried about losing a customer. Marketeers must sometimes "buy" their way into a market by underwriting any potential losses a distributor might sustain, or by joint venturing with a potential competitor. In extreme cases, a company may simply buy out the local market competition completely, taking over their facilities and distribution channels.

NOTE: While "buying a market" can be efficient from a time standpoint, it should be conducted with discretion. Even with smaller companies, it can give the appearance of economic or cultural colonization, with its incumbent consumer resistance or outright rejection. In many countries, such market entry attempts are now subject to government approval.

LACK OF INFRASTRUCTURE

Willing distributors, minimal competition, and eager consumers may not be enough to overcome the lack of infrastructure needed to bring specialized goods or services (those requiring high-tech delivery methods) to market. Refrigerated truck fleets, temperature-controlled warehouses, fiber-optic cables, air-conditioned computer rooms, pipelines, and sometimes even paved roads, bridges or electric power may be in insufficient quantity, quality, or completely absent in the target market.

■ OPTIONS

Infrastructure development Such development is always a combination of public and private efforts. Marketeers may find that their product or project is highly desired in a market of millions (e.g., China) but that physical access to consumers is limited. Part of the marketing plan must be an international lobbying effort to secure the proper infrastructure funding. International aid groups and development banks are always the first to approach (see Chapter 3). Another possibility is the offer of a Build-Operate-Transfer plan wherein the marketeers finance the infrastructure development necessary for distribution themselves (e.g., the laying of pipelines), with the agreement that local governments will buy back the project at a later date while retaining the marketeer's right to distribute. Such BOT projects are set up by large global companies; smaller companies (those unable to finance bridges, pipelines, or power plants) may offer their expertise on behalf of target-market governments to secure the proper funding. Telecommunications gear providers often take this approach when dealing with the emerging markets. Setting up proper first-stage financing and installation of infrastructure has allowed Australia's Telstra to secure long-term relationships with many of Southeast Asia's markets and government ministries.

CHANNEL RESISTANCE

New products may intimidate local channel members, who may be reluctant to take the chance on an unproven product. Even when the product has shown considerable success elsewhere, local intermediaries resist adding it to their distribution chain.

■ OPTIONS

CODISTRIBUTE A marketeer may attempt to distribute its products along with those of another foreign marketeer already operating successfully in the target economy. Kikkoman, the famous soy sauce manufacturer, used this option when its products met resistance during the early 1980s in Mexico (not a traditional user of Asian cooking products). By contracting with successful U.S. food marketeer Del Monte to use its existing channels in Mexico, Kikkoman was able to gain immediate access at a minimal cost.

- LOCAL LABELING When a company is only interested in marketing its products but not advancing its brand name to the public, it may consider contracting with a local company to place their label on the product prior to distribution. This allows the foreign company immediate access and the local company to link its name to quality goods or services. Many big names in Japanese electronics (e.g., Hitachi, Matsushita) have allowed well-established local brands to relabel their products in order to overcome the resistance of distributors against products with Japanese names.
- LOCAL PARTNER As was true in previous cases, resistance can often be overcome by simply buying a piece of the local action. It may take the form of joint-venturing with a local producer or becoming part of the distribution channel.

NOTE: This can meet with varying degrees of another type of resistance to the venture itself; marketeers may find it easier to partner with producers that aren't direct competitors or with distributors on the periphery of the main channels.

- LOCAL BUY-OUT When a marketeer buys out a local producer or distributor in order to gain access to distribution, expense is traded for efficiency. The same provisos that apply to local partnering apply here, with the additional advice to maintain a low profile and keep the local government on your side.
- DIG A NEW CHANNEL Many times, local distributor resistance can leave foreign marketeers no choice but to create their own local channels from scratch. Besides being very expensive, there's a good deal of accompanying risk—but it's usually worth taking. The case of Toys "R" Us is one of the most famous examples of a foreign marketeer creating its own highly successful channel in a local market. In 1990, after close to twenty years of institutionalized channel resistance, Japan finally revoked the law that allowed local competitors to give "permission" to companies wishing to open retail stores in excess of five hundred square meters. Toys "R" Us, a proponent of vertical marketing, circumvented the usually thick intermediary layers of Japanese distribution and opened a five thousand square meter retail store in Niigata. Their market share in Niigata in their first year was 50 percent.

Selecting Teammates: Trusting Others with Your Future

Success may depend on what type of companies a marketeer chooses to work with when overcoming the problems of distribution. Choose carefully as the relationship may last a long time and there's little advantage to disharmony. Here are some attributes, both financial and personal, that should be taken into account when searching out "teammates" for a distribution effort.

CONNECTED

Members of the chain should have the widest network available, one that includes not only those resources needed directly for actual distribution but also the political, diplomatic and public relations connections necessary to a smooth operation. In international marketing, members of the chain may become political, cultural, and legal intermediaries as well as commercial ones—get the best you can afford.

NOTE: Don't take a member's connections at face value. If their stated connections can't be verified, consider them nonexistent. Be discreet during the verification process and solicit recommendations.

FINANCIALLY SOUND

Distribution is a business, and like all businesses it can have money problems. Just like connections, each member of the chain should be able to prove that they can do what they say they can and that they won't go "belly up" a few months into the contract. Keep in mind that in a new market, your image will be directly linked to the quality of the distribution channel.

NOTE: In some developing markets, distributors may be using the prestige of handling a foreign product to leverage financing for other projects. Keep informed about the marketplace to prevent your company's name from being unknowingly used to raise operating funds for channel members.

SERVICE ORIENTED

Distribution is a service, and the level of that service must match the marketeer's standards. Unless total vertical marketing is achieved, much of the service that the consumer sees will be provided by someone out of the producer's direct control. When choosing channel teammates, make your standards clear and reasonable for the target market. Distribution, like the product itself, must sometimes be adapted to each specific segment. Rewards for meeting standards, as well as punishment for not meeting them, should be part of the contractual agreement. Even when certification is present (e.g., ISO 9001), don't assume that your needs and those of the end-user are "understood" by members. Start with quality service and stick with it.

NOTE: Take great care to be specific about service levels when distribution channels are limited or when members have been "assigned" to your project by local governments. It may be best to postpone market entry until the status of the channels improves, if assurances on service can't be found. Don't fool yourself into believing you can "bring them up to par" once you've entered the market. By the time you've corrected the distribution problems, the consumer will be elsewhere.

PROFESSIONAL

This word means many things in many cultures, but it's only the end-user's culture that matters. Marketing research must reveal what constitutes professional standards in the target market, and that must become the hallmark for local distributors. Accept no less and demand no more.

NOTE: Don't apply your home market's level of professionalism or attempt to impress it upon the target market, at least initially. You must get used to the local channels and they must get used to you. Unlike service standards, you can afford to wait and you just may learn a thing or two in the meantime.

FLEXIBLE

Views about contracts vary as greatly as professional standards. However, when a new product enters the marketplace, all members of the channel must be flexible until the "bugs" are worked out. Any intermediaries that show signs of adhering to the "letter of the contract" and nothing more should only be used if no alternative is available.

NOTE: When possible, insert "breaking-in periods" with specific starts and ends to let members know that flexibility isn't perpetual.

STABLE

Some members of the chain may not distribute as their core business or may not approach a chosen segment on a regular basis. Marketeers can't afford "part-time" channel members. Regular and reliable distribution should be the only kind a marketeer seeks out.

NOTE: Although stability is most likely found in members that have been in the marketplace for a long period, newcomers shouldn't be dismissed out of hand, especially if they embody the right attributes.

EAGER

Marketeers should look for teammates that are excited about distributing your products to new markets. Enthusiasm can be contagious; smart marketeers know that it filters directly down to consumers. A great deal of consumer resistance can be overcome by the manner and methods of the distribution chain. Unlike stability, eagerness is most often found in the newcomer who is unjaded by the vagaries of the marketplace. As movement along the chain approaches those links most directly involved with selling, eagerness will take on greater importance.

NOTE: Although eagerness is part and parcel of sales, it plays a role in many other aspects of the channel. For instance, many companies choose to ship their products via FedEx just so the deliveries are handled by the global delivery company's enthusiastic drivers.

FAR-SIGHTED

The international marketplace is full of people who want to make a quick profit. Marketeers should learn to avoid them. A new product in a new market may take some time to become profitable. Distribution chain members must be willing to share the long-term outlook of the marketeer.

NOTE: Potential members who try to have clauses added to contracts that allow them to easily drop an individual product from an entire line (called "cherrypicking") should instead be encouraged to have shorter initial contracts with an option for extension. Place the burden of performance on the distributor, not the product. If they balk at this prospect, look elsewhere.

UNBIASED

The goal of the distribution channel is to assist the producer in getting the product to the consumer—any product, any consumer. Members that demonstrate cultural, ethnic, class, religious or any of the other myriad of negative biases are best left out of the chain. Marketeers should interview members of the distribution chain (especially those with customer contact) as much as time and circumstance allow. This will ensure that they're comfortable with the product line and the target consumer base. Reluctance to deal with "that sort of people" or less-than-subtle remarks about "quality" generally mark potential members as being unable to control their biases; these prejudices won't be lost on consumers.

NOTE: Everyone suffers from some form of negative bias. Marketeers and their distribution teams must simply learn to control them.

OPEN

Marketeers working in global business discover that each culture sets its own values on openness. At one extreme are the groups that "lay everything on the table," including their personal lives early in a business relationship. At the other end of the spectrum are those cultures that reveal good news easily and keep the bad news secret, at least until a more private and opportune moment. Neither extreme is necessarily more "honest" than the other; only the timing and level of intimacy are different. What's important is that the marketeer learn how to access the level of openness they require for business dealings. Much of the needed methodology will be uncovered during the cultural research phase (see Chapter 6).

NOTE: Though you've applied your research, you still may not get the "whole story" from members of the chain unless you've made your requirements known early in the relationship. Keep in mind that 50 percent of the burden of cultural understanding and honesty is on the distribution chain. Members must please producers as well as end-users.

MORAL

This word is one of the most controversial in all of international business. It derives from the Latin *moralis* which means "custom," and every culture certainly has its own customs. Marketeers must look for members that best reflect the level of morality suitable for the marketeer and the marketplace. It will be a compromise and concessions must be made. It's not unusual for a marketeer to find the level of morality unacceptable (too high as well as too low). If so, look for another market. The same may be true of potential channel members. Unless "the fit" is just right, the relationship will fail in the long run.

NOTE: Morality takes in many of the other attributes stated above. To be successful, marketeers must maintain the core of their own morality while reshaping those aspects that are less stringent. Just as a product may require minor alterations to make it acceptable to the new market, so too may a moral code. This isn't a recommendation for moral indifference, just an acknowledgment that self-righteousness is a poor foundation for international marketing.

FINAL NOTE ON DISTRIBUTION: Members of the distribution channel may be the only members of the target marketplace with which the marketeer will have direct contact. Choose them carefully and treat them well. They'll be both your sales force and service representatives. The distribution team will reflect your outlook on the marketplace and determine the level of success or failure. Marketeers are coaches as well as managers in this very competitive game.

CHAPTER 11

Advertising and Promotions

We like to be deceived. — Pascal

ADVERTISING IS GREATLY misunderstood, although the term is used universally in business. To *advert* really means "to turn one's attention toward" and there's little harm in that. Pascal's quotation, above, refers to deception, but *deceive* originally meant "to seize." Advertising, when properly done, does just that: it seizes the consumer's attention. Advertising isn't lying (although it can be in the wrong hands), and consumers really do like to have their attention drawn to products that they find beneficial. Promotion suffers from a similar misunderstanding. Although it has come to be associated with hucksterism, it really means "to move forward," but that sense is rarely made clear when applied to promoting products. This chapter will look at the positive way in which marketeers can advertise and promote their products to the benefit of customer and producer alike. But first, two definitions are in order:

ADVERTISING A form of sponsored public notice that seeks to inform, persuade, and otherwise modify consumer attitudes toward a product, with the object of triggering an eventual purchase.

PROMOTION Any of the various techniques used to create a positive image of a seller's product in the minds of potential buyers. It includes such areas as advertising, personal selling, public relations, and discounts.

Challenges of the Foreign Market: Understanding the Customer

A great deal of effort must be put into determining what motivates consumer purchasing behavior. Some advertising can be used across all cultural lines (e.g., The Marlboro Man), although the positive effects may differ from market to market. Some promotional activities (such as personal selling) may have to be altered or extended, depending on what the targeted consumers consider adequate and positive. What's important is that marketeers adapt their techniques to the new market, just as they would adapt their product lines.

Advertising in the international market increases by more than 10 percent per year and over US$70 is spent each year on advertising for every man, woman, and child on the planet. The United States alone spends more than US$100 billion each year on global advertising. Surely with this much money being spent, there must be a great deal at stake. However, advertising and promotions are much more than just a matter of spending money. In fact some of the most economical techniques are the most effective. Choosing the right technique and format happens once the challenges of the local market have been determined.

THE LANGUAGE CHALLENGE

Language is the primary way in which producers and distributors communicate with consumers. Those involved with personal selling will find that speaking the local language isn't optional but a requirement for success. Besides just being able to get the basic information across to the customer, a salesperson also communicates the company's dedication to the marketplace. All salespeople face an uphill battle when trying to promote a product, but those without the requisite language skills may find that the hill is almost vertical.

Language skills will also come into play when advertising and promotional collateral (brochures, manuals, business cards) are translated. A poorly worded document or mistranslated slogan can sink a sales effort before it even starts. (Wanting to assure their Belgian target audience of the sturdiness of their vehicles, General Motors' marketeers once translated their slogan of "Body by Fisher" into Flemish. The resulting translation read more like "Corpse by Fisher" with embarrassing results. One could question whether, even if it had been properly translated, the slogan would have had the desired effect on the Belgian consumers.) The choice of brand names (see Chapter 9) will also rely heavily on how the translation or logo design will play in the new market.

Prior to distribution, all translated advertising and promotional materials should be reviewed numerous times by native speakers to uncover potential problems. All administrative and sales personnel who will be working regularly in the target market must have a degree of fluency that will permit their marketing skills to be effective over the long-term.

THE CULTURE CHALLENGE

Understanding the target culture is a continuing difficulty, even for major global market players. Pundits may be claiming that the world is becoming more and more homogenized, but there's only scant evidence of it in marketing. Cultural challenges are perceptual, and perception changes regularly. Having a firm understanding of what a culture was like a decade ago is of practically no use today. Cultural research must be continually updated if advertising and promotions are to work.

Even cultures that have had a long-term relationship with each other can have difficulty communicating. For instance, though the Paris-based House of Chanel has been a name brand in the United States for many decades, they were unable to reach the American market with an ad that was hugely successful in Europe. The now-famous Egoiste fragrance ad—featuring women screaming out the brand name from the windows of a Riviera hotel—made very little sense to the U.S. consumer. The ad was just "too French" for the United States and demonstrates a lack of market research. Another Chanel advertising campaign, this one for the Coco line, featured scantily clad European pop star Vanessa Paradis swinging on a trapeze inside of a birdcage. This ad was quite successful, even though few in the U.S. market knew who Ms. Paradis was. In this case, the sexual nature of the advertisement crossed the cultural line. The same ad, however, would have been banned in much of Asia and the Middle East.

Very few advertising campaigns succeed in crossing cultural lines on a global basis. Certain categories of products are more easily "globalized" than others. Those that become part of a "lifestyle" (beverages, clothing, personal care, food) are the most common culture crossers. Thus, Budweiser, Levis, Lancome, and

Mars have all had an easy time making cultural inroads. Because these "lifestyle enhancers" are positioned by the "image" they create, they're intentionally directed at youth, who often prefer to separate themselves from the dominant local culture. Advertising schemes that have the greatest chance of succeeding globally exhibit the following attributes: simplicity, directness, humor and clever imagery. All four components should be as broad as possible in composition for the ad to have universal appeal.

THE REGULATION CHALLENGE

Government regulation has been discussed earlier in the text (in reference to partnerships and distribution rights). However, as many marketeers have discovered, governments involve themselves extensively in advertising and promotions at the municipal or provincial level; this generally takes the form of regulation of signage size, composition, location, and lighting. At the national level, governments control the usage of names and the verification of advertising claims. In Germany, when Yves St. Laurent attempted to market its Champagne fragrance, the company was brought to court by wine manufacturers from the Champagne region of France who claimed it was an unauthorized use of their *appellation.* This same type of regulation prevents California sparkling wine producers from calling their product Champagne.

- ADVERTISING CLAIMS In terms of advertising claims, a government will require that a company "tell the truth" in its ads or face prosecution. The United States has the most detailed advertising regulation (it's also the globe's most extensive advertiser), setting limits for terms such as "homemade," "American made," and even "fresh." However, this hasn't prevented some of its companies from having problems in foreign markets. Coca Cola had to drop its slogan "Coke Adds Life" in Thailand and Norway, where the phrase was considered an overstatement of the product's benefits. Similarly, Kellogg had to drop its claims of vitamin content in order to enter the Netherlands and also remove the depiction of a child wearing a logo t-shirt in a French advertisement because it violated that country's regulations against children endorsing products. Clearly, each market has its own standards. It should also be noted that most countries (the United States being a major exception), have laws against comparing competing products in advertising.

- BRAND NAME REGISTRATION Governments also control who is licensed to use a name for advertising purposes and each name or logo must be registered on a country-by-country basis. Marketeers may even find that they must pay someone in the targeted market for the use of their own company name when advertising, simply because a savvy local entrepreneur beat them to the registry office. While international trademark and copyright law has made some headway in correcting such problems, it's a long way from perfection. In many developing economies, even when a company has registered its name, locals may sometimes adopt its usage for their own purposes without much fear of prosecution. Marketeers should register their brands and logos in as many markets as they can afford to, well in advance of actual market entry. Buying back the rights for them can be extremely expensive, and lawsuits generally create bad reactions in the local population.

- **Cultural Standards** Advertising by foreign firms is occasionally seen as a cultural blight and the thin-edge-of-the-wedge for future breakdown of the local culture. Many countries require that the local language predominate in signage (France); some go so far as to require ethnic quotas when human images are part of the advertisement (South Africa). Vietnam regularly launches a campaign against "social evils" that results in numerous advertisements from foreign companies being torn down or painted over—an attempt to maintain cultural homogeneity. This occurs even though foreign firms observe the guidelines given to them by the government.
- **HEALTH WARNINGS** Governments have a duty to their constituents to be concerned with the health impact that a product might have. In many countries, advertisements for cigarettes and alcohol (when permitted at all) will have to carry health warnings or disclaimers, and even the size and design of those warnings may be regulated. Similarly, advertisements for food products may have to be accompanied by clearly stated ingredient lists and preparation statements. Services may have to have their limitations or warranties listed (a.k.a. "the fine print") and manufactured goods may require warnings and liability statements.
- **DISCOUNTS AND SWEEPSTAKES** Promotional efforts (discounting, sweepstakes, contests, coupons) are also subject to government regulation. This ensures that companies, both foreign and domestic, are keeping things on the "up and up" when attracting customers. Even something as common as a "sale" promotion may attract government intervention. By way of example, the city of San Francisco, California places an extra sales tax on any retail operation that displays a "Going Out of Business" sign within the city limits. This prevents companies from taking advantage of tourists expecting bargains at close-out rates when no actual close-out is planned. Also, since the law only applies to those stores actually displaying the sign, it prevents certain retail districts from appearing to be (even temporarily) unprofitable.
- **LEGALITY** Foreign firms use advertising and promotions to call attention to themselves—a possible liability during times of stress in the local market. Presently, governments in all nations either have legislation overseeing advertising or will readily adopt it as it serves their purposes (both political and economic). The great challenge for marketeers is to abide by legislated standards while still producing effective advertisements and promotional efforts.

NOTE: The landscape can change quickly, and governments rarely give notice. Like other aspects of doing business overseas, staying continually informed about local practices will head off most of these problems.

THE MEDIA CHALLENGE

Media are all the forms of communication through which a marketeer will channel advertising and promotional efforts. (A single component is referred to as a *medium*.) The amount and diversity of the media available in the targeted market will affect advertising and promotions on two separate fronts: the type of effort the local population is willing to accept and the availability of media through which an effort can be projected. The two major types of advertisement selling are the "hard sell," which is very aggressive, and the "soft sell," wherein more subtle forms of persuasion are used. Each culture determines for itself what constitutes a "hard" or "soft" sales pitch and how much of each it will tolerate (e.g,. a soft sell in New York will be seen as a hard sell in Tokyo). For the most part, advertising and promotions exist between these two extremes.

Marketeers coming from technological societies will be used to having a wide variety of commercial media at their disposal, from television to direct mail. However, they may not be able to find this same media mix in a particular foreign market. Equally problematic will be the efforts of a company that hails from a market with few media choices when they attempt to enter an economically advanced, media-rich environment. Such an inability to properly utilize an accepted medium will hold back a foreign product's market entry.

THE CONSUMER HABITS CHALLENGE

Consumer habits encompass the when, where, why, how and how much of understanding the marketplace.

- A shopper in France may go to the grocery market every day, while a counterpart in the United States goes once a week.
- A housewife in Beijing will buy a ten-kilogram bag of rice, while her cousin in London buys a twelve-ounce box with its own flavor packet.
- A car buyer in Munich will seek bank financing for a new Mercedes, while in Jakarta, a similar vehicle is paid for in cash.
- A driver in Copenhagen uses a credit card to buy diesel fuel at the local station, while in Luang Prabang, a dozen eggs are traded for a soft drink bottle full of petrol at a street corner.
- In Montreal, a commodities broker buys steak knives from the "Shopping Network" TV show, while in Kenya a farmer walks two days to a market bazaar to buy a carving knife.

A marketeer must be able to understand the economic restraints, cultural influences, physical limitations, and personal psychology of consumer buying habits in the target market. These habits do change, and they can be influenced by the marketeer's efforts. However, changing a market's habits isn't a strategy for market entry, only a long-term goal. Real change may take an entire generation and a good deal of influence, neither of which a marketeer has when entering a market. The challenge of consumer behavior is the ability to comprehend it and respond to it in a way that will "get a foot in the door." That foot is advertising.

Advertising and promotional efforts will most likely be the first glimpse a consumer has of the marketeer's company and products. If you don't "hit the mark" at this level, a purchase is virtually out of the question, and you have only one chance to make a good first impression.

NOTE: Consumer habits may be influenced by factors well out of the control of the marketeer. Keeping abreast of what's going on in the general marketplace will help you "read" your own consumer segment. A good example is the sudden rise in the usage of credit cards by younger Japanese consumers beginning in the early 1990s. This caught many retailers (both foreign and domestic) by surprise, as they had patterned their promotional strategies around the older generation's disdain for buying on credit. Keep your eyes—and your options—wide open!

Standard versus Adapted Advertising: Different Audiences

When a marketeer is selling a particular product on an international scale, a decision must be made about how much of the advertising campaign will be standardized. (Promotions will be considered at the end of the chapter.) This also applies when the product under consideration has small local adaptations. Complete standardization of advertising was attempted by some conglomerates during the late 1950s with such poor results that companies sought out the other end of the spectrum with very localized ad schemes. Though effective in content, these localized schemes proved enormously expensive and administratively unwieldy. The first recognition that greater standardization could be accomplished effectively was in Europe during the late 1960s. It became apparent to industry observers that despite language differences, most European nations had similar living conditions, finances, and media coverage. Since then, that observation has been expanded to a global scale. Global advertising plans present both problems and substantial potential benefits.

GLOBAL PROBLEMS

- REDUCED LOCAL CONTROL A marketeer may be loathe to remove control of the advertising from company members who are closest to the target audience. This is a very legitimate concern that can be overcome by soliciting the input of the local team during the scheme's development.
- MEDIA ACCESS Even when countries share a border and have similar economic development, the availability of media may differ significantly. Germany has a well-developed commercial television media, but its neighbor Denmark shuns such advertising. Luckily, the use of satellite dish technology is breaking down this particular barrier, although some countries (like China) jam the transmissions from neighboring systems.
- LINGUISTIC FORMATS Though English is fast becoming the international language, many countries still insist on local language content for advertisement. This will most likely be a permanent concern for advertisers, with the only bright spot being that technology is permitting faster and more dependable translation of materials.
- CULTURAL NUANCE This is another on-going problem (covered in some detail earlier) that can affect even domestic advertising. For standardized schemes, these nuances can be dealt with by projecting very broad images with simplistic content.
- LOCAL REGULATIONS Many governments have seen the coming phase of global advertising and have taken measures to ensure a high degree of local input and content in an effort to protect their domestic advertising sector. Brazil and Australia, for example, both have long-standing requirements that all TV commercials be produced within their national borders. Technology will most likely overwhelm their efforts, but not entirely.
- LACK OF GLOBAL AD AGENCIES Advertising agencies don't hold sway globally. Some have tried to set up worldwide offices (notably Saatchi & Saatchi and Ogilvy & Mather), with less-than-stellar results. Cost and lack of access to

the local media have been the main causes of failure. When logistics don't sideline them, regulations do.

GLOBAL BENEFITS

- **CONSOLIDATED TALENT** Advertising talent isn't widespread and it's almost nonexistent in some developing markets. A global plan allows this scant talent to be consolidated in a small area with great increases in ad design efficiency and approval. Of course, this requires that the consolidated members have the requisite talent and that the company be large enough to afford the consolidation.
- **COST CONTROLS** Keeping advertising schemes under a single directive greatly increases the ability to control costs. Such control requires very talented management and a keen knowledge of each of the global scheme's components.
- **IMAGE CONTROL** When advertising schemes are left in the hands of local agencies without direct oversight of the producer, companies run the risk of losing control of their image in the target market. Global campaigns help maintain consistency. By way of example, when Novell (the international network specialist) devised a campaign utilizing the very positive and direct slogan of "Yes!" as its centerpiece, it found that "Hello" had been substituted in the Japanese version by a local agency.
- **BRAND EQUITY** The building of a company's brand equity is an important part of any advertising scheme, and doubly so for international marketing. Global schemes allow for a consistent projection of a brand and tight control of any associations that brand may need to break into a new market.

MEDIA AVAILABILITY & PLANNING: BEING SEEN WHERE CUSTOMERS LOOK

Whether an advertising scheme will be standardized or locally adapted, choices about which media to use, and how often, must be made. These choices may be governed by finances, the level of sophistication of the target segment and, most importantly, media availability. Not all media is available everywhere to the same degree all of the time. An ad campaign that will be used internationally must take into account the fact that different localities may not have the requisite medium available or have made it off-limits for a particular product. A company may find that if they focus on a single media, movement across borders can be difficult. For instance, when Suntory (the Japanese whiskey maker) attempted a large-scale entry in the U.S. market, federal law prevented them from using television for liquor advertising. Much of Suntory's advertising had been tied to TV ads in Japan (upward of US$50 million per year); they had little knowledge of getting their point across in print media, the regular choice of U.S. distilleries.

As will be discussed later in the chapter, not all media have the same level of credibility from market to market. Also, different media are utilized by different segments, and each medium has its own "reach" or extent in each marketplace. Marketeers must plan around these variables when devising standard or adapted advertising schemes. The following is a chart of media types that are available around the world, along with some usage percentages from various markets.

ADVERTISING USAGE PERCENTAGES

Country	TV	Print	Trade	Radio	Cinema	Outdoor	Other
Australia	30.3	47.6	2.6	8.8	1.6	8.1	1.0
Brazil	42.0	22.5	9.5	16.0	0.5	3.5	6.0
Germany	9.6	66.5	-	3.3	0.8	3.6	16.2
Japan	35.5	36.3	10.0	5.0	-	-	13.2
South Africa	19.3	55.7	6.5	12.0	2.1	4.4	-
United States	20.5	35.2	3.4	12.0	-	1.1	27.8

Agency Selection

Marketeers may decide to hire an agency to devise and execute the advertising scheme. An advertising agency, much like a distributing agent, acts as an intermediary between those that sell advertising and those that buy it. The amount of involvement that an agency has in a campaign is up to the marketeer. (The extent of those possibilities will be discussed shortly.) Though there's been a slight decline in the number of truly "international" advertising agencies, the use of agencies is still a major factor in cross-border business. Agencies provide a company that's new to a market with both a ready source of information about the types of media that are most effective and a way to determine the most suitable choice of media, given the product line and finances available. A marketeer may choose from the agency types discussed below.

DOMESTIC ADVERTISING AGENCIES

It's not unusual for a company to choose the same agency that they've used in their domestic advertising when they attempt to go international, even if the agency has no cross-border experience. Of course, when a domestic agency hears that a client is planning to market internationally, they'll be eager to offer their services.

■ ARGUMENTS FOR USING DOMESTIC AGENCIES

- They're already familiar with the marketeer's product and image.
- They have an existing relationship with management.
- They have a greater stake in maintaining brand equity.
- They may be willing to discount their services in order to be given an opportunity to operate on the international front.
- They will be able to give long-term cost savings as domestic and international efforts and staffing are combined.

■ ARGUMENTS AGAINST USING DOMESTIC AGENCIES

- They may have no experience with consumer habits in the target market.
- They may lack the cultural and linguistic skills necessary to reach the segment.
- They may lack the media connections needed to get the best prices.
- They may be unfamiliar with local laws and politics regarding foreign companies.

LOCAL ADVERTISING AGENCIES

Using an agency that's based in the local target market is quite common, and in some countries, it's the only option available to the marketeer. Even when not mandated, local agencies are always eager to service a foreign client, as it brings prestige and possible entry into the client's domestic marketplace.

ARGUMENTS FOR USING LOCAL AGENCIES

- They may have strong local political connections and knowledge.
- They are intimately familiar with the consumer habits of the targeted segments.
- They share the cultural and linguistic background of the consumer base.
- They can offer additional input about local standards for product adaptation.
- They currently operate with all of the necessary media in the local market.
- They may offer substantial discounts in order to sign up a foreign client.

ARGUMENTS AGAINST USING LOCAL AGENCIES

- They may lack the technical sophistication necessary to service the foreign company.
- They have little knowledge of the company's image or management style.
- They have little stake in maintaining the company's international brand equity.
- They cannot always offer the savings that come from the economies of scale offered by large, global firms.
- They may attempt to "gouge" the foreign firm with multi-tier pricing.
- They may be as unfamiliar with the product as local consumers are.

AFFILIATE ADVERTISING AGENCIES

An affiliate agency is a local operation that receives input and support from a large international agency. Sometimes the international group has an equity stake in the local affiliate, or it may just work with them on an "as needed" basis for projects involving global marketeers.

ARGUMENTS FOR USING AFFILIATE AGENCIES

- They already have, or have access to, the level of technical sophistication needed by most international companies.
- They have the necessary cultural and linguistic skills for the new market.
- They have local political and media connections.
- They have a firm grasp of local consumer habits and product needs.
- They may be able to offer the cost savings associated with large scale operations.

ARGUMENTS AGAINST USING AFFILIATE AGENCIES

- They will usually lack familiarity with the foreign company's domestic market image.
- They may find it difficult to work with the marketeer's management team.
- They may wish to take their direction from the international agency rather than the marketeer.

NETWORK ADVERTISING AGENCIES

A network agency system is similar to affiliation in scope but with the complete ownership and oversight of the local agencies by a single operator. While this seemed like a perfect way to set up international advertising, many of the big agencies that attempted full networks have either reduced their overseas offices considerably in favor of "regional offices" or retreated completely. Many of the cost savings that were derived from consolidated advertising and media access were overwhelmed by the labor and lease costs of multiple offices.

ARGUMENTS FOR USING NETWORK SYSTEMS

- They have at their disposal the full range of technical requirements needed for any advertising scheme.
- They may already operate as the marketeer's domestic agency and have total familiarity with image, management style, and finances.
- They have local personnel capable of the proper cultural and linguistic insights.
- They have access to the necessary media, public relations, and political connections.
- They have experience with the local regulatory environment.
- They may be able to pass along the cost savings of a standardized advertising scheme.

ARGUMENTS AGAINST USING NETWORK SYSTEMS

- They're more prone to recommend standardized schemes over adapted ones.
- They may overwhelm a small marketeer with limited resources.
- They have difficulty working on a small scale.
- They can't always produce the cost savings that come from economies of scale.
- They may cause resentment among local competitor agencies with resulting bad public relations for the marketeer's company.
- They may cause the marketeer to have difficulty accessing the local distribution chain due to competitor resentment.
- Regulation may prevent the network from operating in all of the marketeer's targeted countries.

Media Planning: A Word to the Wise Isn't Always Sufficient

Media planning is the process whereby an advertising campaign is matched to the appropriate media in such a way as to maximize the campaign's impact on the consumer. Smaller companies may handle this operation internally, although it's recommended that an agency be consulted for campaigns in new markets, if only on a consultant basis. Although a company may have a clear and correct set of objectives for reaching its target audience, a number of other factors must be considered when preparing to launch a campaign. Some of these factors will be under the direct control of the marketeer (or its designated agency); others may be supervised by external organizations or regulatory bodies.

MEDIA BUYING

Media buying is the practice of purchasing large blocks of media space (or air time) and then reselling those blocks piece-by-piece to clients. Those clients may be either advertising agencies or marketeers handling their own advertising schemes. Like agencies, media buyers are just another set of intermediaries between the marketeer and the customer. (This procedure of bulk media buying was "invented" decades ago by the London-based company, Carat.) Not all media buyers are separate entities, as most advertising agencies have their own media buying departments. Although actual global media buying is still in its infancy, media buyers still dominate most of the major markets. Agencies or marketeers handling their own advertising will find that they may have to deal with media buyers even in smaller markets. Media providers (TV, print, radio) often prefer to sell in bulk to the media buyers because it saves them the cost of setting up their own sales force. There are potential savings for the marketeer as well, because media buyers can sell in multiple markets and protect their clients from exchange risk by locking in prices in advance of actual usage.

NOTE: In some countries, all media is centrally controlled by the government with tight regulation over the buying and reselling of advertising.

SCHEDULING

Choosing the wrong schedule can be just as fatal to a campaign as choosing the wrong advertisement. Ads must be scheduled to reach the target audience when they're most predisposed and financially able to make a purchase. This schedule may be seasonal for some products (clothing), culturally related for others (flowers for the Lunar New Year), or based entirely on the budgetary cycles of the target market or individual company (industrial products). Scheduling may be as broad as running an ad in a monthly publication or as specific as selecting what time of day (perhaps even to the minute) a television commercial will be broadcast. The main external factors that govern the schedule are customer needs and the amount of time it takes for a customer to deliberate about the purchase of the product. Both of these factors require a great deal of cultural knowledge and recognition of local consumer habits. Whereas a Chinese consumer may deliberate for weeks over the purchase of a washing machine, a consumer in the United States may buy one on impulse while watching a TV "shopping network." Similarly, a farmer in Uruguay will purchase his children's winter coats as the weather starts to turn cold, but a shopper in Germany will find the latest winter fashions "on sale" at the end of the preceding summer. These consumption patterns and the level of affluence all dictate the scheduling of an advertising campaign. Internally, of course, an advertising campaign schedule will be dictated largely by the amount of money the marketeer can devote to the required media. Many companies would prefer to run sixty-second ads during the Super Bowl or contract for all the signage around the World Cup Finals soccer pitch, but their budgets just won't permit it. Substantial amounts of money should be set aside for advertising when entering a new market; doubling the domestic ratio is wisest.

REACH AND FREQUENCY

Reach is the percentage of potential consumers that will be impacted by an advertising campaign. Frequency is the number of times each target of the campaign "experiences" the advertising. Marketeers entering a new market that may be unfamiliar with the product tend to concentrate on "reach," as they're trying to create product awareness. Once awareness (and sales) have been established there's a tendency to focus on the "frequency" of advertising as a way of maintaining market share. All advertising, whether it's done at market entry or long-term, is a trade off between reach and frequency. A large part of the trade off will be determined by how much money a given company can spend. The other determining factors will be what type of media is available in the target market and which of them is best received by the target population of consumers. Having wide reach or heavy frequency will do little if the choice in media isn't matched to the consumer and the product line. In South Africa, for example, where the population is largely agricultural, broadcast television ads for farm-related products garner little success, regardless of how often they're shown. Electricity and batteries are scarce in the countryside, making even radio a poor choice of medium. Here, more than 55 percent of advertising is done in print media, which is the most economical and widespread media for these types of products. On the other hand, urban-related products (luxury automobiles, security services, leisure clothing) are best advertised on television, which is far more prevalent in the cities, whose inhabitants are more likely to be able to afford (and to desire) such purchases.

Much like adapting a product line, the reach and frequency of advertising campaigns must be customized to individual markets. Another consideration is the general level of overall advertising present in a given society. Whereas the average U.S. or Japanese consumer is bombarded with advertisements, all competing for their attention, the average Chinese or Peruvian citizen is relatively untouched by such mass media. The relative level of competitive advertising is often called "noise," and the greater the local "noise," the greater the effort the marketeer will have to put forth to gain attention. Getting heard (or seen) above the great din in New York City or Tokyo may require an extended reach, an increased frequency, or both. Of course, the marketeer may be happy to find that the target market is relatively "quiet" and that communication with consumers is relatively easy and inexpensive.

NOTE: Markets can change their level of advertising acceptance, usually as the result of technological changes. Developed markets are seeing a sharp rise in Internet advertising, and most of the industrial societies of Eastern Europe are experiencing a massive increase in TV campaigns as satellite systems become more common. Even in troubled South Africa, the BayGen company is currently selling a hand-cranked radio that operates without batteries or electrical hookup. Originally the radio was designed to keep rural areas apprised of political developments, but savvy marketeers will no doubt see its potential impact on advertising reach and frequency.

Being Believable: Be Careful What You Say

Each society has its own level of acceptance of what they will and will not believe in an advertising campaign, and the level of belief varies with each type of media. It also varies greatly from segment to segment inside of a given market. Some general observations about "types" can be made, but the reader is cautioned to verify any of these generalities in the target market.

ASSOCIATION

Societies that have been heavily exposed to political billboards tend to find commercial ones less believable, as they equate billboards with political sloganeering and unfulfilled promises.

CLASS ORIENTED

Less affluent societies put the greatest sense of belief in those media to which they've had the least exposure (television, cinema, glossy magazines), as they associate these with upper-class behavior.

PERSONALIZED

Segments with higher education are more likely to shun the "mass media" campaigns of TV and radio in favor of specialized print media (catalogs, market specific magazines). These segments can be very discerning and demanding. The product better be exactly as advertised.

IMAGE CONSCIOUS

The more developed markets tend to put greater, or at least equal, stock in how an advertisement is produced than in its content. This type of ad (e.g., Lexus automobiles) relies on emphasizing an image rather than technical aspects. Advertising directed at this group has to entertain and stimulate as well as inform.

SUSPICIOUS

Less educated market segments have a tendency to view all advertising with suspicion, as they fear being tricked by more sophisticated sellers. This can be magnified when the seller is from a foreign, more developed market. Such segments rarely buy a product sight unseen.

PROVINCIAL

Agrarian societies prefer to make purchases from local sellers and have follow-up service provided locally as well. This is due to a sense that, even within their own national market, that which isn't in the immediate vicinity is automatically foreign. Real foreign companies must set up local access with local personnel.

JADED

Affluent urban dwellers in the globe's developed markets often judge an advertisement and the product it describes by the amount of money that was spent on the campaign. These types of ads (e.g., four full pages in the *Wall Street Journal*) may impart the same amount of information as a much less expensive ad but lure the customer by the sheer enormity of its expense.

CHAPTER 12

Making Contact: Different Products and Promotions

SMALL OPPORTUNITIES ARE OFTEN THE BEGINNING OF GREAT ENTERPRISES. — DEMOSTHENES

ADVERTISING COMMUNICATES with consumers indirectly, but it isn't the only way to reach them. Other promotional techniques—personal selling, industrial sales, sponsorships and direct marketing—put the marketeer in closer contact with buyers at all levels.

Personal Selling

Personal selling occurs anytime a marketeer or a marketeer's intermediary meets with a potential customer for the purpose of promoting a product. It takes place on either a face-to-face basis or via telephone lines (nowadays, even email is considered "personal"). Each customer is treated individually and essentially becomes their own separate market segment. This type of promotion is becoming increasingly prevalent in both international and domestic business as product information disseminates, choices widen, and affluence continues to rise, thus making for a more demanding consumer.

SELECTION OF PERSONNEL

Personal selling requires the selection of very specialized personnel when working in the international market. Not only must they have the language and cultural skills mentioned earlier, but they must fully understand the business protocols and methods of the target market. Most importantly, they must be skilled negotiators. While many aspects of the plan will be conducted at some distance from the consumer, personal selling is as close as the marketeer and the consumer can get, and in no other aspect of marketing is proper personnel selection more important.

Many international companies have chosen to recruit their sales forces inside of the targeted market, with supervision by management sent from headquarters or a regional office. Clearly these local personnel will have the language and cultural skills necessary, as well as much of the business protocol information. Often, the use of local personnel may be mandated by law. A marketeer will have to provide considerable training to the local sales force, in regard to both the product line and (in most cases) negotiation techniques suitable to the company's image and financial requirements. Sometimes, a marketeer is permitted (or finds it easier for technical reasons) to bring sales personnel from their domestic market or another foreign subsidiary. This "expatriate" personnel should receive intensive and extensive training in linguistic, cultural, and protocol skills, as well as in local negotiating techniques.

NOTE: International companies are currently scaling back the use of expatriates in favor of local personnel. Much of this is the result of the high cost of transferring staff (and their families) overseas, but it's also related to the salary differential between local and expatriate personnel. In emerging markets, it can be a factor of ten. Other considerations are visa and work permit regulations. A marketeer may find that it's more economically feasible in the long-term to use expatriate sales personnel for training purposes only.

Industrial Sales

The sale of goods or services by one company for use by another company to make a new product is referred to as industrial sales. While this category is similar to the personal selling of consumer products, it has some additional aspects peculiar to business-to-business transactions.

TRANSACTION BY TENDER

Most large projects, public and private, are put up for "bid"—that is, the company looking to make a purchase asks interested parties to submit (or tender) their proposals for inspection. With "tendering," the buyer will weigh aspects of quality, price, financing, delivery, and postal service before making a decision. This permits the buyer to receive the most competitive pricing with the least amount of effort. Marketeers selling products to governments will deal almost exclusively with this form of promotion. A clear understanding of the company's products and profit margins, as well as the purchaser's ability to pay, are necessary if the tender is to be successful.

A company wishing to be part of the tendering process must go through the following stages prior to completing the sale.

- SEARCH During this phase, the marketeer investigates the marketplace to determine when new tendering deals will be open for bidding. Companies that sell industrial products have specific personnel who search out these opportunities.
- PREQUALIFICATION Not all projects are open to every bidder. A marketeer must be deemed "qualified" before a bid can be submitted. During this stage, a company must furnish documentation that proves it can provide the goods or services specified by the purchaser. The purchasing company will often provide its "specifications" months, even years, in advance of the actual bidding.
- SUBMITTAL While many companies participate in prequalification, the purchaser will only invite a small percentage to submit an actual bid. At this point, the marketeer may request additional information that may be needed to prepare a proper bid. Bidding may be "open," wherein each competitor can alter their formal proposal based on the content of their competition. This format requires the marketeer to be a savvy negotiator, as the bidding may take place with all competitors at the same table. Bidding may also be "closed" (a.k.a. "blind"), wherein the purchaser makes the decision without any input beyond the formal proposals.

- PURCHASE ORDER Should it be determined that the marketeer is the winning competitor in the tendering process, a purchase order will be issued with specific delivery dates. The purchaser may also require that the seller either ensure performance and delivery dates or otherwise guarantee the product. Penalties may be assessed for noncompliance.

NOTE: Transactions by tender can take a very long time, sometimes several years, between prequalification and project completion. This may require substantial patience and financial flexibility.

Sponsorships

Technically, a sponsor is a person who gives an assurance for another, but companies use this same technique to promote their products. A company moving into a new market may find that sponsorship is the easiest way to gain quick access to customers. For business, sponsorship works in reverse of the normal circumstance—the sponsoring company actually receives the assurances of the event or program being sponsored. In return for financial input, the sponsor is permitted to associate itself with an event that already has a positive image in the consumer's mind. If that image is lost or damaged, the company withdraws its sponsorship, as its value as a promotional tool has declined. Sponsorships can take the following two forms.

COMMERCIAL

These sponsorships are usually associated with the entertainment industry, television in particular. In this format, a sponsor is permitted not only to display their company name but also to exhibit and (to varying degrees) attempt to sell its products. The sponsor hopes that the popularity of the event will reflect itself with an increase in the popularity of the product line. While this is very much akin to advertising, it can be said to differ by its focus on nonstandard events, such as a sports or entertainment program in which sole sponsorship is maintained (e.g., Winston Cup auto races, Mobil's Masterpiece Theater). When several companies split sponsorship of the event, they'll insist on being designated as "official sponsors" to separate them from standard advertisers. Large sponsors nowadays often seek to have a degree of control over the content of the events they sponsor, in order to maximize the promotional effect.

NOTE: Commercial sponsorship shouldn't be confused with TV or radio "commercials," which are broadbased advertisements sold on the open market.

NONCOMMERCIAL

While money does change hands during this form of sponsorship, the sponsor is only permitted to display its brand name. Beyond that, no selling takes place. The use of company logos on professional team clothing and equipment (Adidas, Umbro, Rossignol) or even the displayed logos of unrelated sponsors (Ricoh Copiers, Guinness Beer, Fuji Film) are now an accepted part of sports events. Art exhibits, community affairs conferences, educational programs, and symphony orchestras regularly seek out this form of "underwriting" in order to assist with the financing of major undertakings. In return, the sponsor gains from the positive (preferably) image of the performers and participants created in the program viewers' minds. Some companies have taken on diverse sponsorships in order to reach as many consumers in as many segments as possible. Beer, for instance, has supplemented its traditional association with athletic events and car races with the sponsorship of global tours by rock groups.

NOTE: Marketeers should be cautious about what type of events they sponsor in new markets. Cultural research is essential for maximizing any sponsorship. Even experienced companies operating in their domestic market have come to rue their decision to sponsor a particular event or celebrity.

Direct Marketing

Direct marketing uses a variety of techniques—direct mail, door-to-door, coupons, telephone solicitation, TV and radio, print media, the Internet—to contact potential consumers in the hope of eliciting a direct, measurable, and almost immediate response. What differentiates it from other forms of promotion is the measurability of its results.

The increased use of computers to gather product preference information on consumers has given rise to a subgroup called "database marketing." Companies sell each other background and contact information about very specific market segments. American Express was a pioneer in this promotional format and has offered information about its membership's buying habits for decades. Internally, companies track their current customers' habits in an effort to further segment the customer base. Much of the information for database marketing is culled from credit card use and consumer response surveys. Such information is usually only available in the developed, more technologically equipped economies.

Even small-scale marketeers working in very limited markets should track their customer's consumer habits. Computers are by no means required for such tracking, even a filing cabinet or a simple Rolodex can be used to create a useful, if less high-tech, database. All of the following forms of direct marketing can make use of (and supply information for compiling) a customer database.

DIRECT MAIL

In this format, a company sends its catalog or "mail piece" directly to the homes or businesses of potential consumers. Mailings are done in highly targeted fashion but in large numbers; most postal systems worldwide provide a discounted "bulk rate" for volume. A direct mailing may be considered successful if it gets only a 2 percent response rate, so it must be produced as cheaply as company image will permit. Some markets (like the United States, where direct mail was first developed) have been so deluged that effectiveness is increasingly limited. The onslaught has even given way to the nickname "junk mail."

Direct mail requires that the marketeer be working in an environment that has an efficient postal system, as both the solicitation and the product will be subjected to the system's efficiency. Although many international delivery systems (such as DHL and FedEx) have improved the level of communication worldwide, they're often far too expensive for the original solicitation. Also required is an efficient means of paying for transactions. Though C.O.D. (cash on delivery) is still practiced in some markets, direct mail marketeers prefer to have their payment made by check or credit card prior to shipment.

NOTE: Most of the world's consumers don't have access to a credible banking system or to credit cards. Direct mail is useful only in developed markets.

DOOR-TO-DOOR

Though associated with a bygone era, the door-to-door sales technique is still used on a regular basis in a variety of markets. Avon cosmetics has made enormous inroads into the gigantic Chinese market by sending out swarms of local salespeople to every small village and farming community. Another technique in this category is the use of the "sales party" where friends, neighbors, and business associates are asked to attend a gathering where products are put on display. Amway, another U.S. company, has used this format to sell its cleaning products for decades around the globe. In Japan, Amway has been hired to market consumer products for Sharp Electronics.

NOTE: Not every society accepts the use of the door-to-door technique or even the selling of products to friends and neighbors. Some localities may even require that each salesperson be licensed as an individual merchant. Local sales tax issues are also a concern. Marketeers must be sure that their supply and distribution lines are efficient before taking orders on the foreign doorstep.

COUPONS

Coupons are vouchers or other documentation that entitles a consumer to a discount, a cash rebate, or free add-on products when making a purchase. Sometimes the coupon goes into effect at the time of purchase; sometimes it requires the consumer to contact the producer *after* the purchase has been made to receive the coupon's benefits. In the United States, where coupons are the primary form of sales promotion, large service companies (a.k.a. "redemption centers") have evolved just to handle the massive volume of vouchers that consumers turn in. Coupons can also take the form of sweepstakes by directly relating a product to the prizes offered, if only in an advertising connection.

These forms of sales promotion, as well as in-store price reductions or gifts, are highly regulated by governments, as they've been frequently linked to consumer fraud. Some countries (Germany, Greece) forbid product coupons altogether, while others (Brazil, New Zealand) restrict their usage on certain products or limit the value of the benefits.

NOTE: Because regulation on sales promotions is so varied from nation to nation (and sometimes city to city), marketeers should seek extensive local input before issuing coupons or sweepstakes-type promotions.

TELEMARKETING

Telemarketing is the use of the telephone to contact potential consumers directly, a form of promotion that saw a major growth surge in the early 1990s. The immediacy of telemarketing has been both its greatest attraction to marketeers and its least attractive aspect to consumers. Many cultures find being solicited at home as a nuisance and telemarketers have seen a rise in regulation—in the form of privacy laws as well as technology (e.g., caller ID) meant to thwart their efforts. But this hasn't lowered predictions about telemarketing's future growth. The greatest successes can be found in business-to-business contacts during regular working hours. Here, telemarketing is used to identify those companies that show some interest in a product and therefore warrant a personal face-to-face sales call. This practice of "qualifying a lead" makes the selling process more efficient, especially where large distances are involved.

Like direct mail, telemarketing depends on having the proper level of infrastructure present. It should be noted that the majority of people on the planet don't currently have access to a telephone; however, there's been explosive growth in telephone infrastructure, especially in the Asian emerging markets. Marketeers (or telemarketers) are quick to follow in the wake of these infrastructure projects. Currently, many companies in Europe and the United States use international direct dialing as a regular means of establishing customer contact for interbusiness promotions. Recent developments in "Internet telephones" (see below) will make telemarketing not only more cost-effective but also less intrusive. All marketeers should give telemarketing serious consideration in those countries that permit its open usage and where the product's positioning is conducive to such contacts.

TELEVISION AND RADIO

Whereas telemarketing provides the consumer with an involuntary immediacy, television and radio give the buyer much more control over when and where they'll be the subject of promotional efforts. Television offers "shopping channels" with direct viewer feedback as well as "infomercials" in which products are given almost documentary attention for up to thirty minutes, all the while soliciting viewers to phone in their orders. Both of these are quite common in the United States but satellite networks are quickly increasing their reach in the global markets. Call-in sweepstakes-type offers have been a mainstay of radio broadcasting for decades, as has been producer-sponsored programming. While many countries lack the necessary level of affluence and infrastructure for widespread television promotion, most nations have substantial radio access.

NOTE: Television and radio come under the direct control of local governments, and even satellite broadcasts can be subject to local regulation. Also, most responses to TV/radio promotions are done by telephone, requiring suitable infrastructure, and product delivery necessitates an efficient postal system.

THE INTERNET

Internet promotions often involve the direct contact of consumers via email for the purpose of selling products. This direct approach shouldn't be confused with the "banners" or cross-link "icons" that appear on many commercial and Internet service provider (ISP) web pages or with the use of a company website in place of catalogs or brochures. These are more akin to advertising or sponsorship and have become a multi-billion dollar industry that has revolutionized and revitalized promotions.

Internet promotions (sometimes called "spamming" when it takes on the nuisance level of junk mail) combine the feedback speed of telemarketing, with a more voluntary consumer contact level. (Promotional email can be deleted from the consumer's electronic mailbox without being read or even "filtered" out before making it to the consumer.) Though some Internet "purists" were dismayed by the commercial use of the medium, such promotions, as well as extensive banner advertising, have become common parts of daily cyber-life. For some companies, the Internet is the sole means of promoting their product line. In developed economies, just about every company has some form of Internet presence.

NOTE: Even tiny companies can afford Internet promotion. Like telemarketing, email is a great way to qualify leads on an international basis for business-to-business contacts before making expensive trips. Databases of potential customers can be purchased from service companies or assembled from internal records. A well-designed webpage costs little to operate and, unlike brochures or catalogs, it can track its viewers.

Push versus Pull: Creating Demand, Creating Interest

PUSH STRATEGY

A push strategy involves a greater reliance on personal selling and direct contact with consumers. The emphasis here is on allowing advertising to generate interest. Push strategies are more common when the product is complex in nature, requires a good deal of after-sale service, and must be marketed in areas where the amount of advertising media is severely limited or too expensive. Thus, these strategies are a common feature in less developed economies or those market segments that place little credibility in advertising. Here, producers and distributors must push products through distribution chains.

PULL STRATEGY

Pull techniques can be applied when a product is widely used, lacks complexity, when the distribution channel is extensive, and when mass communication media are readily available. This strategy is used to overcome the inefficiencies of long distribution chains, as consumers place pressure on those distributors farthest from the producer to deliver the goods or services seen in advertisements. Consumers literally pull the products through the channel. In larger developed markets (Europe, the United States, Japan), marketeers should consider a pull strategy for greatest effectiveness if the other criteria are in place.

NOTE: It's generally easier for a company experienced with push promotions to switch over to pull strategies than the reverse. Marketeers facing the process of switching from an advertising-based marketing plan to one centered on direct promotions will require a substantial change in psychology and customer contact skills. Make sure the retraining is done before entering the new market.

CHAPTER 13

Staffing the New Market

THE FIRST STEP BINDS ONE TO THE SECOND.
— FRENCH PROVERB

THE WORLD'S MARKETS may be crying out for a producer's goods and services with cash in hand, ready to make purchases, but that same producer still faces risk. Preparing to enter a market requires that the marketeer prepare for the next step, which is *managing* the market. The same techniques and personnel that were used in the domestic market may be only partially suited for the foreign project. Proper selection and training of personnel, along with suitable direction from headquarters, will determine a company's long-term success in a foreign market.

Personnel Restrictions: Your Country, My People

All governments have restrictions on foreign persons visiting or working within their national borders. Additional restrictions are placed on foreign nationals owning or operating businesses within those borders. International companies are faced with the choice of training local management and staff for work with the new product line or using personnel from their domestic market to fill positions in the new foreign project. Added to this is the local governmental regulation of how many and how long foreign personnel can be used on a project. And as a market "heats up," marketeers will also find that competition for competent local personnel adds another variable. (Four out of ten local management positions available with foreign companies in Vietnam go unfilled because of the lack of local talent.) From a small trader wanting to set up a representative office in Caracas to Microsoft setting up a programming facility in Bangalore, personnel restrictions are a universal problem in international business.

A company preparing to operate overseas can negotiate a variety of deals with local governments to ameliorate this situation. Under normal circumstances, governments impose regulation in order to protect their human and natural resources from exploitation. Even powerful economies like the United States hound Japanese companies working in America to allow more locals into the upper echelons of management. Marketeers requiring the extensive use of their domestic personnel due to product or distribution complexity should negotiate the project on the basis that locals will be trained for promotion over a reasonable period of time. This may also involve a technology transfer or management training for local managers sent back to the marketeer's domestic market.

Another avenue to pursue is that of tax relief (or "breaks") to cover the inefficiencies and cost of training local staff during a project's early stages. Most governments in undeveloped markets prefer this latter choice because it puts their population to work immediately, not at some later (perhaps years) date.

NOTE: At this stage, marketeers are very vulnerable to being approached with corrupt deals in which "under the table" taxation or the hiring of politicians' relatives are offered for consideration. Like bribery, this should be decided on as an option before negotiating with local governments. This isn't just an occurrence in emerging markets. Don't wait to be surprised at the negotiating table.

Selection Guidelines: The Rules for Expatriates and Locals

The ratio of expatriates to locals will vary from project to project and from country to country. The marketeer can, however, have set guidelines for selecting members of each group that will apply to any situation, in any market. Listed below are some attributes to look for when considering local and expatriate staffing. Marketeers considering working overseas should apply the expatriate attributes to themselves before deciding if they're the best person to run the overseas project.

EXPATRIATE PERSONNEL ATTRIBUTES

- HEALTHY Expatriate life can be physically trying. Going through the trouble and expense to station someone overseas demands a reasonable assurance that they'll be able to endure the environment. Whether you're sending a Canadian manager to Brunei or a Bangladeshi manager to Stockholm, make sure you send a healthy one.
- DECISIVE Even with the advanced state of communications, overseas personnel will be out of contact with their headquarters and regional offices for extended periods. Expatriates must be capable of making decisions (commensurate with their position) without the benefit of much guidance. Expatriates must be decision makers, not order takers.
- LOW MAINTENANCE Local standards of housing and office facilities may not meet the expatriate's domestic market standards. Only those personnel who can work in "less than ideal" circumstances should be considered for overseas work. Anyone who considers air-conditioning a necessity rather than a luxury should be dropped from consideration.
- FLEXIBLE Expatriate management and staff must "wear many hats" when attempting to fill in the gaps left by undertrained locals or by unfilled positions. Simply being able to fulfill the duties of the job title listed on a business card isn't enough. Expatriates should be multitalented and willing to put that talent to use whenever and wherever it's needed.
- TOLERANT Even when an expatriate is familiar with the foreign market under consideration, long-time posting to the foreign country can bring out some previously untested biases. These need to be eliminated *before* the assignment, as they can have disastrous and long-lasting effects on the product's profitability and the company's image. Bigots make poor expatriates.
- LOYAL A competent expatriate working in a difficult market will be extremely attractive to other foreign firms seeking to penetrate that same market. It's not unusual for expats to suddenly find themselves being pursued by lucrative job offers. Should they decide to "jump ship," a marketeer's investment may be at risk and, at the very least, they'll have to start all over again. The loyalty of

expatriate staff will also guarantee that technology or techniques will not become part of the public domain or part of a competitor's product line in the new market.

NOTE: If you're forced to make a choice between sending a highly competent employee or an extremely loyal but average one, err on the side of loyalty. Good attitude is harder to find than high aptitude.

- MORAL Morality is a very relative attribute, but it's best if expatriates reflect the moral code of their employers. The potential for graft or other malfeasance increases significantly over long distances. Marketeers must keep in mind that the image of their company (and perhaps all of its brand equity) will be tied directly to the performance of the overseas staff. While that behavior can't be guaranteed, measures should be taken during the selection process to ensure that reasonable moral standards will be maintained.

NOTE: Many companies now specify in their contracts with expatriate staff that termination may be the result of actions—on or off the job—that reflect poorly upon the project. Expatriates will also need to abide by local moral codes, especially when working in countries with fundamentalist regimes.

- CALM The life of an expatriate businessperson can be tumultuous—ask any who were in Beijing after Tiananmen Square or in New York after 9/11. Even the everyday difficulties of working in a different and sometimes implacable marketplace can try the patience of anyone. Expatriates should be able to keep events (and problems) in perspective and arrive at calm and controlled solutions.

NOTE: In some cultures, the "losing of one's temper" is viewed as an indicator of basic mental instability. Clearly, this is not the type of reputation that will serve a marketeer's efforts well. The word "manager" derives from the Latin for "hand," and expatriates must be able "to handle" both the business and the local environment. Cool heads and cool hearts do the best overseas.

- EXTROVERTED Expatriates, especially managers, will be called on to represent the company on a variety of levels, including social and political ones. This will be particularly true for large, well-known companies in most markets or for virtually any foreign company working in emerging markets. Expatriates must be able to enthusiastically socialize on behalf of the company's interests, whether in the position of host or guest. Shy and retiring types, unless their technical skills are irreplaceable, should be left off the roster for overseas assignment.

NOTE: Many cultures use social situations as the main battleground for negotiations. Expatriates must be extroverted but capable of recognizing when business and pleasure are being mixed. Many a contract has been won or lost at the dinner table or cocktail party.

- TEAM PLAYER Expatriates are usually placed in positions of power in the overseas operation, and they may be placed in charge of hiring all local personnel. This position requires that they be able to assemble and effectively work with a team of decidedly diverse people. Beyond this, it's important that expatriates see themselves as part of the larger international team that is working toward company goals. Expats may be encouraged to act with greater independence than domestic market managers, but they should never believe that they're an entity apart from the company team. Managers who weren't good team players in the domestic market will be even less effective once out of sight of headquarters.

NOTE: Some companies make the mistake of choosing a "lone wolf" as their overseas representative in the false belief that independent spirits need less guidance. The reality is that they tend to refuse any guidance. This "Colonel Kurtz Syndrome" (from the movie "Apocalypse Now") of entrusting the project to a renegade expatriate manager is a common but easily avoidable mistake.

- SELF-MOTIVATED Employees who need to be constantly patted on the back, cajoled, or otherwise rewarded for their work make poor expatriates. Even at the staff level, expatriates must be able to keep their own morale high under generally trying circumstances, as there may be little time or opportunity to pause and distribute praise. Overseas offices, especially new ones, are often hectic and understaffed. On top of this, expatriates are a long way from the normal motivating factors of their domestic market. Candidates for expatriate jobs should be able to recognize a job well done, take pleasure in its successful completion, and be prepared to move on to the next task without fanfare.

NOTE: Having self-motivated employees doesn't relieve upper-management of its duty to give credit where credit is due. One of the biggest expatriate complaints is that when they return to their domestic duties, their overseas work is given short shrift. This is a quick and sure way to lose a valuable employee to the competition.

- COMMUNICATIVE Expatriates can find themselves suddenly thrust into the helm of an exciting new venture in a foreign (often exotic) market where their level of importance is significantly higher than in their domestic environment. Those that let this "go to their head" may suddenly become less communicative with the home office as they concentrate on local matters. Expatriates must be willing to keep headquarters personnel apprised of the foreign operation on a regular and timely basis—the good news as well as the bad. If a candidate had communication problems in his or her domestic duties, these will be magnified overseas with disastrous results.

NOTE: Even with dependable employees, a clearly laid-out plan and reporting schedule should be put in place to ensure that vital information is available to the marketeer in time to make corrections. International business is rife with examples of expatriate managers who withheld information or "cooked the books" in order to protect their positions.

- MULTILINGUAL Speaking the local language will be a major asset, both for business and social situations. Of course, advance technical or managerial skills may require that an expatriate be put in place without the requisite language skills. Only those candidates willing to take the time and trouble to learn the local dialect should be considered. If they can't achieve at least at a conversational level within six months of their assignment, then they aren't trying hard enough.

NOTE: While this may be a trying and expensive ordeal, it must be emphasized as part of the company's long-term commitment to the new market.

- CONFIDENT Besides the confidence required to assemble and manage the venture's team, expatriates must be able to deal effectively with competitors, politicians, journalists, and potentially even local activist groups. Both self-confidence and confidence in one's company are vital to success when entering a new market.

- INFORMED Overseas work can be very absorbing, sometimes too much so. Expatriates must stay informed about what's going on around them, locally as well as globally. While "taking care of business" is an admirable trait, candidates for overseas positions must recognize that business is dependent on a wide range of external factors (e.g., competitors, financial markets, politics). While these may be beyond the expatriate's control, they shouldn't be beyond view. Headquarters also bears some responsibility for keeping their overseas employees informed of company and international events. This may require some financial outlay (especially in the minimal infrastructure emerging markets), but its benefits will be immediately evident. A well-informed expatriate is an efficient expatriate.

NOTE: Some governments (e.g., China) maintain strict control over all communication systems and often over their own commercial information (e.g., Vietnam). Staying informed under these circumstances can be difficult, expensive, and dangerous.

- ORGANIZED Expatriates on their first overseas assignment may find that they have difficulty operating outside the safety net of support personnel present in their domestic operation. Naturally organized persons tend to weather the storms of setting up a new office (and household) in a foreign city better than those with more chaotic tendencies. Employees who need a lot of support to function properly will not have success as expatriates unless the overseas operation has been running smoothly for some time prior to their arrival.
- WELL ROUNDED Expatriates run the risk of becoming "workaholics," due to the demands of the assignment and the lack of familiar diversions. This leads to burn-out and the eventual (and costly) replacement of personnel. Well-rounded candidates with interests outside of business make the best expatriates. They're better at "clearing their head" after a long workweek and can approach difficult projects with a fresh outlook. Workaholics tend to turn a marketing effort into drudgery, with little innovation. Well-rounded employees will find the new market to be more interesting and that will add both to their long-term commitment and possibly to the garnering of social contacts, which can be a very important part of international marketing.
- SOPHISTICATED This word originally meant "to mix with foreign substances." Expatriates should be able to readily mix with the local culture and absorb its nuances for later use when determining local values and motivators. They should also bring with them the full extent of other cultures with which they've mixed; an expatriate should be well traveled and as experienced as possible in intercultural activities. As a representative of a company, he or she must never come across as "provincial" or small minded.

NOTE: Having a passport full of foreign visas does not necessarily result in sophistication. Some people travel an entire lifetime and never benefit by it. Poise is the outward manifestation of sophistication and an indicator of a good marketing expatriate.

- FINANCIALLY SOUND Even when a company covers all of the costs of moving an employee overseas, the process can still be a burden on the expatriate's personal finances—especially when families are involved. Under no circumstances should a candidate be considered for overseas duties if he or she already has financial problems. (Sadly, some may even be hoping to escape creditors with the assignment.) These problems will only distract them from their duties in the new market and even precipitate dishonest behavior.

NOTE: Another common complaint of expatriates is that they get taxed into penury overseas and return with little to show for their efforts. International companies have recently given expatriates the incentives of covering their tax liabilities during overseas assignments and of offering salary bonuses. This enables a company to keep competent personnel on foreign assignments for longer periods.

LOCAL PERSONNEL ATTRIBUTES

- EDUCATED Marketeers should approach local employee interviews with a clear idea of the level of training required to fill each position. This level of training may not be available locally; the company may even need to implement an extensive training program of their own in advance of actual operations. Seek out employees with the highest level of education available to meet the needs of the project. Prior to the necessary training level being in place, hire those who are trainable.

NOTE: Large- and medium-sized companies have underwritten numerous academic programs in emerging markets in order to fill their managerial ranks. Smaller companies, in return for fees or higher wages, can hire from these same business-oriented programs. International hotels in those same markets have instituted their own training programs to raise local standards of customer sales and service, thus benefiting both themselves and numerous smaller operators.

- AMBITIOUS Rarely will even the most successful marketeer wish to keep an expatriate management team in long-term control of a foreign operation. Local staff must be trained to move into these positions and, in some cases, the promotions may be mandated by government. In either case, the local staff must aspire to promotion in order for the training to be effective and the operation viable. Because marketeers are entrepreneurial by nature, they're often shocked by certain cultures in which "ambition" isn't part of the local vocabulary. This cultural, sometimes religious, lack of aspirations must be circumvented by choosing the most ambitious locals available. Often, these are members of minority groups. Care should be taken not to unduly irritate the local majority population, as they may be the customer base as well.

NOTE: In societies where ambition flourishes, a candidate's personal ambition shouldn't be confused with what's needed to advance within the confines of the operation. If candidates want to succeed with the company, fine. If they just want to succeed personally, it's best to continue your search elsewhere.

- CONFIDENT Marketing requires faith in the product, the distribution channel, the customer, and the company. Self-confidence enables the other four levels of faith to function properly. One of the early complaints by marketeers when moving into the promising markets of Eastern Europe was not a lack of education or ambition but the lack of employees confident in their own abilities, a legacy of having lived through years of a centrally planned economy. Unconfident employees (local and expatriate) require greater supervision, work more slowly, and are prone to more production defects—not a very good combination of ancillary attributes. Local employees will come to represent the company in the long-term. Marketeers must make every effort to raise self-confidence when it isn't already present and preserve it when it is.

- FLEXIBLE The rule for local employees is the same for expatriates: If an employee can only work within a narrow job description, the company can't use that employee's services. This definition may be subject to union contract or local regulation, but a marketeer should strive to obtain the most flexible employees possible. It's incumbent on both marketeers and expatriate managers not to abuse this flexibility. Cross-training and job enrichment are standard ways for companies to increase the flexibility of their workforce while maintaining good community relations.

WARNING: Abusive work practices by foreign firms or their intermediaries have caused serious damage to marketing efforts both inside the target market and internationally. Subcontractors for Nike have been taken to task by local governments for this type of abuse even when the parent company made quick resolution of the problem.

- EAGER Unlike ambition, eagerness is an employee attribute that will impact directly on the consumer. Pride in one's work and a desire to do it the right way every time can't help but produce the best possible product. Eagerness to please the customer should start with the marketeer and move through the entire organization.
- CONNECTED Employees can be a marketeer's most important link to the community. Beyond their value to public relations, the connections they have politically and culturally can supply a foreign company with much needed in-roads to the new market.

NOTE: Hiring someone solely because of his or her connections is not recommended (although some employees may be forced on a foreign firm for this reason). However, the connections employees do bring to the organization should be maximized. Supervisory and middle-management personnel can be especially useful when negotiating local contracts.

- LOYAL All employees need to exhibit a degree of company loyalty. Of course, loyalty is a two-way street and marketeers can ask for no more than they're willing to give themselves. When hiring local staff in new markets, it's best to elicit some sense of commitment from candidates. In some cultures, this can be done by checking references, while in others it will have to be derived from a "gut feeling" generated during the interview process. Technologies and information must be secure for the new marketing effort to succeed; therefore, local employees shouldn't receive the implicit trust of their employer until their loyalty can be confirmed. Foreign firms can be easy targets for industrial espionage especially in markets with little court protection.

NOTE: Not all markets permit a foreign company to conduct the hiring of locals with a completely free hand. The recently reformed socialist countries and those with totalitarian governments, tightly regulate the hiring, retention, training, compensation, and termination of local staff as part of standard employment law. Many set clear ratios of expatriate to local staffing and demand thorough training and promotion schedules. These regulations should be thoroughly checked before embarking on local employee interviews.

Overall Management

Marketeers must prepare for the long-term management of their foreign operations far in advance of actual market penetration. Both the overall executive style and the day-to-day technique of operations managers and supervisors should be thoroughly discussed and planned. Unlike the domestic market, the foreign market will most likely give a marketeer only one chance to do it the right way.

There are three basic forms that an organization can take when designing the overseas operation.

MATRIX

This format draws members from disparate parts of the organization together to work on specific assignments related to the overall operation. As each task is completed, new teams may be assembled for new projects or tasks. Members are answerable to their original supervisor as well as to the head of each task group.

UTILITARIAN

This format reflects the same hierarchy that's present in most domestic operations (e.g., engineering, sales, purchasing, accounting). Each section works only on those parts of the project that directly involve them, with little crossover. It maintains standard corporate structure and plants it in the new market.

FOCUSED

This format chooses a specific aspect of the international market (such as the region, the country, the consumer, the product) and uses it as the focal point for all of the organization's efforts.

Marketeers should choose a general style that most aptly fits the target market, the level and quality of the communication system, the scope of the project, and the financial capabilities of the company. Smaller companies will be best served by the "focused" method, especially when it emphasizes the local consumer.

Operations Management

Management and supervisory style may have to be substantially adjusted to match the conditions and regulations of the new market. As the Japanese discovered when they began opening factories in the United States, foreign employees don't always exhibit the same deference, loyalty, or work habits as those found in the domestic market. Or, as Korean managers discovered in Vietnam, local employees will not necessarily tolerate the disciplinary actions of foreign management. (One South Korean manager working in Vietnam was deported for beating her employees across the face with a shoe.)

Although the management of day-to-day operations isn't often considered part of the marketing function, it *will* be when working in a foreign market. Even in a market as large as the United States, the management style of Japanese firms was the subject of great discussion (and often resentment) during the 1980s, and it had a genuine effect on the sale of Japanese products. It even resulted in a Hollywood motion picture "Gung Ho" that focused on the unsuitable management techniques of a fictional Japanese auto manufacturer in the American Midwest. While most marketeers won't receive this much attention, they should be aware that their management style will be a big part of the company's public relations image.

Cultural Training

A company preparing to enter a new market must keep in mind that they will have to play by a new set of rules. The local regulations (previously discussed) are, in most countries, a matter of civil code and can be readily accessed with some translation. But the cultural rules aren't as easily accessed and are rarely written down. Yet these must be abided by as surely as the civil code if a marketeer expects to achieve any level of success.

All levels of management that will be working in or with the overseas operation should receive extensive training in the culture and language of the society they're about to enter. Most of the large, developed economies have companies that provide these service at rates that can fit most budgets. Marketeers with limited finances, or those from locations without cultural training service providers, may have to take this obligation upon themselves and develop their own program.

There are a wide variety of resources available to assist in this matter. Books on the culture and customs of every nation can be found in the business section of most bookstores or ordered via the Internet (e.g., Amazon.com). Also beneficial are published texts on business protocol (e.g., the *Passport to the World series*, World Trade Press). Marketeers will need to have a good understanding of the history of the targeted market, but they should be careful to get a reading of that history from the perspective of the market's natives as well as foreigners. Any information that was compiled by members of the marketeer's culture will add a great deal to the application of that information, as each foreign culture will be received differently.

If professional language training isn't available, a marketeer may have to resort to the use of cassette tapes, videos, interactive DVDs, or online service for lessons. While this isn't ideal, the basics will come through and that will be sufficient for making initial research trips to the target market. Once there, more professional and thorough language training can be sought out.

NOTE: It's important that marketeers and their subordinates learn at least a few phrases in the language of a target market, even during the research phase. Showing even a mild interest in a language can open doors, and conversations meant to aid your pronunciation can bring much greater insights.

Motivating the Overseas Team: Long-Distance Interaction

Expatriate managers on assignment will be communicating with their headquarters over great distances, and often somewhat impersonally with fax and email reports. This can have a severe effect on morale and may endanger the marketing effort. Marketeers must prepare to keep their overseas employees motivated, either in person or remotely, if the project is to succeed. Here are some tips for maintaining high morale.

PAY WELL AND PAY ON TIME

Contrary to much management theory, employees do consider good pay as an indicator of their job performance and their worth to the company. This is even more essential for employees when they're living in a foreign environment a good distance from regular praise. And being paid on time allows them to have a sense of stability in what may otherwise be a very unstable environment. Many companies with international projects create special pay packages for overseas employees, in order to keep their taxable income to a minimum. Not all countries have "double taxation" agreements that prevent expatriates from being taxed both at home and abroad. Wise employers can keep the team's mind focused on marketing by keeping payroll problems to a minimum. This affects local employees in the same manner.

PROFESSIONAL FACILITIES

Besides protecting the company's image, locating the project in functional, comfortable facilities with quality furnishings and equipment can also be a morale builder. When the team is marketing the product and inviting contacts to the facility, it's best if they can take pride in the company and offer a professional image. Local employees will feel this sense of pride as well. Don't skimp in this area, even if your operation requires little more than a warehouse. Get the best facilities that the locale can offer and your budget can afford. In emerging markets especially, foreign companies and their personnel will be judged by how they "appear"—and treated by the local population accordingly. Outside of the professionalism the facilities will demand of the employees, first-class facilities will also show a willingness to put money into the local economy as well as profit from it. The choice of facilities is definitely a case of having to spend money in order to make money.

AMPLE HOUSING

Make sure that everyone on the team is properly housed and has a sense of "home," as this will allow them to focus on marketing instead of their discomfort. Some companies purchase or lease their own housing facilities and provide them, at no cost, to employees. This is quite common in less developed markets, where the company can get a better deal than a solo employee might. Subsidized housing gives the employees a sense that the company is "taking care" of them in this new environment and this increases loyalty as well as productivity. If a subsidy isn't used, compensation will have to be sufficient to cover suitable housing costs, which can be shockingly high in many of the world's commercial centers. In less developed markets, a company may wish to provide housing for locals. If this can be done, the motivational factor is enormous and the loyalty it creates is unshakable. When company housing is used, make sure employees don't get the impression that they have no private space. They should never feel that work is a twenty-four-hour-a-day process.

QUALITY HEALTH CARE

This is an increasingly important issue for overseas staff and their families. Arrangements must be made for local health care and, in less developed markets, emergency medical evacuation. Many health problems occur in the first few months of the assignment (especially in tropical environments) and the company must be prepared to protect its Human Resources investment. Even a simple cut that goes untreated can remove a key member of the marketing effort before that effort even gets off the ground. If this health care can be extended to locals (in cases where it isn't already mandated), the motivational and loyalty effect is similar to that of subsidized housing.

NOTE: Marketeers should send as robust a set of personnel on overseas assignment as possible—and take measures to ensure they stay that way. Sick people aren't very productive.

TAKE CARE OF THE FAMILIES

The number one reason that married expatriates give for requesting a return to the domestic market is that their spouse is unhappy with the new environment. When families are sent along as part of the assignment, the company bears some responsibility for their care and comfort. Suitable schools for children (and a paycheck large enough to afford them), jobs for spouses, transportation, and even social events are all things that keep the family as motivated as the employee. When the family is left behind in the domestic market, this causes problems of its own. Besides ensuring that the family finances are regularly sorted out, a company should provide the opportunity for the family (at least the spouse) to visit the employee at least twice a year. A generous telephone allowance is also a good way to maintain morale. Many marriages head for the divorce court due to overseas assignments. Rest assured that an employee going through a long-distance divorce will be of little use in your marketing effort. Married staff can be a major liability if proper measures aren't taken to keep family matters smooth.

Families of local personnel may also need some attention and this has many morale benefits if done properly. Jobs for spouses, along with educational or daycare facilities for their children can make the foreign firm seem less of an exploiter and more of a benefactor. Along with keeping the employees happy and productive, the public relations benefits should be manifest.

NOTE: Married marketeers working overseas must not allow business to completely overwhelm their family duties. Many cultures consider families a mark of stability and divorce a sign of failure. Personal life can become a public relations issue.

SECURITY

Most overseas marketing efforts will be situated in major metropolitan areas, all of which offer their own particular security risks. Emerging markets can be very dangerous places to operate in, as the rule of law is generally minimal. Sometimes the danger is criminal, other times it's political, and still other times it may be environmental. In any case, a company must make a reasonable effort to provide employee security. It may be the provision of bodyguards for assignments in Russia, a walled commercial compound in Cambodia, or private air transport for evacuation from the Congo. It could even be as simple as providing a chauffeur service for employees in New York City or an earthquake kit in San Francisco. Security literally means "without care" and employees (local and expatriate) who feel secure tend to focus more on their work.

PROVIDE LOCAL LANGUAGE TRAINING

Unless the employee arrives in the new market with complete fluency in the local language, training should start almost immediately. Besides being an obvious business tool, these lessons show the company's commitment to the market and to the employee's position in that market. Similarly, lessons for local employees in the company's mother tongue will help to assure them that advancement is possible.

VACATIONS

All work and no play makes a dull marketeer. Make sure the overseas staff gets ample opportunity to relax and refresh themselves. In-country holidays or leisure trips back home make for much more enthusiastic and productive employees. Local staff should also be encouraged to take vacations.

NOTE: Different cultures have different views of how long a work week is (in much of Asia, it's six days) and what constitutes vacation time (in France, it can be as much as ten weeks). On top of this, there's a vast array of religious and cultural holidays. Foreign companies generally apply local standards to local employees and domestic market standards to their expatriate personnel. Any conflicts are usually settled in favor of local standard—and wisely so.

RETURN TO BASE

Expatriates often feel that they're no longer part of the larger company for whom they work. A wise marketeer will bring the expatriates to the domestic market at least twice a year to reinforce the connection between the overseas operation and headquarters. This also allows the expatriate to bask in the envy of domestic staff who themselves may be seeking the excitement of an overseas assignment.

NOTE: Expatriates who are happy and motivated in their work are great recruiters for the marketeer's other international projects.

VISITATION

Another aspect of expatriate life that's potentially demoralizing is the fact that very few, if any, people from the domestic offices actually see the work that they do. Marketeers should visit all of their overseas operations several times a year—not just to check on progress but also to allow the expatriate and local employees to "strut their stuff" for the big boss. It's human nature to want to take pride in a job well done; sometimes marketeers must put themselves in the position of being "witnesses" to the accomplishments of subordinates. Local employees, too, need to be able to put a "human face" on the often-mentioned "headquarters." Unless some major problem has occurred, these visitations should be used primarily as morale boosters, not as a form of inspection.

NOTE: When problems do occur, and they will, the visitation/inspection should be conducted as discreetly and professionally as possible. Employees of all types take their cues from the top. Angry, shouting, and abusive bosses have negative, long-term effects on morale.

International Specialists: Hot Shots and Hired Guns

While a competent marketeer can market any project, it's not necessarily true that every experienced marketeer is suitable for an international assignment. This difference can come into play when deciding how to manage the new market. A small company with few domestic staff members to choose from, or a large company with no international experience may be tempted to look outside of their respective companies for management personnel to staff the overseas offices or supervise the new market. This can be a very wise decision if conducted within a few parameters. Besides all of the attributes cited above for overseas personnel, the following should be considered when hiring from outside of the company.

- Seek out candidates with direct experience in the target market. That experience should be as recent as possible; experience more than five years old may be of little value.
- Give priority to candidates who can call on numbers of useful and powerful connections in the target market, in both the business and political communities.
- If the target market uses a different language, perfect fluency may not be mandatory. But if a candidate is not at least "conversational," it means that their target market effectiveness will be limited.
- Consideration should be given to candidates who have worked in fields related to the marketeer's product, especially if there is a short-time line for market entry or if the product is highly technical in nature. This isn't mandatory, but it's preferred.
- Marketing specialists need to be skilled in all forms of modern communication and research. Because reporting and data compilation will be such a large part of the job, computer application skills must be of the first order, even in the less technically developed markets of the emerging economies.

NOTE: Candidates who can't be contacted by email or who continue to list telex numbers on their curriculum vitae should go to the bottom of the list.

- As is true with consultants, candidates for overseas positions will have to provide multiple and verifiable references. When these references are contacted, solicit information that's quantitative, not just qualitative. (e.g., "By what percentage were sales increased?," "What survey methods were used?")

NOTE: Experience that cannot be verified should not be considered.

- Candidates must be willing to make a lengthy commitment to the marketeer. If they won't give a firm commitment (a contract may be optional), it most likely means they're only taking the position to get back into a market where they'll start their job search anew. The length of the requested commitment should reflect the cost involved in sending the candidate overseas, as well as the degree of risk the marketeer will take in making the assignment.
- Work permits and visas should be thoroughly checked out before making an offer to a candidate. A marketing effort is too sensitive an issue for a foreign firm to have its management personnel either refused entry or deported for overstaying a visa.

While it's the responsibility of the candidate to secure these documents, a marketeer must be concerned about the diplomatic status of potential employees. This is especially true when they're hired from outside of the marketeer's domestic market.

GOOD CHOICES, GOOD RESULTS

The choice of personnel to manage the foreign office will be a key factor in the success or failure of an international marketing plan. It should be done thoughtfully and well in advance of the projected entry. Whether they're chosen internally or externally, these managers ought to be brought into the planning process as early as possible. If they were hired for their expertise (rightfully so), then that expertise ought to be brought to bear on the problems of the new market at the earliest opportunity.

WARNING: It's a mistake to hire project management after the planning phase has been completed. Besides being resentful of being made responsible for a plan not of their own making, these managers may be reluctant to offer useful suggestions for a plan that has already received the approval of their new employers. Also, if the plan fails, it's hard to hold such managers accountable.

International Divisions: Decentralizing the Decisions

Even with modern communication systems, most large companies have found that attempting to effectively run a far-flung international company from a central location is just short of impossible. Market needs, time zone differences, management styles and local regulation have necessitated a move toward decentralization. Also, the attractiveness of transfer payments—wherein a company sells and buys products among all of its subsidiaries in an effort to gain tax advantages in different markets—has further ingrained decentralization in modern international business.

Initially, a marketeer may be reluctant to give a new operation much autonomy, and that's a reasonable reaction. However, once expatriate (or local) management has proven that they're capable of "working without a safety net," a marketeer will find that decisions are made more quickly and with smoother results if done so at the local level. The new market will be rife with inherent problems that will only be exacerbated by slow decision making or extended debate.

If a marketeer chooses not to run the foreign operation in person, then qualified management should be sought out and employed for that purpose. Once that decision has been made, management should be given the opportunity to act on the marketing plan as soon as possible in a fairly autonomous manner. Not to permit this level of autonomy is to admit that marketeers need to second-guess their own hiring practices. Competent personnel soon grow tired of being "micromanaged," especially when it's done long distance.

NOTE: As is true with consultants, if you hire someone to do a job, let them do it. If you want to personally manage a foreign office from headquarters (not recommended by any means), then you should hire a less decisive, organized, and experienced management team.

CHAPTER 14

Evaluating Performance

TO PERCEIVE THINGS EARLY ON IS INTELLIGENCE.
— LAO-TSZE

NO MARKETING PLAN, nor the management put in place to implement it, can avoid the need to respond to marketplace changes. After all, the marketing plan is simply a forecast of how a company's products will progress in any particular market. No marketeer has ever gotten that prediction completely correct the first time, nor has the market remained unchanged for very long after a plan's implementation. International marketing is a complex issue, even for small companies. Projects of all sizes run the risk of becoming so involved in daily functions that marketing managers fail to audit their progress. When this happens, the ability to plan for the next marketing phase is greatly diminished. The only way to combat this problem is to have a regularly scheduled monitoring and evaluation of the marketing plan.

Sales Analysis: Are You on Course?

Prior to market entry, sales goals must be set in order to determine the level of acceptability of the product by consumers and to provide a base for forecasting revenues and expenses.

Sales goals should be set at realistic levels and determined objectively. Goals should be based on the potential of the new market, not on domestic market experience. Always make conservative estimations of sales growth. Marketeers who have been successful in their home market often forget the amount of time it took them to reach that level of sales revenue. Expecting to duplicate that hard-won success on a compressed time scale in a new market will cause disappointment (or worse) in even the most receptive environment.

A company can divide its fiscal year into whatever size portions it finds easiest to manage while still giving timely information. The most common method is to have twelve periods that correspond to the months of a year. Unfortunately, all of the months aren't of equal length; some companies work instead on thirteen four-week-long fiscal periods per year. This allows marketeers to make more accurate comparisons among the various sales periods to determine where "peaks" and "valleys" truly exist. Much of the decision regarding this matter will be based on the type of product being sold and on consumer buying patterns.

NOTE: Some large retailers have taken advantage of bar-coding technology to track their sales on a minute-by-minute basis. This form of "real time" sales auditing allows for very precise inventory control and consumer feedback.

The key to proper sales analysis is accuracy and consistency. While marketing is rarely mentioned in the same breath with accounting, the two disciplines are closely related. Marketing sets forth the goals of a company and accounting determines if those goals have been met. It's essential that marketeers understand financial accounting in order to track their sales and adjust their marketing plan. Many a company has come to regret the decision not to maintain a firm control of their accounting processes. This can be even more critical when operating on an international scale with few personnel. An old saying in business states that "figures never lie, but liars always figure."

WARNING: Keep accounting internal and keep an eye on it.

Overseas operations should be sending frequent updates to regional offices or headquarters. Weekly reporting is most common although communications technology and computers make more frequent analysis possible. Even a small company or solo marketeer should review sales figures as often as time and input permits. Forecasts may be devised on a monthly cycle, but daily or weekly review of sales figures will allow a marketeer to spot upward or downward trends. There's little value in waiting until the end of the period to discover that adjustments could have been made early on to achieve forecast.

Understanding financial accounting is part of a successful marketeer's "education"; this will keep the company in the marketplace longer and safeguard its resources. Computers and accounting software (much of it in "template" formats for smaller companies) can make the sales analysis process far less time consuming.

NOTE: Sales revenue is the measuring stick with which to gauge the marketplace. Make sure that your gauge is accurate.

Market Share Growth: The Seeds of Expansion

Each company embarking on an international marketing scheme is doing so in the hope of expanding its market segments. Once the larger national segment has been penetrated, the marketeer can turn attention to expanding their share within that market, further segmenting it, or moving into another market entirely. None of this ought to be considered without properly auditing and evaluating the progress of the company to date.

A common phrase in international business is that "to cease to grow is to die," and this psychology certainly points to the competitiveness of the marketplace. Growth may be healthy, but unplanned, unrestricted growth is as deadly as no growth at all. Healthy growth must be laid on top of the profitable and stable foundation of previously successfully market planning. Even large, global "conglomerates" (e.g., Coca-Cola, Matsushita) have had to retreat from expansion as they came to realize that their reach exceeded even their considerable grasp. Such resource draining "retrenchments" can happen on the small scale as easily as on the large.

Most mistakes that occur when a company expands into areas that prove to be quagmires rather than gold mines stem from looking ahead before determining current positioning. The penetration of a foreign market suddenly expands the view of possibilities and the temptation to pursue new areas immediately is alluring—especially when a marketeer has had some early success in the new market. Prospective market segments within a larger national landscape require as much planning as the original market entry. Equally needed is the discipline of knowing that past successes can't always be duplicated in new situations. Proper and unemotional evaluation of the company's current status will make the choice of when to expand a more accurate process. Remember, the word *opportunity* originally meant "in the proper season"; savvy marketeers know that they must plant in spring if they want to harvest in autumn. Evaluation lets you know what season it is and how your crops are doing.

Tracking Satisfaction: Giving Customers What They Want

Another area that requires evaluation is customer satisfaction. Assuming that if consumers are buying the product, they must be satisfied with it is a dangerous bit of logic. Consumer tastes are always in a state of flux. The sudden arrival of a competitor can make a company realize just how dissatisfied consumers actually were. Many companies in markets formerly protected by government edict (e.g., Lada Autos in Russia) came to this realization the first time that local consumers were given a chance to buy foreign products. Brand satisfaction (or loyalty) turns out to be a chimera.

Even in open markets, consumers sometimes continue to buy an unsatisfactory product just because they haven't been exposed to an alternative. Major U.S. breweries like Coors and Miller discovered this when the sudden appearance of microbreweries drained away market share at an alarming rate in the mid-1990s. Consumers wanted fuller-bodied beer but had not been given the option until that point. Megabrewers responded by putting out quasi-microbrews in direct competition with their own products. Some even attempted to disguise the fact that they were behind the marketing of the new products in order to retain a "little guy" image.

What happened in both of these examples is that companies began to believe they controlled their own success. In reality, it's the consumer who calls the tune to which marketeers must dance. The same type of research and analysis skills that brought the marketeer into the foreign market in the first place must be continually deployed to find out what type of "music" consumers are going to play; though companies can certainly make suggestions via advertising and promotions.

The greater the competition in the marketplace, the more often a company will have to evaluate consumer wants, needs and beliefs. Understanding consumer behavior is at the root of all marketing success and it solidifies the link between the buyer and the seller. If a producer isn't willing to evaluate and attend to that link, a competitor will be more than happy to become the new "dancing" partner.

Marketing Audit: Back to the Drawing Board

The marketing audit is a systematic appraisal of an organization's preparation, implementation, status and prospects of its marketing plan. An audit can be a very time consuming (and, if improperly conducted, traumatic) process, with repercussions throughout the organization, as well as in its distribution channels. It often uncovers failings that have been "swept under the rug" or simply forgotten. It involves personnel at all levels and is conducted both inside and outside of the company structure. An audit gathers the data and provides the analysis that allows a marketeer to properly evaluate the marketing plan. Conducting the audit isn't always an agreeable process but it must be done.

WARNING: Rest assured that a competitor—somewhere—is sizing up your company's performance, even if you choose not to do likewise. When a competitor knows more about your company than you do, failure isn't far away.

A detailed outline of the areas covered by a marketing audit is included in Chapter 16 of this book. At this point, some guidelines for the scope and use of the audit need to be discussed.

OBJECTIVITY

Companies of all sizes have a difficult time maintaining objectivity about the value of their own planning processes, especially when the plan is still in effect. Objectivity decreases in proportion to the size of the company, with solo marketeers having the least. Unfortunately, an audit that lacks objectivity is worse than no audit at all, because it has the *semblance* of truth. A company that has the resources may choose to hire an outside service to conduct the audit, but that requires turning over information that may be sensitive. If the company is operating in a foreign market with little in the way of commercial law and binding nondisclosure statements, outside auditing may not be an option.

The reason company personnel lack objectivity is that they fear blame and seek praise, both very human responses. Objectivity must start at the top with the marketeer and infuse all other personnel. The audit should be conducted in an atmosphere that simply takes the facts as they are and makes necessary adjustments to get back on track. Blame and praise shouldn't be part of it. Even a solo operator needs to view the audit as a chance to make course corrections, not jump overboard. For this reason, audits ought to be performed regularly (at the very least, every six months, preferably every fiscal quarter) so that they can be seen as a normal part of an ongoing process. Besides reducing the tension level, frequency of audits makes for more efficiency, as auditing personnel gain greater familiarity with what to look for and where.

NOTE: Unlike financial audits, which are done randomly to uncover surprises, marketing audits are designed to prevent surprises.

INPUT

The marketing audit isn't just an internal assessment. Even those portions that are done internally aren't restricted to management personnel or their functions. Marketing encompasses every aspect of a business organization's dealings. Even when a marketeer is a solo operation, the suppliers, distributors, agents, shippers, freight forwarders, ad agencies, media buyers, retail sales personnel, warehouse operators, and, most importantly, customers will be called upon to make contributions to the auditing procedure.

NOTE: When building the distribution chain, all prospective candidates must be willing to participate in the marketing audit as part of the price of admission. This doesn't mean that they must throw open their financial records to auditor scrutiny, only that they be willing to explain and alter their processes. Some channel members may rely on their ISO 9000 status as a sign that they're open to such outside inquiries.

WHO WILL AUDIT?

Large global corporations with sizable resources will use any one of a number of international consulting groups (e.g., KPMG, Boston Consulting Group, McKinsey) to conduct the marketing audits. Similar services are open to smaller companies that have the necessary resources to fund such external auditing. While these external consultants can certainly lay claim to a great deal of objectivity, they're still outsiders and may cause resentment. Also, external auditors being used for the first time have a slower "learning curve" when it comes to contacting the correct personnel in order to access necessary information.

Most small- and medium-sized companies that operate on a limited international basis use their own internal personnel to perform the marketing audit. Like financial auditors, these personnel must be given unlimited access to the company's records and full cooperation from staff at all levels. It's not recommended that members of the market planning team be used for the audit unless they're overseen by management from another department. Company executives should avoid becoming involved unless company size dictates otherwise; it's wiser to use strong middle-management personnel to oversee the process.

An audit can be very expensive (especially when consultants are used), but the results can more than pay for themselves if the audit is thorough and the analysis keen. The cost can be distributed among all departments as an administrative cost or charged directly to the marketing account. Whatever the case, it should be budgeted as part of normal business planning and given sufficient funding to get the job done correctly.

WARNING: An incomplete audit done "on the cheap" is more costly in the long run than one done properly.

ACCOUNTABILITY

Accountability isn't the same as blame; it's more akin to responsibility than fault finding. When evaluating the results of the audit, a marketeer must assign responsibility for fixing problems rather than pinpointing those who made mistakes. (Only when mistakes are absolutely egregious or intentional should any punishment be doled out to internal staff. Also, in some markets, politically sensitive relationships with distribution chain members may preclude any immediate actions, should those members prove to be part of the problem.) Ultimately, upper management (or the solo marketeer) must be fully accountable for the design and implementation of the marketing plan. If the audit proves that the plan is indeed effective and well implemented, much is to be gained by spreading credit for that success throughout the organization and distribution channels. If major problems come to light, it's best for the executive(s) to take full responsibility and then turn attention immediately toward remedial action.

NOTE: Marketing efforts and their implementers must remain highly motivated to get the job done right. Savvy marketeers won't succumb to the urge to sacrifice long-term success for short-term retribution.

EFFECT ON FUTURE PLANNING

A proper audit and evaluation of a marketing scheme can pay benefits well beyond the project it was designed to survey. Problems, successes and potential innovations that are uncovered can be applied to other ongoing projects or to planning market entry elsewhere.

The evaluation will be of particular use to companies that have only just recently embarked on the international marketing scene. Lessons can be learned from successes as well as failures, and marketing plan evaluations should be kept as part of a company's performance records (a.k.a. knowledge database). While no two markets are exactly alike, a good audit of current planning will prevent the marketeer from having to "reinvent the wheel" for every new national market or market segment.

NOTE: All people and companies need to learn from experience. The evaluation serves as a clear record of that experience.

CUSTOMER COMMITMENT: KEEPING YOUR PROMISE

Making a commitment to the customers of each market segment is the essence of a good marketing plan. It's very easy indeed to make that commitment early in the planning process, but it can be difficult to maintain it as time goes by and the relationship becomes all too familiar. The customer may have the right to take the marketeer's commitment for granted, but the marketeer must constantly renew the relationship.

Keeping a focus on the needs and wants of customers is the determining factor in whether a company achieves long-term success in the marketplace. When operating internationally, that focus will require additional effort right from the start. Understanding the cultural, economic, political, and historical motivations of each targeted segment requires considerable research and insight. This effort is just the beginning of a much larger commitment to those new customers to grow with and service their needs over many years. More than an obligation between a company and a market segment, it's a promise among people. The willingness to make this commitment brings with it the excitement of opening up new markets and expanding revenues and global relationships. Most importantly, it brings the satisfaction of a job well done and a promise kept.

CHAPTER 15

The Marketing Plan

Take time to deliberate . . . stop thinking and go in.
– NAPOLEON BONAPARTE

THE FOLLOWING is an outline for developing a basic international marketing plan. While such a plan requires a good deal of research, the marketeer is cautioned against "overplanning" and thereby missing an opportunity at market entry that may not come again. Conversely, while not every aspect of this outline will be relevant for every size project, don't take too many shortcuts. As Napoleon admonished: Think it through, but be prepared to act.

Guideline for Marketing Success

I. INTRODUCTION

A summary of the long-term and short-term objectives of the marketing plan as well as a brief description of the target market

II. PRODUCT DESCRIPTION

Evaluate the product/product-line from the perspective of the target market based on the following categories:

1. Marketplace advantage
2. Innovation
3. Cultural compatibility
4. Perceived complexity
5. Willingness to adapt
6. Current familiarity
7. Potential resistance
8. Potential share size

III. TARGET MARKET

A. Summarize the cultural and economic research of the target market for the following areas:

1. History
2. Geography
3. Politics
4. Current government
5. Family roles
6. Education levels
7. Legal environment
8. Philosophy and religion
9. Language
10. Culinary
11. Housing
12. Labor
13. Health
14. Economics
15. Population profile
16. Income distribution
17. Agriculture and industry
18. Technological development
19. Transportation
20. Energy
21. Communications
22. Environmental concerns
23. Distribution channels
24. Advertising Media

B. Profile local consumer buying habits

1. Usage patterns for similar products if available
2. Shopping habits (place, time, frequency)
3. Methods of payment

4. Product differentiation and feature choice

C. Describe local pricing strategies
   1. Markup techniques
   2. Availability of discounting promotions
   3. Levels of retailer discretion
   4. Estimation of governmental intervention on pricing
   5. Influence of taxation

D. Estimate the size of the target market
   1. Determine industrywide sales specific to the product for the national market
   2. Estimate the amount of sales of the product during its first year
   3. State reasons for the level of initial market penetration

IV. COMPETITION ANALYSIS

For each direct or indirect competitor, compile the following information:

1. Competitor name
2. Country of origin
3. Presence in target market
4. Presence in neighboring markets
5. Overseas operations
   a) Total number
   b) Estimated revenues
6. Domestic operations
   a) Total number
   b) Estimated revenues
7. Directly competitive products
   a) Pricing
   b) Features
   c) Packaging
8. Indirectly competitive products
   a) Pricing
   b) Features
   c) Packaging
9. Local advertising
10. Local promotional efforts
11. Local distribution channels
12. International distribution channels
13. Governmental connections
14. Strategic partnerships
15. Joint ventures
16. Importer relationships
17. Estimate of current market share
18. Potential for future competition

V. GOVERNMENT REGULATION AND AGENCIES

A. Role in domestic commerce
   1. Internal tariffs
   2. State-owned enterprises

B. Role in foreign trade
   1. Import/export controls
   2. Tariffs
   3. Quotas
   4. Customs process
   5. Licensing process
   6. Embargo restrictions

C. Trade finance assistance
   1. Access to public and private funding sources
   2. Usage rates

D. Foreign investment policy
   1. Property ownership rights
   2. Business ownership rights
   3. Entry/exit visa policies
   4. Permanent resident policies
   5. Taxation rates
   6. Foreign-owned businesses
   7. Expatriate workers
   8. Profit repatriation rates
   9. Expropriation and domestication risks

VI. SEGMENT SUMMARY

Summarize the potential market segment problems that will require attention prior to market entry. (A great deal of this information can be derived from the experience of other foreign operators in the target market.)

VII. PRODUCT STRATEGIES

A. Objectives
   1. Sales projections over five years (monthly or period breakdown)
   2. Initial market share for one year after penetration by period and four successive years by quarter
   3. Operating profits over five years (monthly or period breakdown)

B. Adaptation

Describe how the product will be adapted for the new market in the following categories:
   1. Product content
   2. Product name
   3. Product label
   4. Service component
   5. Packaging design
   6. Local usage

C. Advertising

Describe how the advertising for the product will be designed for the new market in the following categories:
   1. Design
   2. Media mix
   3. Reach
   4. Frequency
   5. Impact/message
   6. Estimated costs

D. Promotional effort

Describe how the promotional effort will be implemented for the new market in the following categories:
   1. Public relations
   2. Personal sales
   3. Industrial sales
   4. Sponsorships
   5. Sweepstakes
   6. Coupons/discounting
   7. Telemarketing
   8. Other direct marketing

E. Strategic partnerships

List possible partnerships and their influence on the marketing strategy.

F. Brand Equity

List information regarding the current brand recognition in the market and plans for its development. Additionally, list any information that would interfere with the establishment of copyright or trademark rights within the target market.

VIII. DISTRIBUTION STRATEGIES

A. Modes for distribution

List modes of transport available, most suitable and respective costs for the various modes of import, export and internal shipping.

B. Ports of entry

Describe the available ports and their respective cost benefits or problems.

C. Packaging requirements

Review the regulations and cultural standards that will affect packaging along with the effect such requirements will have on cost.

D. Shipping requirements

Define the regulations that will affect the shipping and internal transport of the product in bulk format and the accompanying costs.

E. Insurance needs

List information about the availability of insurance in the local market and the projected costs for insuring the distribution effort.

F. Documentation

Catalog all documentation, method of acquisition, and processing costs that will be required for import, export, or internal transport of products or their components in the new market (bills of lading, air bills, pro forma invoices, etc.). Also, note the proper government agencies that must be contacted, along with their location.

G. Freight forwarding

Review all freight forwarders available for use in the new market along with their price proposals. If internal freight management will be utilized make note of the regulations regarding their performance in the new market and all necessary licensing.

D. Warehousing

Include information about the availability and suitability of local warehousing with an emphasis on cost and quality control. Also note any regulations that prevent or discourage foreign ownership.

E. Inventory controls

Delineate plan for controlling inventory from raw materials through finished product to end-user. Make note of local rates of and attitude toward pilferage.

F. Distribution channel design

List all required and contractual intermediaries (agents, retailers, wholesalers, distributors, etc.) along with a cost-benefit analysis for their usage. Make note of other potential disadvantages beyond direct cost of operating the distribution channel as an internal process.

G. Taxation

Provide information on the current tariffs, customs duties, local transportation taxes, documentation fees, handling charges, levies, value added taxes or other fee structures enforced by local government regulation.

IX. PRICING STRATEGIES

This section is used to elaborate on the company's projections and methodology for setting its prices in the local market. It should include:

1. Wholesale markups
2. Retail markups
3. Discounts
4. Rebates
5. Bulk purchase rates
6. Projected market entry price schedule

X. REVENUE STRATEGIES

This section will define the methods by which the company will accept payment for its products in the new market. Methods to consider are:

1. Cash (local currency and foreign substitutes)
2. Exchange rate risk
3. Banking facilities and rates
4. Credit extension to customers
5. Credit card usage and terms
6. Bartering
7. Mixed compensation
8. Buy-back strategies
9. Build-Operate-Transfer

XI. FINANCIAL STATEMENTS

The following documents should be prepared as part of the marketing plan:

A. Marketing budget (five-year projection)

1. Product cost
2. Selling expenses
3. Regulatory costs (applied to marketing effort)
4. Advertising expense
5. Promotions expense
6. Distribution costs
7. Auditing costs

B. Pro Forma Income Statement (P&L) (five-year projection)

XII. FINANCIAL RESOURCE REQUIREMENTS

This section should provide detailed information about the amount and source of financing that will be required to penetrate the new market. Since the marketing plan will eventually be included in the overall business plan for a company, this section may be a sub-section of the overall financial projections.

XIII. PERSONNEL REQUIREMENTS

All general and specialized requirements for personnel needed to implement the marketing plan and staff overseas offices should be listed here. A schematic (flow chart) of the project's organizational chart along with lines of communication and authority should be included. Each position listed is best accompanied by a brief job description and wage scale. Housing and transfer benefits may also be listed here.

XIV. SECURITY ISSUES

All concerns about the security needed for personnel, product, buildings, equipment, and other assets of the company to be sent overseas as part of the marketing effort can be stated in this section. Security issues for intangible assets such as goodwill, brand rights, and public relations can also be included.

XV. MARKETING PLAN SUMMARY

Plan designers should summarize the main points of the plan and make concrete recommendations for its implementation, as well as both short-term and long-term ramifications. Its projected effect on other current company marketing schemes (foreign and domestic) ought to be included. Finally, projections about its effect on future marketing efforts, both in the target market and otherwise can be stated here. This summary is often placed at the beginning of the plan and designated as the Executive Summary.

CHAPTER 16

The Marketing Audit

PROSPERITY HAS NO FIXED LIMITS.

— HENRY MORGENTHAU

THE PURPOSE of a marketing audit is to gather the data and provide the analysis that allows a marketeer to properly evaluate progress in implementing the marketing plan. It allows a company to ensure that it is reaching the benchmarks it set for itself. The following is a guideline for the preparation of a marketing audit:

The Marketing Audit

I. LOCAL MARKET SURVEY

Make detailed lists for the following categories:

A. Economic
1. The major changes in the local economy since the market plan was devised
2. Actions the company has taken in response to these developments

B. Demography
1. Major changes to the local demographics
2. Responses to those changes

C. Technology
1. Changes that have occurred in product technology that have affected the marketing plan or will do so in the foreseeable future
2. The company's reaction to those technological developments

D. Environmental
1. Any changes that will affect the company's impact on the local environment
2. Any environmental activity or changes that may influence the marketing plan

E. Government
1. All developments in local politics that may affect the marketing plan
2. Any laws that have been passed or are being considered that could impact the plan in the long- or short-term
3. Description of the company's current relationship with the local government
4. Potential problems or changes in that relationship

F. Labor
1. All information regarding changes in the attitudes of local labor
2. Reactions of expatriate personnel to local standards and employees

G. Advertising and promotions:
1. Statistics supporting the effectiveness of advertising schemes
2. Information about the company's promotional efforts
3. Information that profiles the company's public relations image

H. Culture
1. Current local opinions regarding foreign business

2. Any changes in the local lifestyle, culture, or values that might affect the plan
3. Status of relationship with the local community

I. Marketplace
1. Statistics regarding the current size of the local market
2. Growth trends of the market
3. All segments currently being served
4. Potential segments

J. Consumers
1. Description of consumer buying habits
2. Consumer opinions regarding:
   a. Product
   b. Postal service
   c. Pricing
   d. Competitive products
   e. Sales personnel
   f. Brand image

K. Competition
1. Names of direct and indirect competitors along with their respective
   a. Size
   b. Market share
   c. Ad and promotional schemes
   d. Effectiveness of positioning
   e. Pricing strategies
   f. Brand image
2. Impact of the company's market entry upon competition
3. Description of possible future competitors and reasons for market entry

L. Resources
1. Effectiveness of current suppliers of materials
2. Reasons for original selection as suppliers
3. Potential problems in supply linkages
4. Pricing structure and potential changes
5. Back up systems and possible alternative suppliers

M. Financing
1. Current level of financing
2. Anticipated needs for remainder of plan implementation
3. Potential resources
4. Potential exchange risks and counter strategies
5. Current status of accounts payable and receivable

N. Distribution channels
1. Members of channel with an analysis of their efficiency
2. Alternative cost saving or service improving systems
3. Any potential changes to the retailing component
4. Any potential changes to the transportation component
5. Current status of warehouse facilities

II. STRATEGIC

1. Mission of the company
2. Objectives of the marketing plan
3. The following questions should be answered in detail:
   a. Are the company's goals reflected in the objectives of the marketing plan?
   b. Does the marketing plan reflect the company's resources and the level of competition?
   c. Has management put forth clear strategies for achieving the objectives?
   d. Does the marketing strategy match the local state of the economy?
   e. Does the marketing strategy account for a realistic product cycle?

f. Has the company pursued its originally targeted market segment?

g. If so, have results matched forecast?

h. Has the company pursued additional segments?

i. What have been the results of those pursuits?

j. Has the company achieved the positioning as set forth in the marketing plan?

k. If not, what are the reasons for not having attained the original positioning?

l. Have sufficient financial and material resources been put at the disposal of the team?

m.If not, what additional resources need to be allocated?

n. Can those additions be fiscally justified?

o. Is the current strategy sufficient to meet the objectives of the plan?

p. Have those objectives changed?

q. What changes to the strategy need to be made in order to achieve the objectives?

III. STRUCTURAL

1. Define the current structure of the marketing team, including the lines of communication and levels of authority.
2. The following questions should be answered in detail:

a. Does the structure of the marketing effort reflect an efficient flow of information from producer to end-user?

b. Does the structure reflect a task or departmental orientation?

c. Does the current structure match the one originally proposed in the marketing plan?

d. If not, why not?

e. Does the structure take into account all internal business relationships?

f. How can the lines of communication be characterized?

g. Does management have authority to control the structure?

h. What are the current conflicts among the internal sections of the structure?

i. How can they be improved?

j. What potential conflicts can arise among the internal business groups?

k. How can these problems be avoided?

l. What are the current conflicts with the external sections of the structure?

m.How can they be improved?

n. What conflicts could arise with the external business groups?

o. How can these problems be avoided?

IV. TACTICAL

A. Research

1. Did the company have sufficient access to information to make proper marketing decisions at inception of the plan?
2. If not, what areas were lacking? How has this affected the implementation of the plan?
3. What is the current method for acquiring marketing data?
4. Have sufficient personnel and finances been allocated?
5. What steps have been taken to improve information gathering?

B. Planning

1. What system does the company use to forecast sales?
2. Has this system proved to be accurate?
3. If not, what are the alternatives?

4. What systems are in use for:
    a. Measuring market share?
    b. Designing sales quotas?
    c. Determining prices?
    d. Monitoring the competition?
    e. Segmenting the market?
5. Have these systems proven to be sufficient? If not, what alternatives can be brought on line?

C. Management Oversight

1. How often does management monitor:
    a. Prices?
    b. Competition?
    c. Distribution?
2. How often does management monitor the sales force?
3. Has this brought measurable improvements?
4. By what method does management monitor and control product quality?
5. What problems have been uncovered?
6. What solutions are in place?
7. Has quality improved after these solutions were put in place?
8. How often are marketing costs monitored?
9. What cost-saving measures have been put in place?
10. What quality-improving measures have been put in place?
11. How often does management monitor customer satisfaction?
12. What steps have been taken to improve customer satisfaction?
13. What effect, if any, has this had on market share?

D. Product Development

1. What system does the company use to determine what new products should be developed?
2. What financial resources are devoted to research and development?
3. Is this a sufficient amount?
4. What products has the system developed since the implementation of the marketing plan?
5. What system is used to test these new products in the marketplace?
6. What has been the reaction of the marketplace to these products?
7. Have any of the recently developed products been "rolled out" in the actual marketplace?
8. What have been the results?

V. ELEMENTS

This section looks at the suitability of the marketing components as separate issues.

A. Products

1. Does the current product line meet original objectives?
2. Has sufficient customer surveying been done to determine if the product line is meeting market needs?
3. What are the specific opinions that customers have regarding the product line?
4. Should the line be expanded or contracted?
5. Is the company financially prepared to develop new products?

B. Pricing

1. Has current pricing met the objectives of the marketing plan?
2. Do consumers find the pricing to be competitive?
3. Do consumers believe they receive the correct value for the price?
4. Has the elasticity of demand been tested in the marketplace?
5. What were the results?
6. What input do external members of the distribution chain have upon the price to the end-user?

7. Is this effect considered exorbitant?
8. What discounting methods are open to the company?
9. Will discounting improve market share?
10. What cost changes will be affecting pricing in the near future?
11. If costs are rising, will consumers be sympathetic to these cost increases?
12. If costs are declining, will the savings be passed along to consumers or retained as profit?
13. Does the company need to redesign its pricing structure?

C. Distribution

1. Is the current distribution deemed sufficient?
2. Which members of the chain are the least efficient?
3. Can the company keep distribution completely internal?
4. Will this increase efficiency?
5. Does the end-user absorb excessive distribution costs?

D. Sales team

1. What is the composition of the sales team?
2. Have they proven to be effective?
3. Do they have clearly stated objectives?
4. How are the sales quotas developed and distributed?
5. Does the team need to be expanded to meet sales goals?
6. Have they received sufficient training?
7. Do they have sufficient product knowledge and sales technique?
8. Are they properly compensated by marketplace standards?
9. Are they local or expatriate?
10. What percentages of each?
11. What steps are taken by management to maintain morale?
12. Are they regularly evaluated?
13. How do competitive sales forces rank compared to the sales team?

E. Public relations

1. What image does the company currently have in the marketplace?
2. Does the public's image of the product line match the objectives of the company?
3. Are there sufficient financial resources devoted to advertising, promotions, and goodwill development?
4. What external factors are affecting the company's image?
5. Can these external factors be controlled? If so, how?

VI. PROFITABILITY

Present financial statements that detail the profit or loss of each product for the market in comparison to the forecast from the original marketing plan. All costs from the marketing effort should be taken into account, although some (e.g., goodwill, pre-entry research) may be amortized over an extended period.

VII. REPORTING

The report should be presented objectively, and even when the audit is performed internally, it should have the tone of external observation. Medium-sized companies may consider assigning segments of the audit to various departments to investigate areas outside of their normal authority. Small companies may wish to conduct the audit in a seminar fashion, with results being presented at a management meeting.

CHAPTER 17

Glossary

ABSOLUTE ADVANTAGE (economics) The advantage of a company, economy or other economic unit over another in the cost of producing goods using the least resources (physical and human).

ADOPTER A consumer who is willing to purchase a product. Adopters range in grade from innovators to laggards.

ADVERTISING A form of public notice that seeks to inform, persuade and otherwise modify consumer attitudes toward a product, with the objective of triggering an eventual purchase.

ADVERTISING AGENCY An organization that specializes in the research, design, creation, and management of advertising for a company. They may supply creative services as well as media buying, ad distribution, logo design and information on brand building.

ADVERTISING CAMPAIGN A planned set of advertising messages repeated in a variety of media. The goal of an advertising campaign is to inform consumers about new products or innovations to old ones, improve the image of a product or a company, and trigger actual purchases of products or services.

AGENTS Members of the distribution chain that represents a company's products without ever taking actual possession. An agent's role is to establish contact between buyers and sellers for a fee. Some nation's require that agents be native to the marketplace.

A.K.A. An acronym that stands for "also known as."

ARTIFICIAL DEMAND The creation of consumer demand through the promotion of goods or services for which the marketplace has not expressed a previous interest. See PRODUCT DRIVEN

ATOMIZATION The marketing strategy that treats each individual as a separate segment. Disorganized attempts at atomization can result in SPLINTERING.

AVERAGE RETURN PRICING A technique for pricing products that uses the average amount that a company expects to profit above product costs for its entire line as the percentile to markup new products. An unreliable pricing method as it doesn't account for questions of PERCEIVED VALUE or COMPETITION.

BARTER A trade system whereby goods are exchanged for other goods and services, rather than for money. It's the oldest form of commerce. See COUNTERTRADE.

BILL OF EXCHANGE (a.k.a. draft) An unconditional order by which one party instructs another party to pay a specified amount to a third party. It's often used in foreign transactions as a means of financing.

BRAND EQUITY The value a company derives from the fact that their product name is recognized and well-thought-of in the marketplace.

BRAND EXTENSION The introduction of a new product or service by associating it in promotion with an already existing and well-established brand name.

BRAND NAME A name, symbol, logo, design or combination thereof which is recognized in the consumer's mind beyond the product itself.

BRAND REPETITION An advertising technique designed to trigger a purchase by the constant repetition of the brand name to consumers, either visually or orally, until it's firmly implanted.

BREAK-EVEN PRICING A pricing methodology whereby the sale price of a product covers all costs of manufacture, but with no profit. Break-even pricing is often used to keep prices low during market entry of a new product.

BREAKING INTO A MARKET The process of introducing a product into a new market.

BROKER An individual or company that negotiates contracts with a third party on behalf of a principal. Typically a wholesale intermediary who facilitates sales.

CAPITAL-INTENSIVE A business that requires significant capital input or investment, especially during a start-up period before profits are realized (e.g., manufacturing, bio-technology and infrastructure projects).

CAVEAT EMPTOR Latin for "let the buyer beware." A business expression which implies that a buyer bears responsibility for determining a product's quality and suitability prior to purchase.

CAVEAT VENDOR Latin for "let the seller beware." The author's updated version of the more famous caveat emptor, reflecting the marketplace's belief that sellers are responsible in both the long- and short-term for product safety and quality.

CHANNEL The pathway and the intermediaries necessary for moving products from the producer to the seller. It may include distributors, agents, shippers, freight forwarders, warehouses and retailers.

CO-BRANDING A strategy of building brand equity that combines two or more brand-name products into a single new product, with the goal of benefiting from each participating brand's reputation. (e.g., IBM computer with Intel Inside label)

COLLATERAL MATERIAL A category of marketing materials that includes brochures, catalogs, booklets, charts, press releases, films and even computer diskettes that are used to reinforce a media campaign.

COMMODITY Any article exchanged during trade. More commonly, it's used to refer to raw materials (e.g., minerals or grain).

COMPARATIVE ADVANTAGE (economics) An economic theory which holds that a a company or nation should sell and export those goods or services that it produces more efficiently than other companies or nations and buy or import those goods or services that it produces less efficiently that other companies or nations.

COMPETITION A company or group of companies that markets like goods or services within a given market.

COMPONENT COST PRICING A pricing methodology that takes a major component of a product's cost (e.g., labor, or a key material) and increases it by a standard percentage to arrive at a market price. See MARK ON.

CONSUMER PRODUCTS Goods purchased by individuals or households for their personal use, as opposed to products purchased by businesses.

CONSUMER SOCIETY A national economy characterized by a high purchasing rate of non-essential goods and services, a low personal savings rate and extensive use of credit by individuals and households.

COST-BENEFIT ANALYSIS A decision-making methodology that is based upon a calculation and analysis of a) the total cost of a business option and b) the total benefit of the business option. If benefits exceed costs by a reasonable amount, the decision is deemed worthwhile.

COST-PLUS PRICING A pricing methodology that adds a set profit percentage to the total unit cost to arrive at the sales price. This process relies on costs remaining relatively stable, as large fluctuations are difficult to absorb. See COMPONENT COST PRICING and AVERAGE RETURN PRICING.

COUNTERTRADE Trade in which the seller accepts goods or other instruments of trade (e.g., bills of exchange) in partial or whole payment for its products. Types of countertrade include: BARTER, MIXED COMPENSATION and OFFSET TRANSACTIONS.

COUPON A promotional certificate that entitles the bearer to a cash discount at the time of purchase. Coupons are used to trigger purchases and undercut competitor prices. Not legal in all countries.

CREATED MARKET A market where a product is placed on offer with no previous demand. See FOUND MARKET. Customers are persuaded of the need for the product via advertising and promotion.

CULTURAL ANALYSIS The process whereby a marketeer studies the target culture in order to gain insights into the wants, needs and buying habits of the local population prior to market entry. This analysis enables the company to formulate product design and promotional efforts to please (rather than offend) local tastes.

CULTURE The sum total of behavioral patterns and intellectual achievements of a particular human society that's transmitted from one generation to the next. It includes art, work, leisure, institutions, family units and beliefs.

CUSTOMS BROKER An individual or company licensed by a government to handle import documentation and other formalities for importers.

CUT A DEAL Slang term for negotiating a contract.

DATABASE MARKETING The use of computer records of past customer buying habits for use in making new sales.

DECISION MAKER The individual capable of making a purchase decision for a company.

DEMAND A market's combined willingness and ability to purchase a given product or service at a single point in time. It's the quantity of goods and services that customers want to buy. See ELASTIC DEMAND, INELASTIC DEMAND and UNITARY DEMAND.

DERIVED DEMAND Demand for a product that's directly related to the sale of another product (e.g., DVDs and DVD players).

DIRECT MAIL A solicitation of customers by use of promotional materials sent directly through the mail. While common in the United States, some countries have barred its usage as a violation of privacy, others have inadequate postal systems to facilitate its use.

DIRECT MARKETING A system of marketing that uses a variety of communication techniques to contact potential customers in order to elicit a measurable and almost immediate response. It includes DIRECT MAIL, DATABASE MARKETING, DOOR-TO-DOOR, and COUPONS.

DISCRETIONARY INCOME An individual's income left over after paying for essentials such as food and shelter.

DISTRIBUTION CHAIN (see CHANNEL).

DISTRIBUTION DENSITY The number of sales outlets expressed as a function of population or other distribution factor. Optimum distribution density will depend upon local buying habits and product type. The more outlets, the greater the density.

DISTRIBUTION LENGTH The number of intermediaries required to move a product through the marketplace to the end-user. The more intermediaries, the greater the length.

DISTRIBUTOR A company that undertakes to purchase products from the manufacturer for resale in a given market.

DOOR-TO-DOOR SALES A form of direct marketing whereby sales personnel go to the homes of consumers or business offices without appointments to make sales calls.

DUMPING 1) The export of goods to a market for sale at a price below actual production cost in an effort to gain market share. 2) The flooding of a foreign market with discounted goods in an attempt to transact business before a major devaluation of the exporter's currency.

ECONOMIES OF SCALE The process whereby the cost of producing a single product unit drops as the number of total units being produced increases.

EFFECTIVE DEMAND The desire of consumers to buy accompanied by their financial ability to make the purchase.

ELASTIC DEMAND A market state where percentage changes (+/-) in price result in greater percentage changes (+/-) in demand.

See INELASTIC DEMAND and UNITARY DEMAND.

END-USER The last person or company to take possession of a product. The end of the distribution chain.

EXCHANGE RISK The risk associated with the potential for a change in the market value of currencies that occurs between the time an international contract is agreed upon and when payment is actually made.

EXPLOIT 1) To make full use of a resource. 2) To take advantage of a market's lack of sophistication to profit in ways that would otherwise be unlikely if all parties were fully informed.

EXPROPRIATION (a.k.a. nationalization) The forcible takeover by a local government of a foreign business operating within its borders. The seizure generally happens without payment. Usually the result of political turmoil rather than wrongdoing by the foreign firm.

FIELD TESTING The trial of products on a limited basis with a small number of consumers from the target market, in order to solicit feedback. Done just prior to full market entry to verify previous research and product development.

FIXED COST Costs arising from production that are the same without regard to the number of units produced.

FORFAITING The selling off (at a discount) of long-term promissory notes or other debts incurred by a foreign buyer to a third party, so that the seller may receive immediate payment.

FOUND MARKET A market wherein consumer demand initiates the development of goods or services to meet that demand. See CREATED MARKET.

FRANCHISING The granting by a company (franchisor) of a license to another company (franchisee) to sell the franchisor's goods or services in return for a fee. The franchise agreement binds the franchisee to specific standards of operation, in return for which they gain the value of the franchisor's brand recognition.

FREIGHT FORWARDER A company that acts as an agent for the trans-shipping of freight to or from a foreign country on behalf of another company. The process may include some of the duties of a CUSTOMS BROKER.

FREQUENCY (of advertising) The number of times each target of an advertising campaign is impacted by advertisements for a particular product or service.

GENERIC BRAND A brand of product so popular that its name has become the designation for all products of that type in the marketplace (e.g., Kleenex, Coke).

GRACE PERIOD A brief period following a billing due date during which the debtor has the opportunity to make payment without penalty.

HARD CURRENCY National currencies that hold an internationally stable value over an extended period and have great ease of exchange (e.g., U.S. dollar, Japanese yen, Swiss franc). Opposite: SOFT CURRENCY.

HARD SELL Aggressive sales, marketing, and promotional techniques. See also SOFT SELL.

HIERARCHY OF EFFECT The stages of a successful marketing effort that a product must pass through, including: AWARENESS, AFFINITY, PREFERENCE, CONFIDENCE and PURCHASE.

HORIZONTAL MARKETING SYSTEM A distribution system where two or more companies combine their marketing efforts and distribution channels to the benefit of all participants.

IMPLIED WARRANTY An unstated guarantee that a product will perform properly in the capacity for which it was designed. Only recognized in societies with a high level of commercial law.

IMPORT DISTRIBUTOR The business of importing and taking full possession of foreign goods for further distribution domestically or for potential re-export.

INCONVERTIBLE CURRENCY National currencies that have no value outside their national boundaries (e.g., Vietnamese dong).

INDUSTRIAL MARKETING The sale of goods and services to companies that will use the products to make other goods and services available for sale to end-users.

INELASTIC DEMAND A market state wherein percentage changes (+/-) in price result in lesser percentage changes (+/-) in demand. See ELASTIC DEMAND and UNITARY DEMAND.

INFORMATION GATHERING The structured acquisition, sorting and analysis of specific data for the purposes of market research.

INNOVATORS The first group of consumers in a market to purchase a new product. A form of Adopter distinguished by their willingness to take chances on unproven products. See ADOPTER.

INTERNAL MARKETING The marketing of goods and services of one department to another department inside of a company's operation. Or, the process that occurs when a company attracts, hires, trains and retains employees. All other marketing is considered external.

INTERNET PROMOTIONS The use of the Internet as an advertising platform or for direct marketing.

LAGGARDS The last group of consumers to decide to purchase a new product. A form of Adopter that requires the greatest amount of convincing and have the least confidence in new products of any of the adopters. See ADOPTER.

LICENSING AGREEMENT A contract whereby the holder of a trademark, patent, or copyright transfers a limited right to another person or company to use a process, sell or manufacture a product, or provide specific services covered by the license.

LOCKED MARKET A market from which all but the present participants have been excluded by government edict or local business practice.

LOGISTICS The planning and provision of services, personnel, equipment and supplies for an organization or its specific operations.

MACRO-MARKETING The provision of goods and services in a manner that provides for the satisfaction of a society's wants and needs. See MICRO-MARKETING.

MANUFACTURER'S REPRESENTATIVE A sales person whose product line represents a particular manufacturer or manufacturers. The representative may be either in direct employ of the manufacturer or an independent broker working on commission.

MARGINAL COSTS The incremental increase or decrease in cost incurred when a company produces one more or one less unit.

MARGIN COST PRICING The pricing of goods below the actual cost to the producer in the hope of driving competitors from the marketplace. Profits will be recouped once sufficient market share has been established and prices raised.

MARKET AUDIT The systematic and formal review of all areas of a marketing plan after its implementation to examine the current environment, strategies, tactics and results.

MARKET SHARE (a.k.a. brand share) The amount of sales a company has as a portion of the entire market it has targeted.

MARKET-BY-MARKET PRICING Pricing scheme whereby prices are customized to each target market, based upon that market's perception of value, service, relative local costs, and the ability to pay. See UNIFORM PRICING.

MARKET DRIVEN 1) A company that produces goods, services or modifications based upon what consumers demand. 2) An economic system in which supply, demand and price are the determinants of which products will enter the marketplace. See PRODUCT DRIVEN below.

MARKETEER A person or company that promotes the sale of goods and services.

MARKETING PLAN A detailed, heavily researched and organized plan of a company's goals and objectives for the development, production, promotion, sale and service of its product line. It defines specific strategies and timelines for which the appropriate personnel will be assigned responsibility.

MARKETING MIX The combination of the marketing elements of product, price, place and promotion to generate the sale of goods or services.

MARKET RESEARCH The objective and systematic process of locating and analyzing information for making decisions about a specific market or product.

MARKET SHARE The proportion of sales in the total market claimed by a company's product.

MARK ON The percentage added to the cost of a product's main component (e.g., labor or primary material), by the producer, in order to establish a sale price. Used in COMPONENT PRICING.
See MARK UP.

MARK UP The amount added by middlemen (intermediaries) to the price of a product before it's passed along to the next member of the distribution chain or is offered for sale to consumers. Expressed in units of currency or as a percentage.

MEDIA An advertising industry term used to describe all forms of communications that can carry advertising and promotional messages. Includes print, radio, television, direct mail, billboards, the Internet and even skywriting.

MEDIA BUYER A person or company in the business of purchasing media time and space for the purpose of advertising and promoting products. A media buyer may be an independent making purchases on the behalf of another or a member of an advertising agency.

MEDIA MIX Any combination of advertising and promotional outlets used during an advertising campaign. A company varies its mix based on quantifiable results and product positioning.

MERCHANDISING The activities of a marketeer's sales force, distribution chain, and retailers that promote the sale of goods to consumers.

MICRO-MARKETING The provision of goods and services to very specific groups within a society while maintaining a responsible attitude to the target society at large.

MIDDLEMAN An intermediary that works outside of the producer's company to promote and sell products to the end-user. All external members of the distribution chain are considered to be in this category.

MIXED COMPENSATION A form of countertrade wherein goods or services are exchanged for a mixture of other goods and services, as well as currency.
See COUNTERTRADE.

NICHE MARKETING Marketing strategy in which a company focuses its entire effort on a small, specialized segment of a larger market. Niche marketing is usually practiced by small companies after significant research into the long-term profitability of the niche.

OBSERVATIONAL RESEARCH A method of acquiring information about consumer habits where market researchers observe the behavior of consumers without any direct interaction.

OFFER 1) The presentation of a proposal for acceptance or refusal. 2) The elements of a proposal.

OFFSET TRANSACTION A special form of countertrade wherein the seller agrees to make a commitment to make purchases from the buyer of finished products that have, in turn, been made possible by the purchase of the seller's raw materials or components. See COUNTERTRADE.

ON-THE-GROUND Research or information acquired in the actual market that's the subject of the research. This is the best form of research for cultural studies.
See RBWA.

PACKAGING The exterior container of a product or service as seen by the purchaser. The package may serve to advertise, describe, promote, deter the theft of, or set portion controls for the product. Packaging is used to create brand awareness.

PENETRATION The degree to which a product and its promotion have attained market share in any targeted market segment. Usually describes a company's first effort in any particular marketplace.

PERCEIVED VALUE The benefits (tangible and intangible) beyond the monetary value that a consumer expects to receive from the purchase of goods or services.

PERSONAL SELLING Person-to-person communication between a buyer and a seller that may include face-to-face meetings, telephone conversations, faxes, email or other direct correspondence.

POSITIONING The way that customers perceive a company's product in relation to that of its competition. It may be based on quality, size, price, brand recognition, packaging or a host of other "subjective" features that affect consumer decisions.

PRICE CAP The maximum that will be charged for a product in a given market. Instituted to protect market share and only reconsidered when rising costs eliminate all profit.

PRICE COMPETITION Competition between producers or sellers of like products which are of roughly the same quality, based on price alone. At this point, competition and consumer preference is based strictly on the price of the product.

PRICE DECLINE The drop in the amount that customers are willing to pay for a product as demand decreases. Sets in after a product reaches maturity.
See **PRODUCT MATURITY**.

PRICED OUT OF THE MARKET (to be) The failure of a product in a given market based upon its price being either too high or too low for that market.

PRICE DRIVEN A method of positioning a product in the marketplace based primarily on its price as compared to that of the competition.

PRICE GOUGING The extreme rise in prices that can occur during sudden increases in demand or shortage of supply; may be due to natural disasters, wars or seasonal changes. In some societies, price gouging is considered a criminal offense and may be punishable by imprisonment or execution.

PRICE LINING The setting of prices for an entire product line within a range of price points deemed attractive by customers. The range of the price lining may cover several subgroups of a segment.

PRICE POINT The standardized price used by a marketeer at the retail level for several similar products that have slightly different wholesale costs. Based on the theory that profit lost on the more expensive items will be regained on the less expensive ones without offering consumers too many variables from which to choose.

PRODUCT Goods or services offered for sale.

PRODUCT AFFINITY The favorable attitudes that a customer exhibits toward a product or a company, as a result of positive experiences with the product, advertising, or public relations efforts.

PRODUCT AWARENESS The degree of perception that a customer has regarding a product, as established by advertising and promotional efforts.

PRODUCT CONFIDENCE The belief that customers have in a product and its value. Confidence is most often engendered during the promotion of a product rather than after its first usage, since customers rarely buy what they believe is useless.

PRODUCT DRIVEN A marketing method where products are developed without the benefit of consumer feedback in the hopes that demand can be "created" artificially through promotion and advertising.

PRODUCT LIFE CYCLE The series of stages through which a product passes, including development, introduction, growth, maturity and decline.

PRODUCT DECLINE The phase of the product life cycle where demand tapers off due to competition, technical advances or economic changes in the marketplace. Decline can occur quickly or be drawn out over several decades after a product reaches maturity.

PRODUCT DEVELOPMENT The period during which a product is formulated, created, or altered to conform to design specifications or customer requirements. Usually includes a great deal of research and is followed up with a period of trials, during which a selected group of customers test the product prior to its full-scale introduction into the market.

PRODUCT GROWTH The phase of the product cycle after introduction during which customer demand increases and market share expands.

PRODUCT INTRODUCTION The period that follows product development when a product is placed in a market for general consumption by the targeted segment. Also referred to as product "roll out," it has no set time limit prior to growth.

PRODUCT LINE The full array of goods or services offered by a company for sale via the distribution chain or directly to end-users.

PRODUCT MATURITY The state at which demand for a product consistently absorbs allocated supply, with all pricing objectives being met by the marketeer. A product may remain mature for some time before decline begins to occur.

PRODUCT PREFERENCE Customer choice of one product over that of another similar product. Preference may be the result of actual usage, brand recognition or effective advertising and promotion.

PRODUCT PURCHASE The transaction stage in the HIERARCHY OF EFFECTS during which a customer buys and retains the product.

PROMOTION Any of the various techniques used to create a positive image of a seller's product in the minds of potential buyers. Includes advertising, personal selling, publics relations and discounts.

PULL STRATEGY A market-driven (vs. product-driven) marketing strategy that seeks to inform, persuade and otherwise modify consumer attitudes before they reach the point of purchase. Usually accomplished through large-scale mass-media advertising, resulting in increased demand for products or services.

PURCHASE POINT Any area at which a buyer and a seller transact business.

PUSH STRATEGY A product-driven (vs. market-driven) marketing strategy that seeks to inform, persuade and otherwise modify consumer attitudes by offering incentives and discounts to members of the distribution chain. Results in intermediaries actively selling, rather than just responding to consumer demands.

QUALITATIVE RESEARCH Research that relies on interviewing, surveys and personal interaction to gain insights into consumer behavior and potential demand.

RBWA (Research by Wandering Around) A phrase coined by the author to describe research conducted directly in the environment to be studied. Yields better results than second-hand accounts or simple statistical review. See ON-THE-GROUND.

REACH (of advertising) The percentage of potential consumers that will be impacted by an advertising campaign.

REPRESENTATIVE OFFICE (a.k.a. Rep Office) A subsidiary office located in a foreign country that's not authorized by the local government to conduct transactions. It serves only to solicit business for other offices outside of the target country. These offices may also be used to research the target market, establish local relationships, or demonstrate interest in opening a full-scale operation.

RESEARCH PLAN The formal statement of objectives, propositions and limits on market research as a means of controlling the scope and depth of research activity. Avoids the haphazard acquisition of data and false conclusions.

RETAIL The sale of goods and services to the public. Members of the distribution chain that work in direct contact with consumers are said to be working at the "retailer" level.

RFP (request for proposal) A formal letter sent out by a purchaser requesting that purveyors submit bids for supplying a product or service based on specific details that are included in the letter.

ROLL-OUT Marketing term used to describe a product introduction. Applies to new products as well as the introduction of old products to new markets. See PRODUCT INTRODUCTION.

SALES PEAK The culmination of an extended period of sales increases that occurs just prior to a decline.

SALES VALLEY The lowest level of an extended period of sales decline that prefaces either a new period of increases or the absence of consumer demand and the withdraw of the product from the marketplace.

SEGMENTATION A strategy wherein a large market is subdivided into ever smaller pieces, with each new segment being the focus of its own marketing plan and effort.

SERVICE Post-purchase assistance offered by the seller of goods in order to maintain the product in working order over an extended period.

SERVICE COMPANY A business that sells expertise, assistance or information rather than a tangible line of goods. Services are the other form of products besides goods (merchandise) that marketeers can offer for sale. Most companies sell a mixture of goods and services.

SERVICE DRIVEN 1) A company that specializes in service products.
2) A company that focuses on customer service before and after the sale as a means of differentiating itself in the marketplace.
3) An economy where the bulk of its national product or its highest rate of growth is in the production of services rather than goods.

SLIPSTREAM (information) A term applied to information gathering. Indicates that the acquisition of data becomes easier as researchers determine proper resources and relative dependability.

SOFT CURRENCY National currencies that have an unstable international value and are difficult to exchange, due to the issuing nation's lack of recognized reserves (e.g., Malaysian ringgit, Polish zloty). Opposite of HARD CURRENCY.

SOFT SELL Subtle, nonaggressive sales, advertising and promotional techniques. See HARD SELL.

SPAMMING (Internet) The unsolicited dissemination of advertising and promotions via email. (Derived from a well-known, lower-quality meat product, Spam.)

SPIKE IN DEMAND A sudden, unsustainable increase in consumer demand created by a natural event, political upheaval or advertising. Spikes often lead to GOUGING and are followed by rapid declines.

SPLINTERING The over-segmentation of a market until a company's marketing efforts are so dispersed that they become ineffective.

STATISTICAL RESEARCH A method that utilizes data and measurements to determine consumer behavior and potential demand.

STRATEGIC BUSINESS UNIT (SBU) A product line, brand name or production division within a company that focuses on a specific market or methodology. Its members are drawn from various sectors of the main company and are assembled, by virtue of their specialist talents, for specific tasks.

SUPPLY The amount of goods or services produced by a company, group of companies, or economy for sale. Producers often restrict supply in order to maintain profits when demand stabilizes.

SUPPLY LINE The distribution line that supplies a company with the raw materials or services needed to produce goods and services that will eventually be fed into their own distribution channel.

TECHNOLITH A term coined by the author to describe the large, technological, national powers that dominate international business and the global economy. It's the highest level of economic development.

TELEMARKETING The use of telecommunications to contact, track and sell to consumers. A form of direct marketing that's restricted by many national governments and requires considerable infrastructure in order to be effective.

TRANSFER PAYMENTS Payments made to and from various subsidiaries of a larger single company for the sale and purchase of goods and services across national borders. The ultimate goal of transfer payments is to distribute profits to the subsidiary in the nation with the most advantageous tax structure.

TURNKEY OPERATION A business that is offered by the seller completely ready to operate or produce for the buyer. Can range from a manufacturing plant to a franchise. The buyer needs only to "turn the key" to start the operation.

UNIFORM PRICING A pricing methodology wherein prices in each national market are matched to a single rate (allowing for foreign exchange differentials) without regard of other factors. The opposite of MARKET-BY-MARKET pricing.

UNITARY DEMAND A market state where percentage changes (+/-) in price result in equal percentage changes (+/-) in demand. See ELASTIC DEMAND and INELASTIC DEMAND.

VARIABLE COSTS Production costs that change in direct proportion to the number of units produced.

VERTICAL MARKETING SYSTEM A distribution system wherein all parts of the chain come under direct control of the producer. There are three types: 1) Corporate: The company owns all areas of the distribution channel, including shipping and retail outlets. 2) Contractual: Distribution channel members are under long-term contract to the producer and must perform to exacting standards set by that producer. 3) Administrative: The producer, through dominance in its market segment, oversees all areas of the distribution channel. Members willingly participate due to the amount of business generated by the producer.

VERTICAL INTEGRATION A form of Vertical Marketing. The producer controls both the distribution chain and all supply lines necessary to operate the company.

WHOLESALE Describes all the activities of distribution intermediaries between the original producer and the retailer. Some companies act in both retail and wholesale capacities.

WORD OF MOUTH A form of advertising in which consumers make recommendations to each other regarding the quality, value and desirability of products. Often touted as the "best form of advertising," it's also extremely subjective and prone to uncontrollable rumors.

CHAPTER 18

Resources

Aaker, David A. *Managing Brand Equity*
Free Press, New York, New York. 1991.

Breen, George & Blankenship, A.B. *Do-It-Yourself Marketing Research*
McGraw-Hill, New York, New York. 1989.

Cateora, Philip. *Strategic International Marketing*
Dow Jones-Irwin Inc., Homewood, Illinois.

Das, Dilip K. *Migration of Financial Resources to Developing Countries*
St. Martin's Press, New York, New York. 1986.

Fraser, Robert. *The World Financial System*
Longman Group, Essex, United Kingdom. 1987.

Goetsch, Hal. *Developing, Implementing and Managing an Effective Marketing Plan*
NTC Publishing Group, Lincolnwood, Illinois. 1993.

Hendon, Donald. *Classic Failures in Product Marketing*
Quorum Books, New York, New York. 1989.

Hinkelman, Edward G. *Dictionary of International Trade*
World Trade Press, San Rafael, California. 1997.

Jeannet, Jean-Pierre & Hennessey, Hubert. *Global Marketing Strategies*
Houghton Mifflin Company, Boston, Massachusetts. 1992.

Kotler, Philip. *Marketing Management*
Prentice-Hall, Engelwood Cliffs, New Jersey. 1991.

Lamprecht, James L. *ISO 9000 - Implementation for Small Business*
ASQC Quality Press, Milwaukee, Wisconsin. 1996.

Linneman, Robert & Stanton, John. *Making Niche Marketing Work*
McGraw-Hill Inc., New York, New York. 1991.

Mitchell, Charles, *A Short Course in International Business Culture*
World Trade Press, San Rafael, California. 1999.

Porter, Michael E. *Competitive Strategy*
Free Press, New York, New York. 1980.

Sandhusen, Richard. *International Marketing*
Barron's Educational Series, Hauppauge, New York. 1997.

Savidge, Jack. *Marketing Intelligence*
Business One Irwin, Homewood, Illinois. 1992.

Shippey, Karla C. *A Short Course in International Contracts*
World Trade Press, San Rafael, California. 1999.

Vernon-Wortzel, Heidi & Wortzel, Lawrence. *Global Strategic Management*
Wiley & Sons, New York, New York. 1985.